Twentieth-Century Composers

Twentieth-Century
Composers

Edited by
Anna Kallin and Nicolas Nabokov

Twentieth-Century Composers

VOLUME II

Germany and Central Europe

H. H. Stuckenschmidt

Holt, Rinehart and Winston
New York   Chicago   San Francisco

Contents

Illustrations

Twentieth Century Composers

Acknowledgments

The author and publishers wish to thank all those listed below who have kindly contributed photographs for this book: 1, 10, Bavaria-Verlag; 31, Rudolf Betz, Munich; 45, 47, Czechoslovak News Agency; 4, Photo Ellinger; 23, Klaus Hennch, Zurich; 36, 37, 39, 40, 42, 43, Hungarian News and Information Service; 38, Interfoto MTI, Budapest; 30, Heinz Köster, Berlin; 21, Osterreichische Nationalbibliothek; 22, Percy Paukshcta, Berlin; 5, 6, 28, Radio Times Hulton Picture Library; 16, Susanne Schapowalow, Hamburg; 32, Werner Scholz, Cologne; 11, 18, 20, 24, B. Schott's Söhne, Mainz; 3, Kevin Stephens; 19, 25, Foto Studio Sabine Toepffer, Munich; 7, 8, 12, 13, 14, 15, 17, 33, 46, Universal Edition, Vienna.

Foreword

Geographical concepts are flexible. Lines of demarcation shift with the course of history; peoples and civilizations migrate, merge and go their separate ways again, forming new national sentiments and borders. The term 'Central Europe' fuses Germanic, Slavonic, Gallic and Tartaric elements in an area repeatedly disrupted by armed conflict and intellectual hostility. Although the oneness of the European way of life is an idea that is often put forward, it is extremely difficult to reach agreement on the notion of Central European music. Even when an obvious *rapport* exists, as between the musicians of Austria and Germany, there are always elements of diversity, as there has been between these two countries since Wagner.

If one considers the composers representative of the various trends in Germany and Central Europe one arrives at a sum of cross-connections and influences that transcends geographical boundaries and nationalities. Bavarian composers like Richard Strauss and Max Reger have many technical and stylistic characteristics in common with Gustav Mahler, who came from the province of Moravia in Austria, though each of them speaks in his own unmistakable musical idiom. Together with this group belongs the name Hans Pfitzner, a remarkable figure standing apart from the main tradition of Central European music.

The dramatic Franz Schreker, the ideological sectarian Josef Hauer and the promethean genius Arnold Schoenberg, three outstanding Austrian composers, have each exerted a considerable influence, particularly on the techniques and theories of Webern, Berg and Křenek; these musicians, in their turn, have had a marked influence on a modern generation of composers even beyond Central Europe.

In the works of Hindemith the rebellious atmosphere prevailing after 1918 is clearly manifested, even though he cannot be dissociated from the Strauss-Reger tradition. The same spirit of rebellion, rejecting in principle anything that might be called romantic emotional indulgence, assumes the roles of social criticism and political agitation in the works of Kurt Weill and Hanns Eisler, while other composers, such as Carl Orff, and Werner Egk, Rudolf Wagner Regeny and Gottfried von Einem devoted their attentions more to the stage, taking over and remoulding Stravinsky's consciously stylized neo-classicism.

Boris Blacher's contribution is a radical asceticism in which rhythmic experimentation is pre-eminent. Modern bathos finds its place in the symphonic writing of the Bavarian composer Karl Amadeus Hartmann, while the political engagement of Paul Dessau evolved a new style of vocal writing influenced by the verse and dialogues of Bertodt Brecht. Vladimir Vogel, too, opened up new paths in the field of vocal writing.

The new ideas and ideals of the post-war years produced composers like Wolfgang Fortner who influenced a rising generation of composers including Klebe, Henze and Stockhausen. And the picture is incomplete without consideration of the folk elements which influenced Bartók and Kodály in Hungary, and Leoš Janáček, as well as the quarter-tone exponent, Alois Hába, in Czechoslovakia.

Switzerland occupies a central place in Europe both geographically and culturally; she has absorbed and independently adapted the life and culture of neighbouring Italy, Germany and Austria. The Swiss composers Honegger and Martin stand midstream between French and German influences, and even so Germanic a phenomenon as Othmar Schoeck was moulded in part by southern influences.

Artists, thinkers and composers move from one country to another, profiting where they may from what any country has to offer, but without losing their identity or their ties with the cities and countries of their birth. They determine the paths taken by art, writing and music and create for themselves a universal identity, a sense of belonging to all men. In this process the great musicians of Germany and Central Europe have played and continue to play a formative part.

1 Richard Strauss

If ever a composer was the embodiment of the time and country
in which he lived it was Richard Strauss. He was born in Munich
in 1864 and died in 1949 in Garmisch in the elegant villa which he
had owned since 1908. As a child he lived through the formation
of the first German Reich under Bismarck in 1871 and as a young
man he witnessed the accession of Kaiser Wilhelm II in 1888. The
celebrated creator of *Salome, Der Rosenkavalier, Till Eulenspiegel*
and *Ein Heldenleben* survived all the German and Austrian
political tragedies from the First World War to the collapse and
capitulation in 1945.

These two countries vied with each other in honouring Strauss,
Austria by appointing him to the directorship of the Vienna Opera
House in 1919 and Germany by organizing Strauss Festivals in
Berlin, Breslau, Dresden and Munich in celebration of his sixtieth
birthday in 1924. It was not until the advent of Hitler and totalitarian government that Strauss, as a politically disinterested
composer, found himself in conflict with the powers-that-be and
temporarily treated as a *persona non grata*. He survived the Nazi
dictatorship as a sceptic, not as a resistance fighter. Only when
his idyllic existence in Garmisch was threatened did he openly
rebel. He retreated with his family to his villa to wait for the end
of the war. Here, during thirty-seven hard-working summers, the
major part of his *oeuvre* originated.

Strauss' father was a brilliant horn-player with the *Hofkapelle*
in Munich; his mother came from the Pschorr family, owners of
the famous brewery. At the age of four Richard began piano
lessons and at eight he started to learn the violin and attempted
to compose. He studied musical theory, composition and instru-

mentation in addition to attending the *Gymnasium* which he left on matriculation in 1882.

His father held no brief for artistic revolutions; he was ultra-conservative by nature and brought up his son in the spirit of classicism; he was repulsed by the thought of having to play first horn in the world première of *Tristan* in Munich in 1865. Heinrich Levi engaged this outstanding horn-player for the world première of *Parsifal* in Bayreuth in 1882. His son Richard went with him, and was both fascinated and revolted by Wagner's music. A few years earlier after a performance of *Siegfried* he had written to a friend,

I was bored to tears . . . it was dreadful . . . not a trace of connected melodies . . . chaos . . . Wagner even uses a trumpet mute to make it all absolutely and unspeakably dreadful. My ears were buzzing with those ugly chords, that revolting wailing and howling of a seventh down to the ninth below and then back up again . . . words fail me to describe to you just how frightful it all is.

In 1884 Strauss met the famous conductor, Hans von Bülow, who engaged him a year later as musical director in the small historic town of Meiningen. Here he came into contact with Alexander Ritter, a musician who was one of the most fervent devotees of Wagner and Franz Liszt; in no time he had won Strauss over to the cause of the 'Modern German' musical movement. The composer of chamber music and symphonic works in the traditional idiom suddenly became the creator of symphonic poems and Wagnerian music-dramas. Strauss, a tall slim young man with bright blue eyes, had shown from his childhood an inexhaustible wealth of musical ideas which he realized with success and facility. As a pianist, even in his advanced years, he was a delight to listen to, as, for instance, when he accompanied the recitatives in Mozart's *Così fan Tutte*. While still at school he played the violin in an amateur orchestra founded by his father, rejoicing in the untranslatable Bavarian name of 'Wilde Gungl'. He made his debut as a conductor at the age of twenty in Munich—with a performance of his own *Suite for Wind Instruments*.

When the *Hofoper* in Munich appointed him as third conductor in 1886 Strauss was under the influence of his new-found admiration for Liszt and Wagner. A year later he produced the first of his symphonic poems, *Aus Italien*. Tchaikovsky in a letter of January 1888 writes about this new musical idiom: 'In Berlin I heard a new work by the new German genius, Richard Strauss ... in my estimation no-one has ever displayed such a scandalous, pretentious lack of talent.' About this time Strauss met Gustav Mahler, and the opera-singer, Pauline de Ahna, whom he married in 1894. He left Munich in 1889 to take up an appointment as conductor of the orchestra of the Grand Duchy of Weimar. About the same time he began his long-standing involvement in the Bayreuth Festival.

During the next few crowded years, Strauss composed the tone-poems *Don Juan, Tod und Verklärung* (Death and Transfiguration) and *Macbeth,* as well as many songs with piano accompaniment; these works established his reputation outside Germany's borders, and at festivals of music by national composers his work reigned supreme as the very epitome of modern German music. But the strain on his constitution led to a serious deterioration in health. In 1892 he had a severe attack of pneumonia and had to withdraw to Greece, Egypt and Sicily to convalesce. While lying in bed he said to a friend that it would be quite pleasant to die then—but before that he would still like to conduct *Tristan.*

On his recovery Strauss became *Hofkapellmeister* in Munich and regular conductor of the Berlin Philarmonic Orchestra. Other nations, too, had begun to show an interest in this young conductor and from 1896 journeys abroad took him to Russia, Belgium, Spain, England and France. In 1898 he was appointed senior *Hofkapellmeister* in Berlin. Shortly before that his most famous orchestral work *Till Eulenspiegels lustige Streiche* (1894) had appeared. It was followed shortly after by *Also sprach Zarathustra* (1896), *Don Quichote* (1897), and *Ein Heldenleben* (A Hero's Life) (1898), not to mention innumerable songs. His first attempt to write an opera—*Guntram*—sank under an excess of Wagnerian pathos, from which he fortunately managed to free himself in the humorous Bavarian *Feuersnot* of 1901.

The years in Berlin were decisive in Strauss's career, not only as the most famous composer of the 'Modern German' school but also as a conductor. His debt to opera and concert life in Germany was immense, for it provided incomparable opportunities to musicians. The artistic rivalry between some sixty opera-houses in small towns and cities throughout Germany as well as in such thriving bourgeois centres as Frankfurt, Hamburg and Leipzig, promoted the interests of a rising generation of composers and furthered the careers of gifted performers. Moreover, in an era of social and economic change, this towering German was the ideal representative of the progressively-minded middle-class youth of his time. His rise to fame symbolized both the prosperity of Germany under Kaiser Wilhelm and the emergence of 'resistance groups' in the spheres of art and philosophy.

But even when he was virtually the unique representative of the German music of his time, critical assessment of Strauss was clouded by scepticism and misunderstanding. His platform image of the youthful victor was 'Wilhelminian' rather than 'Bismarckian'. In 1888 Kaiser Wilhelm succeeded to the throne; in the same year *Don Juan* was composed. If one listens carefully, ignoring the horn theme in a brilliant C major with that irresistible leap of an octave, the sense of victory is questionable. Following the *Zeitgeist* Strauss ended his *Macbeth* with a triumphal march for Macduff. Hans von Bülow, his most influential champion, managed to persuade him how alien this was to Shakespeare's intentions, with the result that the tone-poem was given the subdued ending now familiar to us.

Romain Rolland, one of the first to appreciate Strauss's genius, understood the undertones of much of his music better than did his German contemporaries. In Strauss, scepticism and self-doubt hide behind the calm of the doyen of musicians and most respected of citizens. Indeed it was his very triumph that carried with it unrest and malaise. 'To what end have I triumphed?' is the formula which Rolland detects in all German intellectual life from 1871— and no-one, not even Gerhart Hauptmann, evokes this mood more clearly than Strauss. If one listens to the ending of the symphonic poems from *Macbeth* through to *Ein Heldenleben* and beyond, one asks 'what becomes of triumph?' At best the idylls remain; is that what the struggle was about?

The idyllic became the focal point in the private life of this apparent iconclast. In elegant apartments in the fashionable west end of Berlin Strauss lived in exemplary conjugal bliss. Here, in 1897, his son was born and, later, brought up. Here too his famous *skat*-parties would regularly take place of an evening, as Strauss relaxed after the rigours of work. His domestic life was protected and his prosperity skilfully increased, for Strauss was as shrewd a businessman as Handel and Gluck before him. In 1898 he founded the *Genossenschaft Deutscher Tonsetzer* (Incorporated Society of German Composers) and succeeded in securing rights for intellectual property until long after the death of the composer. His self-confidence defied even the Kaiser, who suspected Strauss of being a sort of revolutionary snake in the bosom of the Prussian *Hofoper*. Resistance only added impetus to his rise. In 1903 a Strauss Festival was held in London with the Concertgebouw Orchestra of Amsterdam, and in the same year Heidelberg conferred on him an honorary Doctorate. Together with his wife he made his first concert tour of America in 1904, which involved him in thirty-five orchestral concerts and song recitals, including the world première of his *Sinfonia Domestica*; Busoni said of this that the score reminded him of the streets of New York. Yet the work describes the idyllic family life which Strauss so often had to forego in the interests of his career.

Between 1903-5 Strauss composed *Salome* after the play by Oscar Wilde. It was first performed in Dresden in 1905 and was the first great resounding stage success to have undertones of scandal associated with it. The audience was wildly enthusiastic, though the experts and critics had reservations which were not entirely concerned with the use of biblical material to convey sexual perversion. Strauss's declamatory style was more forceful than that of Wagner; the strange orchestral dimensions he employed, his complete lack of inhibition in the use of dissonance and his disregard for normal concepts of tonality had a profoundly disturbing effect. In Berlin Henry Thode, an art-historian and husband of one of the daughters of Cosima Wagner, held a lecture directed against the debasement of music to a vehicle for perverse modes of behaviour. In Berlin, too, the Kaiser himself forbade the work to be performed until the manager of the opera-house shrewdly thought of having a Star of Bethlehem rising at the end of the work. In consequence *Salome* was performed fifty times in a single season. Ten other opera-houses bravely followed suit and soon Strauss could afford to have a villa built in Garmisch in the *art nouveau* style. In the same year, 1908, he was appointed senior musical director of the *Hofoper* in Berlin. He began his work there with one year's leave of absence to complete *Elektra*.

It was in 1900, at one of the Lamoureux concerts in Paris, that Strauss met the Austrian writer Hugo von Hofmannsthal, whose play *Elektra* had greatly impressed him when he saw it in Berlin with the famous actress, Gertrud Eysoldt, in the title-role. In the spring of 1906 Strauss played parts of the incomplete opera to Hofmannsthal. On 25 January 1909 the opera was given its world première in Leipzig under Ernst von Schuch. The critics wrote of ultimate anarchy and polluted art: the success with the audience was hardly less than it had been for *Salome*. After the dress-rehearsal Strauss called out in satisfaction 'I liked it'. Later he himself was surprised by what he had written: *Elektra* was even bolder than *Salome*. In fact, almost at the same time as Schoenberg and his school in Vienna, Strauss had freed himself from the restraint of tonality. The famous 'blood' chord in *Elektra* intertwines bitonally E major and D major, and the vocal lines often pursue their own course without reference to the harmonies of the accompanying orchestra, which was itself astoundingly new in structure. Strauss himself felt that he had gone too far, and after *Elektra* the tendency is towards greater simplicity. Deterred by his own boldness he left his new discoveries to the Schoenberg generation. With *Der Rosenkavalier*, Strauss turned his back on new sound effects, on dissonance and disturbed major-minor tonality and gave the history of modern music its first act of voluntary self-correction. A similar trend was shown by Stravinsky with his classicism, Hindemith with his pedagogic approach and the censured Shostakovitch, all of whom rejected the stylistic innovations of their youth. Strauss was the first and it represents a remarkable act of integrity from such an individualist.

In his famous correspondence with Hofmannsthal we can trace the growth of *Der Rosenkavalier*, the finest of modern musical comedies. Strauss was captivated by Hofmannsthal's idea of a comedy set in Vienna in the mid-eighteenth century. To his first objection on the grounds that the text was 'perhaps a shade too refined for the majority' the poet replied: 'A real and lasting success is achieved by its effect on both the coarse and the refined members of the audience—the latter provide the prestige without which one is just as lost as without popular appeal.' Once again the world première was held in Dresden to be followed by one success after another all over the world. An important factor in its success was Hofmannsthal's libretto, with the ageing Countess and the Page, Octavian, as enchanting central figures, the grotesque Baron Ochs, and the aristocratic and well-to-do society of Vienna at the time of Empress Maria Theresa. In its music,

Mozartian delicacy triumphs over Wagnerian pathos, and new vocal lines blend with the soft sensuality of the orchestral colour. Even anachronistic waltzes seem to be in keeping with their baroque environment.

A similar combination of refinement and simplicity is found in *Ariadne auf Naxos*. The huge orchestra of earlier works is pruned down to thirty-six solo players; elements of comedy and *opera seria* are intertwined. An aura of aestheticism and experimentation surrounds the work, and these elements have survived, despite subsequent modifications of the score. The lucid gaiety of *Der Rosenkavalier* remains unique in the works of Strauss; it surpasses *Intermezzo* (1917-23) which, to Strauss's own libretto, illustrates his idyllic life in Garmisch (with its slightly clouded conjugal bliss), and *Arabella* which, for the last time, combines a bitter-sweet libretto by Hofmannsthal with the magic of Viennese love-duets (1933). *Die schweigsame Frau* (1935), *Die Liebe der Danaë* (1940) and *Capriccio* (1942) cannot compete with *Der Rosenkavalier* in this respect.

During the First World War Strauss ended his cycle of symphonic poems in which organ and wind instrument vie with each other in portraying nature. The oriental, mystical *Die Frau ohne Schatten* (Woman without a Shadow) recalls the harmonically rich polyphony of *Salome* and *Elektra*, though the sheer élan of these earlier, iconoclastic works is missing. The *Aegyptische Helena* of 1928 is also an echo of earlier sounds rather than an original work. In neither libretto does Hofmannsthal manage to rise above a jaded, though still subtle aestheticism. Finally *Daphne* and *Der Friedenstag*, twin works to texts by the theatre critic, Joseph Gregor, only served at their world première in 1938 to emphasize how great a loss the death of Hofmannsthal had been to Strauss's inspiration as a composer.

The sparkling, gay libretto of *Die schweigsame Frau* resulted in Strauss's first conflict with the Nazis. The text is by Stefan Zweig, whose name, being Jewish, could hardly be printed for the world première in Dresden in 1935. After three highly successful performances under Karl Böhm the work disappeared from the repertoire of German opera-houses for the duration of the Hitler régime. Strauss was appointed by Hitler and Goebbels as President of the *Reichsmusikkammer* (Reich Chamber of Music). In Berlin and Bayreuth he replaced Bruno Walter and Arturo Toscanini as conductor, both of whom had refused to have any dealings with the Third Reich. A letter to Zweig on 17 June 1935 clearly reveals how little aware Strauss was of the political implications of his move: 'For me there are only two types of person, those that have talent and those that have not, and a people only exists when it becomes an audience. Whether this consists of Chinese, Upper Bavarians, New Zealanders or Berliners is all the same to me.' Hitler's secret police, whose censors read the letter, saw in this a mockery of Hitler's racial policy. Strauss came under pressure and withdrew from the Presidency of the *Reichsmusikkammer.* From then on he lived in relative freedom and isolation, with Strauss Festivals in Germany and Austria to mark his seventy-fifth and eightieth birthdays. He fell between two stools, being branded abroad as an opportunist who cringed before authority, while authority, fully aware of his indifference, showed its disapproval. The number of performances of his works was drastically reduced and the press were given strict instructions not to devote much space to him.

After Germany's collapse in 1945 Strauss went to Switzerland, resigned to his lot and without means. England was the first to break the spell of political malevolence directed against him by inviting him to London in 1947, at the age of eighty-three, to conduct concerts with the Royal Philharmonic Orchestra and the BBC Symphony Orchestra. Among his final works is one that is endowed with a sublime nobility rarely encountered elsewhere in his works—the tragic mood of the *Metamorphosen* for twenty-three solo strings, which quotes, as an act of farewell, the *marche funèbre* from Beethoven's *Eroica* Symphony.

Strauss was the great individualist, the deliberate isolationist who nevertheless, felt the need for critical acclaim. He inherited from the nineteenth century a belief in the autonomy of art which to him, as a non-believer, replaced religion. In his early years Strauss was influenced by the anarchism of Max Stirner which probably accounts for his naïvely materialistic attitude. In 1903 for example, he did not hesitate to conduct a concert in the Wannamaker store in New York when a huge fee was offered. The abusive song-cycle *Der Krämerspiegel* to texts by Alfred Kerr was motivated simply by a financial difference of opinion with his publishers. At the same time he acted swiftly and successfully to safeguard the interests of all composers in Germany. His realistic outlook, his matter-of-factness, enabled him to see in the musical profession a link in the chain of economic possibilities and opportunities of which he made use throughout his long life.

He died in 1949, shortly after returning to his villa in Garmisch, crowned in his advanced years with a multitude of honours. The last text he set to music was Hesse's *September,* which ended with these words:

Summer smiles and marvels at the dying garden dream. For a long while he stands by the roses, longing for repose. Slowly he closes his tired eyes.

The setting is in D major, the rhythm simple, four in a bar.

2 Gustav Mahler

Gustav Mahler was born four years before Richard Strauss in the Jewish provincial atmosphere of West Moravia, which in those days belonged to Austria, though it is now part of Czechoslovakia. A local newspaper from the small town of Iglau contains the following entry for 16 October 1870: 'a nine-year old boy, the son of a local Jewish tradesman by the name of Mahler, gave his first public piano recital. His great success was well-deserved, and one is left only wishing that an instrument to match his playing had been placed at his disposal.'

In later years Mahler was to say that the only artistically fruitful impressions are those made between the age of four and eleven. The boy whose piano-playing had met with much approval had attended the *Gymnasium* in Iglau since 1866, where his father, a grocer and *schnaps* distiller, had set up business after moving from the neighbouring village of Kalischt soon after the birth of his son. A school report says of him: 'Religion and Singing excellent; German and History commendable.'

The excellence of his singing had already been noticed by his parents, for their rather delicate son had learned some two hundred songs while playing near the parade-yard of the barracks. The insight of the teacher who had observed how 'excellent' he was at religion and singing is remarkably relevant, for with Mahler all music can be said to embody a powerful statement of faith; for him metaphysics found expression in fervent song. At the age of fifteen Mahler entered the Conservatory in Vienna. His professors were Julius Epstein for piano and Robert Fuchs and Franz Krenn for counterpoint and composition. One of his fellow-students was Hugo Wolf, with whom he shared a room near the opera-house.

The two men both loved the music of Wagner, and went together to hear *Götterdämmerung*. They also shared a great admiration for Anton Bruckner, whose friendship and personal example exerted a great influence on Mahler as a man and as a musician.

As pantheists in the Wagnerian mould Mahler and Wolf were both strict vegetarians—at least in those early days. In a basement room on Wallnerstrasse they would meet bearded cranks in shabby clothes, the apostles of Nature, and socialists such as Victor Adler of the German National Movement, who later founded the Viennese workers' newspaper.

On graduating from the Conservatory in Vienna the young music student won first prize playing the scherzo of a piano quintet. His insatiable appetite for work also made him find time to attend Anton Bruckner's lectures at the University.

In 1880 he was appointed to his first conductorship, at Bad Hall, Laibach (now Ljubljana) and later at Olmütz. He also conducted the choirs of the Italian repertory opera companies at the *Carlstheater* in Vienna. One can well imagine that the 'instrument to match his playing' of his early recital in Iglau was likewise found lacking with these early posts. But after 1883 one good appointment followed another: Kassel, the German *Landestheater* in Prague—where Angelo Neumann allowed him to conduct Wagner—and Leipzig, where he assisted Arthur Nikisch and came into contact with such people as Ferruccio Busoni. The slight schoolboy from Iglau with the wide, thin-lipped mouth and piercing eyes had matured into a young artist with strong views of his own. A large bushy beard covered his face, though later, during his Prague appointment this was trimmed down to a mere moustache.

The year 1888 was a crucial one for Mahler, for it was then that he was appointed musical director of the opera-house in Budapest. This post lasted only two and a half years, but in that short space of time he worked wonders, entirely transforming the ensemble, the repertoire and the morale of the establishment. Six years in Hamburg in company with Hans von Bülow added the final polish to the young operatic conductor.

In 1897 he made his debut at the *Hofoper* in Vienna, conducting *Lohengrin;* he held this post until 1907. The composer Franz Schmidt, who was a cellist in the orchestra at the opera-house at that time, wrote of him: 'His years as Director hit the opera-house like a natural catastrophe. An earthquake of staggering intensity

1

4

2

3

1 Richard Strauss (1864–1949), at the age of thirty-four. This photograph was taken shortly after he had been appointed to the post of Kapellmeister at the Berlin Opera House.
2 A silhouette of Richard Strauss and the poet Hugo von Hofmannsthal. Strauss's career as an operatic composer was greatly influenced by his meeting with Hofmannsthal. During the period 1900 to 1929 they collaborated on such well-known works as *Elektra*, *Der Rosenkavalier*, *Die Frau ohne Schatten* and *Arabella*.
3 Strauss, with his wife, former opera singer, Pauline de'Ahne and his son. Strauss' relationship with his wife was a dominant influence in his life.
4 Richard Strauss and the opera-singer Lotte Lehmann.

5

5 Like Strauss, Gustav Mahler
(1860–1911) was trained as an operatic
conductor. His first important
appointment made him musical
director of the opera house in
Budapest, a post he held for two and a
half years, following this with six
years in Hamburg and then ten at the
Hofoper in Vienna. But he wrote
nothing for the stage himself,
composing almost exclusively Lieder
and symphonies.

6 Mahler at five. He gave his first
concert recital at the age of nine, in
the small town of Iglau in West
Moravia, near where he was born. One
of his school reports says that he was
'excellent' at singing and religion, a
prophetic comment, for there is a
strong religious element in all his work.
He was born into a humble Jewish
family but was converted to Roman
Catholicism in 1896.

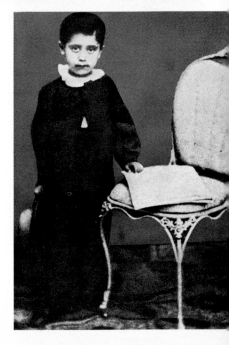

7

9

7 Mahler stayed in this house on the shores of Lake Wörther when he was Director of the Hofoper in Vienna. He rid the opera house of most of its old and outdated elements and paved the way for many innovations, including the first productions of Tchaikovsky's *Eugene Onegin*, and Puccini's *La Bohème* and *Madame Butterfly*.

8 A page from the autograph score of Mahler's *Das Lied von der Erde*, one of his most important works. It is a song-cycle based on a series of Chinese poems, with new verses by the composer.

9 A silhouette of Mahler conducting. He conducted with a combination of religious devotion and fanatical perfectionism which made some of his performers idolize him and others detest him. When he left the Vienna Opera in 1907 he wrote in his farewell letter: '. . . at all times I have devoted my full energy to it, have subordinated my person to the cause and my own inclinations to duty.'

10 Max Reger (1873–1916) was one of the strongest influences on the course of modern German music up to the beginning of the First World War. Although he died at the early age of forty-three, he wrote as many as 146 numbered works, plus another forty unnumbered ones.

and duration shook the whole edifice from top to bottom. All that was old, dated, or in any way lacking in vitality fell by the wayside and was swept away once and for all.'

Mahler conducted this body of performers with religious devotion and fanatical zeal, for him the two essential factors behind any musical performance. He found himself idolized by some and detested by others, and was ruthless in his treatment of mediocrity, though humble in his attitude towards a work of art.

Mahler, whether conducting or composing, was able to comprehend music only as one part of an integral whole. When he spoke of his great artistic experiences he was referring to books. On one occasion he said to Arnold Schoenberg, 'Let the young people that come to you read Dostoyevsky—that is more important than counterpoint'. Nietzsche exerted a powerful influence on him, less however as the author of *Also sprach Zarathustra*, than as the philosopher with the notion of the 'superman', and the radical thinker who set out to reverse accepted values. Mahler's personal tragedy lies in his lifelong attempt to aspire beyond the bounds of his restricted and restricting environment. His first symphony was to be entitled *Titan*, and a 'Nordic' symphony was also planned.

As the son of a modest Jewish family his conversion to Roman Catholicism in 1896 was distasteful to many—but for him religion was something supra-denominational; his God was an integral part of himself and Pantheism and Buddhism found their place in his religious concept of life. The god Pan lives in his music side by side with the *Creator Spiritus* and the 'supreme sovereign lady of the world'. Indeed, Mahler loved Nature, and understood it as only few artists of his generation did, he also remained deeply attached to his native Moravia, visiting his parents there every summer for many years.

For all that, the atmosphere of his scores is far-removed from the sentimental *Heimatkunst* of the time. They contain cries of solitude such as are only experienced by the city-dweller, and the term *Heimat* spelt for him a narrow parental home and the ghetto-like surroundings of which reflected a disturbing narrowness of outlook. The *torah*-scroll and the *hanukah* candlestick were brought out at appropriate times in the year, though the family considered themselves liberal in their beliefs and desired to see themselves as integrated members of society. It was from such an environment that Gustav Mahler emerged. The idea of the 'chosen race' meant nothing to him and he looked down upon the 'dirty Polish Jews' as alien stock. Family was no absolute notion for him—he had no time whatever for his brother, but each day carried his ailing sister, who acted as his house-keeper, up three flight of stairs to his apartment in Budapest.

The heights of emotion and passion of which he was capable found their expression in his marriage with Alma Maria Schindler, herself a composer and twenty years his junior, whom he married in the Karlskirche in 1902. Mahler, that 'strangely unerotic creature', was moved to write her the most impassioned poems. That their marriage worked is little short of a miracle, for not even the intellectual and aesthetic basis they had in common could bridge the enormous differences between them—on the one hand a man of Jewish peasant stock completely governed by things of the spirit, and on the other the socially superior young woman, receptive to the good things of life and brought up in a well-to-do artistic environment. An aura of the severe Old Testament prophet surrounded Mahler; as for Alma Maria—or 'Almschi' as he affectionately called her—she seemed to reflect the gaiety and brilliance of the comedies of Schnitzler and Hofmannsthal. To see Mahler in perspective one must remember the splendour and gaiety of Imperial Vienna at the turn of the century, with court balls and trips to the *Prater*: and in contrast one must also remember the Austrian Workers' Movement locked in conflict with the Christian Socialists, the Pan-Germans and the antisemites; the explosion of preconceived ideas of 'modesty' and the separation of the sexes in the writings of Siegmund Freud, Alfred Adler and the short-lived Otto Weininger; not to mention the struggle for emancipation by the first generation of university-educated women.

In this context it is interesting to recall what had been accomplished elsewhere in the scientific world of Europe at that time: Max Planck's quantum theory, the investigation of cathode rays, the application of radioactivity as a result of the disintegration of the atom. The contemporary world of ideas was dominated by monistic theories, just as technology was dominated by the airships of Count Zeppelin and the flying kites of Orville and Wilbur Wright.

Gustav Mahler

Although Gustav Mahler now represents an integral part of his Austrian milieu and era, he was regarded by his contemporaries as a sort of foreign body. His rejection of compromise inspired both hero-worship and hatred—and it was to the forces of hatred that he finally succumbed.

In 1907, after a heroic struggle against jealousy, spite and intrigue, he left the post he had held for ten years at the *Hofoper*. During that time he had not only sought to eradicate slovenliness and self-interest but had altruistically smoothed the path for innovations in the opera-house. Under his direction in 1897 many first productions took place: Tchaikovsky's *Eugene Onegin,* Anton Rubinstein's *Demon,* Umberto Giordano's *Fedora,* Puccini's *La Bohème* and *Madame Butterfly,* Hans Pfitzner's *Rose vom Liebesgarten* and Hugo Wolf's *Corregidor.* He also presented familiar works by Mozart and Wagner in a new light, in performances that were daring in their disregard for convention and some of which he directed himself with sets by Alfred Roller.

In his letter of farewell to the members of the *Hofoper* he wrote:

I leave behind, instead of something whole and self-contained as I had dreamed, a patchwork, incomplete, as is man's lot . . . My intentions have been honourable and my sights set high. My efforts were not always crowned with success. No-one is more exposed to the unresponsiveness of matter, the whim of the inanimate object than the performing artist. But at all times I have devoted my full energy to the task, have subordinated my person to the cause and my own inclinations to duty. I have not spared myself and have consequently allowed myself to demand from others the full and wholehearted application of their resources.

From then on there was no peace for Mahler. After 1907 he was an ever-welcome guest conductor at the New York Metropolitan Opera, and also conductor of various American orchestras, not to mention the Vienna Philharmonic. All Europe was fascinated by this slight man who could impose his artistic will on singers and instrumentalists alike and who, in private life too, lent his commanding personality to the furtherance of such unpopular causes as the works of Schoenberg and his pupils. In contrast to Richard Strauss, whom he admired and championed as a friend, Mahler was never motivated by considerations of material reward or advantage and he frequently offered generous assistance to struggling artists.

Ultimately his frail constitution proved unequal to the excessive work and utter asceticism he inflicted on himself. In March 1911 Mahler was struck down by a streptococcal infection. The French doctors whom he consulted in Paris were unable to offer any cure and on 18 March he died in Vienna.

Mahler's music comprises a tremendous range of works, all the more astonishing in the light of his relatively brief career as a composer. He wrote nine huge symphonies and a tenth that was almost completed. In addition there is *Das Lied von der Erde* and forty-two songs, either single or in cycles, that represent the essence of the composer's being. He uses strange juxtapositions of idyllic or exuberant folk elements, gay tunes from fairy tales, with macabre visions and biting satire.

Among the early songs—in all probability deriving from his years in Budapest or Hamburg—the one that is most characteristic of Mahler is the *Tambourg'sell*. Here one finds the folk element, drawn from the collection of poems known as *Des Knaben Wunderhorn*. It is the ballad of a soldier 'in the vaults' who awaits the gallows ('the high house') and takes his leave of marble-stone, hills and mountains, and of officer, corporal and musketeer of the guards. This is the tragedy of a deserter such as may well have been enacted at the barracks in Iglau. The music is sketched in bold strokes with detail added by the finest of brushes—a bass trill 'in imitation of a military drum', the interval of a fourth in dotted rhythm, the key of E minor wandering into the archaic Phrygian mode with its flattened second. At the words 'Tambour von der Leibkompanie' the music becomes reminiscent of the song of the good comrade; at the markings 'molto alzata' and 'con tutta la forza' the vocal part surges to its climax, then subsides into a slower middle section in D minor. Here, in embryo, are all the *marches funèbres* and cortège-like passages that recur in the symphonies—the coda to the final movement of the second, the opening movements of the fifth and seventh. The mournfully intoned sixth at the words 'Von euch ich Urlaub nehm' (I take my leave of you) prepares for a striking motif that reappears as an *idée fixe* in the sixth symphony—minor following immediately upon major.

Mahler's innovations in the spheres of harmony, melody, form and orchestral timbre are innumerable. He wrote in a kind of melodious counterpoint which had no precedent, and the thematic wealth in his development of contrapuntal ideas though never arbitrary, leaves the mind confused. His writing for brass is perfectly moulded and the expressive force of his harmonic modulations truly dramatic.

The unique effect of these symphonic blocks and the songs is determined, however, by a sphere beyond that of the written page. It derives from an exalted didactic idea that has taken musical form, a sort of religiously sublimated 'super-art' which makes Mahler's music stand out above all else in his generation. The writer Gerhart Hauptmann, with whom Mahler stood on close personal terms despite great differences of temperament, described it as 'demonism and the morality of fire', and Thomas Mann, after the world première of the eighth symphony in Munich, spoke of him as the 'most earnest and sacred artistic force of our time'.

The great vocal symphonies (numbers two, three, four and eight) are not the only ones concerned with love and death, resurrection and faith. These same elements appear equally often in the nocturnal sections of the seventh with its transcendental sounds of guitar and mandoline. Even the theatrical pathos of his enormous orchestral forces, the two hammer blows in the finale of the sixth, and the protracted length of all his orchestral movements are to be interpreted as the fruits of this sense of religious fulfilment.

Mahler's career is characterized by iron discipline and self-instruction. Hans Pfitzner and Guido Adler, two friends of his in Vienna, have described his development as conductor, from his explosive, terrifying gesticulations as a young man to his magical control over the orchestra through an ever increasing economy of movement.

At a time when he was rising to fame as an interpreter as well as a composer he yet remained an example of humanity and fanatical devotion to the music he was interpreting. His rigid, idiosyncratic readings of Mozart and Beethoven were probably a creative protest against a misguided tradition as well as the logical realization of the process of empathy and self-identification with the spirit of the scores.

The resigned melancholy that pervades *Das Lied von der Erde* reflects the shadow that lay over his final years in America. Success brought no fulfilment—a similar case to that of Busoni who spoke of the great mistake of his own virtuosity. These two great musicians came into close contact in America. Following the highly successful première of Mahler's incidental music for *Turandot* Busoni wrote in an enthusiastic letter, 'Your presence purifies'. The 'purifying' effect of contact with him was something felt by all those who really knew him and it bore testimony to the things that he stood for as a musician. His spiritualized approach to music lived on in Otto Klemperer, as did his exuberance, in Bruno Walter.

Alma Maria Mahler outlived her husband by more than half a century. There were two children of the marriage, Maria Anna who died in infancy, and Anna Justina who became quite well-known as a sculptress. Mahler's wife was always regarded by him as a sort of higher being, one whom he looked up to with utter devotion. He shared with her his artistic problems and she served as a link with the outside world. He himself needed few contacts apart from those that arose from his work. She, however, was an extremely sociable character, willing to experience any new intellectual or social venture, and as such she happily complemented Mahler's intellectual and emotional temperament.

The story of her marriage with Mahler has been published in her book of reminiscences and letters. She ends with the drafts of his tenth symphony which she found after his death. The work contains some of Mahler's finest inspirations, as in the third movement, entitled *Purgatorio,* and in the scherzo that follows it—a mad, demonic dance of incomparable tragic intensity. In the middle of the sketches for the work—in the finale—Mahler twice wrote, 'To live for you! To die for you! Almschi!'. This ecstatic confession of total love is the final statement in the life of a man who belongs both to the classical and the romantic humanist tradition.

3 Max Reger

The south German provinces, and especially Bavaria, are historic cultural centres: their cities developed a particular style of Baroque church architecture; their stone-masons and wood-carvers have been amongst the best in Europe since the Middle Ages. The Catholic core of Bavaria has produced a wealth of church music, and its capital, Munich, offered excellent working conditions to such composers as Orlando di Lasso during the Renaissance. Bavaria (together with Franconia, which later became part of it) is still the home of great composers, and great musical progeny can also be claimed by neighbouring regions such as Salzburg and the Tyrol as well as Bohemia and the Danube region of Passau.

Along with Richard Strauss, Max Reger determined the course of modern German music up to World War I. Reger, however, nine years younger than Strauss, came from a totally different background; his career, too, followed a completely different course. Strauss was a city dweller, born in Munich and living for many years in Berlin; intellectually he belonged to the modern progressive and industrial world; he was also a free-thinker, a man of the theatre and a shrewd businessman.

None of these characteristics can be ascribed to Reger. He was born on 19 March 1873 in the village of Brand near the small town of Weiden in northern Bavaria, not far from Nuremberg and Bayreuth and it was here that he spent his childhood. This countryside, which had produced Christoph Willibald Gluck in the eighteenth century, is predominantly agricultural, with dense forests and a few small-scale industries, of which porcelain and glass-making are the most important.

On both his father's and his mother's side Reger came of peasant stock. The social rise of the Regers and of the Reichenburgers, his mother's family, had brought with it modest wealth and a desire for higher education. Joseph Reichenberger, his maternal grandfather, was an inventor, whose most daring projects always ended in failure. Joseph Reger, the father, was the village schoolmaster and an enthusiastic amateur musician who played the organ and piano, as well as several string and wind instruments. One year after the birth of their eldest son, christened Johann Baptist Joseph Maximilian, the family moved from their village to Weiden, where Reger received his schooling and, from 1886, trained as a teacher at the local training-college, in compliance with his father's wishes.

Reger started piano lessons at the age of five but showed no particular interest in the instrument until an excellent teacher, Adalbert Lindner, later to be his biographer, took over from his mother. Lindner also encouraged Reger's interest in the theory of music and his talent for composition which showed itself at an early age. Lindner, modelling himself on the piano teacher Hans von Bülow, was unusually progressive, both for his time and for the social background. But Richard Wagner was also an important influence on Reger's early development. In his father's library he found books on Wagner as well as some of his works, and in August 1888 he attended performances of *Parsifal* and *Die Meistersinger* at Bayreuth.

Nevertheless, opera, and the virtuoso piano pieces which he mastered very early, were only of subsidiary importance for Max Reger's intellectual development. It was the organ which influenced him most. Between the ages of thirteen and sixteen he was already deputizing for his teacher Lindner as organist at the Parish Church of Weiden, gaining experience that was to be invaluable to him in his later development. Indeed, it is impossible to imagine either the composer or, later, the pianist and conductor without this early training at the organ. During these years as church organist he also learnt the art of free improvisation which in turn prepared the ground for his own compositions in the form of variations.

Reger remained a devout Catholic throughout his life, as his parents expected of him, but he was sufficiently tolerant to look beyond the limits of his own creed. The protestant chorales of Bach, whom he idolized, had a great influence on him.

In 1888 Adalbert Lindner sent one of Reger's scores, the *Overture in B minor,* to the famous German musicologist, Hugo Riemann. Riemann's opinion was favourable and two years later he accepted Reger as his pupil. Reger was warmly received at Riemann's house in Wiesbaden. Imagine him as an uncouth and somewhat provincial giant, over six foot tall, with unruly, slightly wavy fair hair, a strikingly protruding mouth, very short-sighted eyes and a small nose on which he wore a pince-nez. In a letter of June 1890 he described to Lindner an evening at Riemann's house:

> To start with, a first-class dinner in the dining room, then a cosy get-together in the drawing room with plenty of music-making. Dr Riemann tells stories, the Hamburg students and I tease each other, much to the amusement of our host and hostess . . . And at eleven-thirty or twelve you wander home, only to turn up again at noon the next day.

Reger felt completely at home there and was allowed full use of Riemann's library and collection of music. Amongst Reger's fellow pupils in addition to those who had followed Riemann from Hamburg, there were also students from Russia, Mexico and Holland. During these studies Reger was introduced to the works of Brahms and Bach, with Riemann using his own highly controversial 'phrased edition' of the *Well-tempered Clavier.*

Reger's life in Wiesbaden from 1890 to 1898 was decisive for his development. Here he matured as a musician and a composer of individual stature. Here, too, he met and became friends with Richard Strauss and Ferruccio Busoni. In 1896, at the age of twenty-three, Reger was appointed to a teaching post at the Wiesbaden Conservatory, but shortly afterwards he was called up for military service. About this time he also met his future wife, Elsa (née von Bagenski), whom he married in 1902 after her divorce from her first husband.

Riemann had made several attempts to interest German publishers in Reger's early compositions, particularly his chamber music and songs, but without success. Taste in the nineties was so exclusively devoted to Wagner and the North German school of composers that Reger's stylistic form with its sonatas for two or three instruments was considered outmoded and old-fashioned.

c

It was difficult even for Brahms to assert himself, and a successor to Brahms, which is how Reger was regarded, obviously had no chance at all. An English publisher, George Augener, had foresight enough to recognize Reger's promise. From 1893 his London firm published the early works, the *Trio in D minor* (Opus 2), the *Songs* (Opus 4), and the *Sonata for 'cello and piano,* (Opus 5), and as well as numerous later works for piano, for two and four hands; choral works and songs and scores for organ such as the *Suite in E minor* (Opus 16). Thereafter almost all major German publishers acquired his works.

Both as man and artist Reger lacked moderation. Letters written during the Wiesbaden years reveal with what excessive zeal he would devote himself to composition and his teaching duties, so much so that he would generally eat his first meal of the day at nine in the evening; he would often work through five nights in a fortnight, and frequently would not get to sleep until five in the morning. Added to this excess of work was a strong tendency towards heavy drinking, especially after the Riemann family had left Wiesbaden. Reger became stout at an early age, so stout in fact that his relatives in Regensburg used to say of him: 'When Max arrives, we'll have to take the door off its hinges.' He also overestimated his physical powers while on military service and suffered first from a foot ailment and then from a serious throat infection. Reger's appetite was legendary. While staying with friends he is said to have consumed a whole ham down to the bone in one night. On the other hand, during periods of creative work he could forget his bodily needs for days at a time. Truth and fiction combine in stories about Reger's love of alcohol. From his father he had inherited the well-known Bavarian thirst which manifested itself particularly after strong physical work or after virtuoso performances at the organ or piano. But Reger had enough self-discipline to stop drinking altogether for two years in 1911 and thereafter to restrict it until the end of his life.

He produced music with the same lack of moderation. He only lived to the age of forty-three, but a catalogue of his work runs to 146 opus numbers, with a further forty unnumbered works, not to mention innumerable arrangements of works by other composers such as Bach, Brahms, Beethoven, Chopin, Corelli, Richard Strauss, Richard Wagner and Hugo Wolf.

After a breakdown in 1898 Reger returned to Weiden for three years. Here he found the peace and isolation which had been denied him during his time in Wiesbaden. In this small-town provincial atmosphere, where neither his parents nor his former teacher were able to keep up with his intellectual development, Reger produced more than forty compositions. Amongst these are works for organ such as the fantasia on *Ein' feste Burg, Freu' dich sehr o meine Seele,* and *Wie schön leucht uns der Morgenstern*; about seventy songs; innumerable pieces for piano and much chamber music notably the *Piano Quintet* (Opus 64), as well as several choral works including, amongst many others, the *Hymn to Song.*

In the organist Karl Straube, Reger found an enthusiastic interpreter. The two men met for the first time after Straube had already become a keen advocate of Reger's organ works. From this first meeting grew a lifelong friendship, to which Straube's letters, when he was choirmaster at St Thomas's, Leipzig, bear most touching witness.

In 1901 the idyllic life at Weiden came to an end. Only on rare occasions had it been interrupted, as in the summer of 1899 which Reger spent at the house of Baroness von Seckendorf at Berchtesgaden together with her niece Elsa von Bagenski. One of the joys of his provincial life at home was a new grand piano which the firm of Blüthner had placed at his disposal. When Reger's father retired in the spring of 1901, the whole family moved to Munich. Here Reger found plenty of work as a teacher and this finally led him to the Imperial Bavarian Academy of Music. In 1902 he married Elsa in the village of Boll near Göppingen in Württemberg. The churches of both denominations in Bavaria had refused to marry the Protestant bride and her Catholic bridegroom and both families had strong reservations about the marriage. But the perpetuation of antithetical doctrines was as alien to Reger's spiritual life as to his music, in which a synthesis of Gregorian chant, counterpart and protestant chorale is frequently achieved.

The years spent in Munich from 1901 to 1907 were extremely productive of new music. Reger was also very active in his teaching and in playing the piano. In addition to all this he took over the direction of the Porges Choir, which gave him valuable experience for his later career as a conductor. In 1902 his friend Straube was appointed choirmaster of St Thomas's in Leipzig and this gave great authority to his active support of Reger. Reger and his wife lived quietly and happily in Munich. Strauss, with whom he got on well despite their totally different aesthetic ideals, lived in Berlin, but often lent support to his young friend. Reger made arrangements of Strauss's songs but in spite of professing an 'almost unbounded respect' never wanted anything to do with the rising tide of 'programme music'. It was only when *Salome* became the object of a series of spiteful attacks that Reger became his colleague's whole-hearted ally, maintaining that the opera could only offend the religious sense of those who had never known what religion was.

In 1905 the Music Academy in Munich appointed Reger as teacher of counterpoint, and he took up the position in 1906. His excellent relationship with Felix Mottl, the well known conductor of Wagner operas and director of the Academy, smoothed his way with other colleagues who were less well-disposed towards him. But soon his reputation as a composer and teacher had grown to such an extent that he was greatly sought after in Leipzig.

In 1904, in a letter written to Straube from a place called Berg, on the Starnberger See, Reger described his work:

My Variations and Fugue on a Theme of J. S. Bach (Opus 81) . . . the best thing I have ever written . . . a devilish piece of music . . . and also (Opus 82): *From my diary* . . . (exquisite music). At present I am working here on the men's choruses (Opus 83), and the *Variations and Fugue on a Theme of Beethoven* (Opus 86). The *Sinfonietta* is definitely going into print at the beginning of January.

With the first performance of the *Beethoven Variations* the boycott of Reger's music was temporarily broken, even in Munich. However at the first performance of the *Sinfonietta,* which Mottl conducted in Munich, there was loud protest. The supporters of Strauss took their revenge on Reger because he had withdrawn from the Munich Liszt Society.

In 1907 Reger moved to Leipzig as director of music to the University and principal teacher of composition at the Conservatory. This old city had become a musical centre of the highest traditions owing to the choir of St Thomas under Straube the Conservatory founded by Mendelssohn, and the Gewandhaus concerts under the direction of Nikisch. It is one of the paradoxes of musical history that this rather conservative city understood Reger so much better than the more generally non-conformist Munich. Perhaps some of the triumphant successes which Reger had achieved as pianist and conductor in many other countries, notably in St Petersburg, were contributory factors.

During his Leipzig years Reger's music underwent a transformation. The burst of explosive energy in Weiden and Munich was followed by a more reflective period. Large-scale forms predominate more and more. The *Variations and Fugue on a Theme of J. A. Hiller,* which is one of the most successful works, establishes a link between the Munich and Leipzig periods. Reger wrote no organ music in Leipzig; instead he turned to the solo concerto, with two powerful works: one for violin and orchestra (Opus 101), the other for piano and orchestra (Opus 114).

The chamber music written during these years is on the same large scale: a piano trio (Opus 102), two string quartets (Opus 109 and 121), a string sextet (Opus 118), and sonatas for piano with clarinet (Opus 107), violoncello (Opus 116), and violin (Opus 122).

In 1909 Reger reached the height of his achievement as a composer of choral music with a setting of the 100th Psalm (Opus 106) for mixed choir, orchestra and organ, whose great, dramatic final fugue is one of the wonders of all polyphonic music.

The change of style is clearly seen in the *Symphonic Prologue to a Tragedy* (Opus 108), for large orchestra. It shows his development from pure form to programme music; and the portrayal of moods of depression, traces of which could already be detected in his earlier music, become evident.

During this Leipzig period Reger's controversy with Hugo Riemann took place. Riemann's essay 'Degeneration and Regeneration in music' was answered by his former pupil with an attack which analyzes the concept of progress and ends with the much-quoted words 'I am moving continuously towards the left'. The supporters of the Liszt faction thought rather differently. Reger himself embodied the conflict between a completely free, harmonic mode of thought and a growing admiration for old music.

As a teacher Reger had wide influence. Among his pupils were Josef Haas and Othmar Schoeck, Jaromir Weinberger and Alexander Jemnitz, the violinist Adolf Busch and the conductor

Fritz Busch, the musicologist Hermann Grabner and the music historian and conductor Fritz Stein.

Beside composing and teaching, Reger still found time for engagements as a pianist and conductor, which during the 1910-11 season alone included more than one hundred and fifteen concerts.

In 1911 Count Georg II of Saxe-Meiningen summoned him to be director of the famous *Hofkapelle,* where once Hans von Bülow had worked for Brahms and Richard Strauss. The beautiful city of Meiningen, which had taken over from Weimar as the theatrical capital of Germany, both stimulated Reger's development as a conductor towards an individual, indeed, almost exemplary style and also led him, in his close association with the orchestra, to a new understanding of Wagner, Strauss, Bruckner and Debussy.

Out of a meeting with Debussy there emerged a new style full of delicate nuances and restrained passion. Apart from the *Romantic Suite* (Opus 125), and the *Ballet Suite* (Opus 130), the best examples of this final period are the *Four Tone Poems after Arnold Böcklin* (Opus 128). The muted trumpets, the changing tone colours and the usual tonality of the harmonies give this score a unique place in German orchestral music.

This incessant work and innumerable journeys with the orchestra overtaxed Reger's health. In March 1914 he suffered a stroke and was forced to undergo a long period of convalescence. He asked the count to release him from his post, and in the summer of 1914 he wrote one of his most vivid and masterly works, the *Mozart Variations for Orchestra* (Opus 132).

In the famous Thuringian university city of Jena, Reger bought the house where he was to spend his last years. He composed most of the time but still gave many concerts in German and Dutch cities. Once a week he taught at the Leipzig Conservatory. Reger's marriage was childless, but there were two adopted daughters living in his house and many friends enjoyed his hospitality. The terrible events of the Great War caused few shadows to fall on Reger's pleasant life in Jena. Here he completed the series of works in variation form with his *Piano Variations on a Theme of Telemann* (Opus 134), and composed chamber music, religious songs and choruses, as well as the bombastic *Patriotic Overture* and small pieces for the organ. This tremendous stream of musical production ends with the *Clarinet Quintet* (Opus 146), a delicate work, with a delicate theme which fades into the distance.

On 10 May 1916 Reger was teaching his class at Leipzig. He felt unwell but despite this met some friends in a restaurant; but he grew worse, and a doctor diagnosed weakness of the heart. That night Reger died of a heart-attack.

Like Brahms, Reger had a brilliant capacity for bringing to life forgotten forms and styles. His fugues are the spiritual successors of Bach and his motets are reminiscent of early polyphony. In the passacaglias, chaconnes and variations, tonality triumphs once more over chromaticism. This continuous struggle between innovation and tradition is what gives Reger's music its tension. His harmony seems to be trying to escape from simplicity: Bach's counterpoint fuses with *Tristan*'s harmony. A musical prose becomes the precursor of the language of Schoenberg. Schoenberg and Berg admired Reger, but he himself could not accept the rejection of tonality in Schoenberg's piano pieces, although he had undoubtedly paved the way for them.

The secret of Reger's music lies in its inherent contrasts. Basically religious, it is the product of mathematically inspired combinations and an intellectual treatment of his material. Straube has spoken of Reger's demonic genius, of his terrifying outbursts, of the astonishing range of his dynamics from *ffff* to *pppp*. Reger delighted in the same extremes in his organ and piano-playing. His characteristic gesture as a conductor was one of horror at excessive noise, a calming movement of the left hand to his lips.

In contrast to his serious philosophical conversations and extensive visits to museums, Reger also had a taste for vulgar jokes. When a princess at Meiningen asked him whether the bassoon-player produced the bass notes with his mouth, he replied 'I certainly hope so, your Highness'. He was well-read and a connoisseur of painting, particularly the baroque period; his favourite painters were Max Klinger, who suggested the titles for several of his works, and Arnold Böcklin. But his taste was not always impeccable, as the texts of many of his songs and choruses prove.

Through the richness of his harmony and polyphony, and the abruptly changing moods of his musical language, Reger's influence extended far beyond his pupils. The Society for Private Musical Performances under Schoenberg in Vienna rehearsed more than forty of his works. As a conductor Reger found in Hindemith one of his most ardent supporters. And there are links between Reger and the classicism of Ferruccio Busoni on the one hand and the neo-baroque movement on the other. Outside Germany his organ and orchestral works have been well-received, principally in England, Holland and Russia.

4 Arnold Schoenberg

Around the turn of the century an avant-garde literary circle
was active in Germany, producing cabaret shows in the Parisian
style. These miniature theatres, with their progressive ideas and
very high artistic standards, quickly established themselves in
Munich and Berlin. They modelled themselves on such places as
the *Chat Noir* in Montmartre whose clientele and performers
included Erik Satie and Claude Debussy. When the *Elf Scharfrichter* (Eleven Executioners) was founded in Munich in 1901,
one of its members was Frank Wedekind, who had already
achieved notoriety with his adolescent tragedy *Frühlings
Erwachen*. Contemporary with the *Elf Scharfrichter*, was the
Überbrettl, founded by Ernst von Wolzogen who, together with
his wife, Elsa Laura, developed a new type of German cabaret
chanson. Wolzogen's *Überbrettl* had a sister company in Berlin
known as *Buntes Theater*, whose members met in an *art nouveau*
house.

In the course of 1901 Wolzogen apponted a twenty-seven-
year-old musician from Vienna as musical director and resident
composer. His name was Arnold Schoenberg. With him he brought
his wife Mathilde (née von Zemlinsky) whom he had recently
married. In his native Vienna Schoenberg enjoyed the reputation
of an ultramodern composer. His close acquaintances were the
young writers and painters of the bohemian coffee-bars to which
he had been introduced by his friend and musical adviser,
Alexander von Zemlinsky, who later became his brother-in-law.
His lieder—even in 1898—had produced a tremendous furore in
Vienna. Their texts were taken from modern lyrical poets like
Richard Dehmel and Johannes Schlaf. The songs displayed an

incredibly rich sense of harmony not unlike Wagner's and complicated polyphonic textures betraying Brahmsian influences. For Wolzogen's cabaret, he wrote a series of *chansons* to texts by Wedekind, Gustav Falke and other collaborators in the *Buntes Theater*. But all this while he was preoccupied with a work which he had begun in Vienna in 1900 and which he was not to complete until 1911. It was the score of the *Gurrelieder* for solo voices, chorus and orchestra, to poems by Jens Peter Jacobsen. This monumental oratorio greatly interested Richard Strauss, to whom Schoenberg showed the work. As a result Strauss did much to help Schoenberg over a number of years, securing for him both the Liszt Scholarship and a teaching post.

While he was in Berlin Schoenberg also wrote a symphonic poem to Maeterlinck's *Pelléas et Mélisande,* a play which Strauss had recommended to his young colleague as potential opera material, unaware that Claude Debussy had already used the text for the opera that had its world-première in Paris in 1902.

Wolzogen's cabaret was a short-lived affair and in 1903 Schoenberg parted company with the *Überbrettl* team and returned disappointed to Vienna. He was engaged to teach harmony and counterpoint at the progressive grammar school organized by Eugenie Schwarzwald, in company with Zemlinsky. By now the circle of people who appreciated Schoenberg's talent had begun to widen; the most influential among them were Gustav Mahler, the director of the Viennese Opera, and Arnold Rosé, leader of the Vienna Philharmonic, who arranged the first performance of the string sextet *Verklärte Nacht* (Transfigured Night), based on a poem by Dehmel, which had been composed in 1899.

In 1904 four young musicians became private pupils of Schoenberg: Alban Berg, Heinrich Jalowetz, Erwin Stein and Anton von Webern. These formed the nucleus of the Schoenberg circle and they devoted themselves fanatically and resolutely to defending their vilified and hated teacher. In close cooperation and friendship with them Schoenberg carried out the development which achieved its first goal in 1907-9 with the elimination of tonality and complete emancipation of dissonance.

Important intermediate stages led to this achievement. In *Verklärte Nacht* and *Pelleas und Melisande* Schoenberg had composed illustrative music in the spirit of Liszt's symphonic poems. This trend ended with his Opus 7, the single-movement

Arnold Schoenberg

String Quartet in D Minor (1904-5) and the chamber symphony for fifteen solo instruments, completed in 1906. The works of Wagnerian inspiration requiring huge forces—like *Gurrelieder*—had given way to a more concentrated style for solo performers. The second string quartet, written in 1907-8, introduces a soprano into the last two of its four movements who sings settings of two poems by Stefan George. In these two movements tonality as such is rejected, apart from final triadic cadences. In this next work, however, fifteen poems from *Das Buch der Hängenden Gärten*, also by Stefan George, even this tradition is discarded. 'Now...I am aware of having broken through all the barriers of a dated aesthetic ideal' are Schoenberg's words in his programme note for the first performance.

The following years in Vienna are among his most productive. The number of his pupils grew from year to year and he wrote his unconventional *Theory of Harmony* stretching to some five hundred pages. It was in this period, too, that he produced the majority of his fantastic oil paintings which were much admired by Kandinsky and exhibited at the *Blauer Reiter*. He composed the *Three Piano Pieces* (Opus 11) and the *Five Orchestral Pieces* (Opus 16) first performed by Sir Henry Wood in London in 1912, the monodrama *Erwartung*, the three small pieces for chamber orchestra and six piano pieces lasting only seconds each.

By now opinions were divided among those that had shown interest in him. Richard Strauss and Max Reger rejected what he stood for. Mahler remained faithful though he could not come to terms with the score of the *Orchestral Pieces*. It was Mahler's resignation as operatic director and his departure from Vienna for the United States of America that strengthened Schoenberg's own decision to leave Vienna again. In the autumn of 1911 he returned to Berlin, where he lectured on aesthetics and the theory of composition at the Stern Conservatory whilst continuing with his diverse work as a composer and writer.

Much interest was aroused in Berlin by the arrival of this controversial figure. Busoni and his circle of pupils were fascinated by his music, as was the famous theatre critic, Alfred Kerr, as well as some of the influential music critics, notably Max Marschalk of the *Vossische Zeitung*. Schoenberg maintained contact with his friends in Vienna; Webern came to Berlin for a few months in the winter and there was an intensive correspondence with Alban

43

Berg and others. In October 1912, in the intimate Choralion Room, Schoenberg directed the first performance of one of his most characteristic works, the monodrama cycle *Pierrot Lunaire* for narrator and eight instruments, commissioned by the actress Albertine Zehme. Having freed himself completely from all traditional concepts, Schoenberg re-introduced into this work such time-honoured forms as the passacaglia, fugue and crab canon. After the first performance Schoenberg took the ensemble on tour, travelling round Germany as well as to Prague and Vienna. Countries abroad became interested and invitations to conduct his own works were accepted from England, Holland and Russia. A book, written by pupils and friends, paying homage to him as composer, teacher and painter was published in Munich. Among its devoted contributors were Berg, Webern, Kandinsky and Paris von Gütersloh. Shortly before that, Universal Edition in Vienna had published his *Theory of Harmony,* dedicated to the memory of Gustav Mahler who had died in 1911. It opens with the characteristic sentence 'I have learned this book from my pupils'.

After the outbreak of the First World War Schoenberg returned again to Vienna and shortly afterwards was called up for military service. However the state of his health was very poor and he was put on lengthy leave. His return to service in 1917 was short-lived and he was finally discharged.

During these years Schoenberg, who for years had been a freethinker, became deeply involved in religion and metaphysics. In his youth he had rejected his Jewish faith in favour of Protestantism. The need for some kind of higher spiritual bond is clearly expressed in the texts he chose to set; this was anticipated, in fact, by the libretto chosen in 1910 for the opera *Die Glückliche Hand* (*The Lucky Hand*), though the music was not composed until later. The religious texts include the *Totentanz der Prinzipien* (Danse macabre of Principles), the very late *Requiem* and above all *Jacob's Ladder.* This oratorio, influenced by Balzac, Swedenborg and Schopenhauer, represents a turning point in his musical development. It is his first work with a main theme consisting of twelve different notes—as such the forerunner to his twelve note technique that was finally realized in 1922. Although *Jacob's Ladder* remained a fragment it nevertheless lasts for three quarters of an hour and shows the full expressive and dramatic potential of the idiom.

Arnold Schoenberg

In the last year of the war Schoenberg moved to Mödling, a small town on the outskirts of Vienna. Here renewed close personal contact with his former pupils led to their mutual involvement in the Society for Private Musical Performances, founded and directed by Schoenberg. Members of the Society took part in rehearsals and performance of innumerable works by contemporary composers, either as performers or as listeners. By now there was a new generation of pupils, including Hanns Eisler, Karl Rankl, Max Deutsch and Josef Rufer.

The twelve-note technique which was first applied in the *Five Piano Pieces* (Opus 23), the *Serenade for Baritone and Seven Instruments* (Opus 24) and the *Piano Suite* (Opus 25) brought new order into the dangerous state of total freedom produced by Schoenberg's first steps towards atonality in 1908. Twelve-note melodies had already been used by Josef Matthias Hauer, for many years a close acquaintance of Schoenberg's. It was only through Schoenberg's invention of the tone-row and is three mirror images (retrograde, inverse, inverse-retrograde) that it was developed into a compositional technique. It is typical of Schoenberg's conservative attitude in these years that he applied this new technique to such historical forms as suites, sonatas, da capo songs and rondos.

These were the years when, as a consequence of the war, Austria was in a very impoverished state. Schoenberg and his circle lived in a ceaseless battle against material need which affected intellectuals in particular. By that time he had achieved international stature and his works were being performed abroad. Then, in 1923, his wife died. There were two children by this marriage—a daughter, Trudi, who married the composer Felix Greissle and died in New York in 1947, and a son, Georg, who is still alive today in Mödling. In 1924 Schoenberg married Gertrud Kolisch, the daughter of a Viennese doctor and the sister of Rudolf Kolisch, the violinist and a pupil and performer of Schoenberg's music since 1908.

In 1924 Busoni died in Berlin and Schoenberg was appointed his successor as professor of the master-class for composition at the Prussian Academy of Arts. Early in 1926 he moved for the third time to the German capital, where he found such friends as Franz Schreker, who had conducted the first performance of the *Gurrelieder* in 1913 and was now director of the Academy of

Music. A few pupils followed him from Vienna, and his new pupils included the Spaniard Roberto Gerhard, Walter Goehr, Peter Schacht and Adolphe Weiss, followed later by Norbert von Hannenheim, Erich Schmid and the Greek composer, Niko Skalkottas.

Meanwhile Schoenberg's mode of existence had changed considerably. Gone was the man with predictably unassuming clothes; in his place emerged the gentleman of sartorial elegance who enjoyed visiting bars with his friends and listening to jazz. His wife, Gertrud, liked social gatherings, and their house was frequently the scene of lavish hospitality. They travelled a lot, more often than not to the south, to Switzerland and Spain, where Schoenberg found relief from attacks of asthma, which were often severe.

This new, fashionable way of life in no way affected Schoenberg's preoccupation with religious problems. In his correspondence with Kandinsky in 1923 he had already dealt with the problem of anti-semitism: 'How will anti-semitism end if not in violence? Is it so difficult to see this happening?' In 1926 the Zionist drama *Der Biblische Weg* appeared and in 1928 he wrote the text for his opera *Moses und Aron*, composing the music for the first two acts between 1930-2. The polemics and aesthetic matters which occupied him continuously found expression in the choral pieces that comprise his Opus 27 and the *Three Satires* for mixed choir (Opus 28), that were directed against such contemporary musical phenomena as the cult of folk-music, Classicism—and above all Igor Stravinsky. The strangest product of these years is the comic opera *Von Heute auf Morgen* (From One Day to the Next), whose operetta-like text had been written by his wife Gertrud, under the pseudonym of Max Blonda. It is one of Schoenberg's strictest expositions of the twelve-note technique.

Wilhelm Furtwängler was at this time conductor of the Berlin Philharmonic Orchestra. The galaxy of famous conductors in Berlin during the Weimar Republic is surely unique. The two State Opera Houses shared between them Erich Kleiber, Otto Klemperer, Leo Blech and Georg Szell. The Municipal Opera was under the direction of Bruno Walter, who also conducted a series of concerts throughout the year with the Philharmonic Orchestra. Furtwängler took a personal interest in Schoenberg: without having a complete understanding of his music he was well able to recognize his greatness. With the Philharmonic Orchestra he conducted the *Variations for Orchestra (Opus 31)* in 1928, shortly after they had been completed in Roquebrune. The conservative audience reacted to this highly complex work with perplexity rather than comprehension. But by now Schoenberg had come to be treated with respect and taken seriously by the critics. The only hostility came from the nationalistic papers which launched a campaign against him as a Jewish composer. This hostility became much more apparent following the world première of the comic opera *Von Heute auf Morgen* by Hans Wilhelm Steinberg in Frankfurt and Klemperer's performance in Berlin in the same year (1930) of his *Begleitmusik zu einer Lichtspielszene* (Musical Accompaniment to a Film Scene), *(Opus 34)*. Schoenberg refused to take a political stand. The path chosen by his ex-pupil, Hanns Eisler, who joined the Communist Party and wrote works for massed choirs would not have suited him. Music for him was an autonomous entity; if it were to voice arguments there must be problems of a higher kind. When Berg set Georg Büchner's *Wozzeck* to music Schoenberg disapproved on the grounds that music should depict angels and not officers' valets.

The main work to be composed in his final years in Berlin was the opera *Moses und Aron*. Although only two of the three acts were fully completed it remains Schoenberg's *opus summum,* as an expression of his intellectual and religious convictions and as a work of art. Its first concert performance was not given until after his death, taking place in Hamburg in 1954. Stage performances were then held in Zürich and in West Berlin. It created a tremendous impression wherever it was heard—in Vienna, Milan, Paris and the United States.

Hitler seized power in 1933 and Schoenberg became undesirable both as a Jew and as an exponent of 'degenerate' music. Even before the Nazis had dismissed him from his life appointment without any legal justification he had left Germany with his wife and daughter, Nuria, who had been born in Barcelona in 1932. After a short stay in France, Schoenberg accepted an appointment to the Malkin Conservatory in New York and Boston.

Musicians and intellectuals across the Atlantic received him as one of the greatest artists of the century. Materially he was starting again from scratch—like many refugees he left Germany without money or means—and life was a hard struggle for the sixty-year-old composer. The state of his health was unpredictable but his sense of purpose as a composer was undiminished. An older European composer once said sorrowfully to him, 'You too will have to make compromises over here'. To this Schoenberg retorted, 'I'm more likely to destroy America'.

This tremendous sense of assurance was based on religious conviction. In 1933 he had openly returned to his Jewish faith. 'I am only the mouth-piece of an idea', he once said at an interview in New York. He was utterly shocked by the political events in Europe, especially after 1939 with the annexation of Austria and Czechoslovakia and Hitler's victories in France, Poland and elsewhere. He had always looked upon himself as a representative of Germany's great cultural tradition; now, in his own words, he had become 'not only homeless but speechless'. On the positive side, after a long period of illness due to the New York climate, he obtained a teaching post and a house in Los Angeles. His artistic integrity was intact. He turned down an offer of fifty thousand dollars to write the music for a Hollywood film because of the inevitable compromises that it would involve. To the surprise of his devotees he started to write tonal works again—the *Suite for Strings for College Orchestra* in 1934, *Kol Nidre* in 1938, *Variations for Organ* in 1941 and *Variations for Wind Orchestra* in 1943. But even these represent not a deviation from his chosen course but rather a technical mastery that is able to express complex ideas in simple terms. At the same time Schoenberg produced works in his own radical idiom—the *Fourth String Quartet* in 1936, the *Violin Concerto* in 1935 and the *Piano Concerto* in 1942.

He found himself more and more emotionally involved in the Jewish problem. Before composing *Kol Nidre,* an old Hebrew liturgical melody, he did private research into early religious rites. Gradually his attitude towards politically orientated art changed. His *Ode to Napoleon* for speaker and piano quintet, composed in 1942 after a text by Byron, unequivocally reflects his hatred of the dictator who had unleashed the Second World War. In 1948 Schoenberg wrote to the present writer, 'Lord Byron, who previously had much admiration for Napoleon, was so disappointed at his simple acceptance of things that he heaped nothing but scorn on him—and this I think I can be said to have done in my composition'.

An even clearer political confession is his *Survivor from Warsaw* of 1947, for speaker, male voice choir and orchestra. The text is about Jewish prisoners who are commanded to march to execution but undismayed begin to sing the ancient prayer 'Sh'ma Yisroel'. In the same year Schoenberg was awarded the one thousand dollar prize of the American Academy of Arts and Letters. In his letter of thanks he said that he had felt what it was like to fall into an ocean of boiling water. His virtue had been that he had not given up, but had struggled on. His opponents deserved to be thanked, because in fact they had helped him.

This is an astonishing confession—as astounding as the whole life of a man who was for ever forced to renew the battle against a hostile world. In 1946, during a serious illness, his heart stopped beating but a doctor managed to resuscitate him with an injection, and shortly afterwards he finished his *String Trio in one movement (Opus 46)*. He explained to Thomas Mann that the highly expressive nature of the music helped him to overcome the memory of the illness. Later a rift was to develop between the author and the composer, because Mann, in his novel *Dr Faustus*, ascribed to the fictitious composer Adrian Leverkühn the discovery of the twelve-note technique, much to Schoenberg's annoyance.

Schoenberg's eyesight was severely affected by his illness. When the present writer visited him in his beautiful home in Los Angeles in 1949 he was writing music on paper specially printed for him with staves the width of one's hand. He was a slight, lively man with dark brown eyes and a bald head like a monk's (he went bald relatively early in life), and by this time he had lost a considerable amount of weight. In conversation he showed the same sharp, slightly aggressive wit as ever. Despite all his troubles he said he hoped to live to a hundred and twenty-five to witness his own universal acclaim. He asked many questions about musical life in Germany and planned to attend the International Holiday Courses for Modern Music in Darmstadt during the summer. His doctors eventually prevented him from going.

His final years were devoted to the *Modern Psalms*. Here too, in strange prose texts, Schoenberg dealt with questions of religion, Judaism, racial theory, superstition and in-breeding. Faith is described as the superior counterpart to perception and Christ is extolled as the most noble person ever to have lived. Only the first of these texts, for narrator, mixed choir and small orchestra, was ever set to music. The fragment breaks off at the words 'and

D

notwithstanding I pray'. The man who revolutionized musical values had found his way to God. He died on 13 July 1951. Apart from his wife, Gertrud, who survived him by fifteen years, he left his daughter Nuria and two sons, Rudolf Roland and Adam Lawrence, aged fourteen and ten respectively.

The chaos into which Schoenberg threw the musical world at the beginning of the century has still not been resolved. But the demonic force and truth of his music have made their mark on contemporary intellectual thought. His former antagonist, Igor Stravinsky, has come to Schoenberg's way of thinking in his old age and adopted his twelve-note technique. Even the young generation in the USSR, where for years Schoenberg was rejected as a bourgeois decadent, has recognized in his work the model for a new attitude towards musical expression.

5 Anton von Webern

Anton von Webern lived nearly all his life in peace and quiet and provincial solitude. It was not until after his death in 1945 that this fragile figure became the idol of a generation and that his posthumous fame became cluttered with misconceptions. Analytical studies and biographies have thrown very little light on his character. The Weberns were a family from the Austrian administrative aristocracy that originated in South Tyrol but settled down in Carinthia. The father, Dr Carl von Webern, declined a baronial title; he was a mining engineer by profession and ultimately became a departmental superintendant in one of the ministries—a highly esteemed and respected civil servant of Imperial Austria. He died in the year following the dissolution of the Austro-Hungarian Empire in 1918. Webern's mother, Amalia Antonia Gehr, was born the daughter of a butcher in the province of Styria.

Anton was the second of three children. Shortly after he was born, in Vienna, on 3 December 1883, his father was transferred as mining inspector to Graz and here it was that Anton attended school from 1890-4. His mother gave him piano lessons. The family's next move was to Klagenfurt, where Anton went to the local grammar school and matriculated in 1902.

In Klagenfurt the boy took piano and cello lessons from a versatile musician, Dr Edwin Komauer. He joined an amateur orchestra and played both the standard works of the orchestral repertoire and also music by Gustav Mahler, for whom he had developed an admiration that lasted throughout his life. Almost at once he began to compose; the earliest surviving songs are dated 1899. Fourteen of these early works together with the ballad

Siegfrieds Schwert for baritone and orchestra and an idyll for orchestra *Im Sommerwind* were not discovered until many years after his death. The ballad for baritone and orchestra was inspired by Webern's meeting with Wagner in Bayreuth in 1902 where he had travelled with his cousin, Ernst Diez, a student of philosophy at Graz.

In autumn of the same year, 1902, Dr Carl von Webern was transferred to the Ministry of Agriculture in Vienna and Anton entered the University as a student of music. The Professor of Music was Guido Adler, the successor of the famous writer on musical aesthetics, Eduard Hanslick. Professor Adler, a friend of Gustav Mahler's, belonged to the new school of musicologists and introduced Webern to both Mahler and Schoenberg. His other professors were the composer Hermann Graedener, for harmony, and Dr Karl Navratil for counterpoint. In addition, Webern sang with the *Akademischer Wagnerverein* and performed frequently as a pianist and cellist.

Webern wrote to his cousin Ernst Diez pointing out that learning mensural notation and reading a book by Hugo Riemann on early music struck him as deadly boring occupations. What he did enjoy was a lecture on practical philosophy in which the lecturer spent more time discussing literature. His diary talks of the surfeit of concerts in Vienna, the indiscriminate applause given by audiences, the poor programmes, and the cult of the virtuoso.

More important for Webern's development was that he, as a composer, learned about medieval polyphony under Adler. He was rejected as a pupil by Hans Pfitzner in Berlin and consequently chose Schoenberg as his teacher. The latter had returned from Berlin in 1903 and started courses a year later, held in the Schwarzwald grammar schools. His fellow pupils were Alban Berg, Egon Wellesz, Heinrich Jalowetz and Erwin Stein.

In 1904 he met his cousin Wilhemine Mörtl for the first time, and they soon became engaged. In 1906 his mother died on the family estate in Preglhof, and from then on, until spring 1910 Webern lived with his father, finding occasional work as repetiteur and conductor.

The first two years of tuition under Schoenberg were extremely arduous, for he was a teacher who tolerated no half measures. Webern's development as a composer very quickly showed that he followed Schoenberg's instruction with the utmost concentration.

At the same time he was working for his doctorate under Professor Adler. Having successfully transcribed a choral work *Sacris Solemnis* by Johannes Brassart, he was given the *Choralis Constantinus* by Heinrich Isaac as the subject for his thesis. The degree of Doctor of Philosophy was conferred on Webern in June 1906. As a result of his thesis Webern published the second part of the *Choralis Constantinus* in 1909 in the *Denkmäler der Tonkunst in Osterreich.*

He remained a pupil of Schoenberg's till the spring of 1908. The last of his early works are represented by a few songs and chamber works such as the *String Quartet* and the *Slow Movement for String Quartet* of 1905 and the *Piano Quintet* of 1906-7. His 'graduation piece', written in his own hand, is the *Passacaglia for Orchestra* (Opus 1), composed during his final year under Schoenberg.

His period of apprenticeship over, Webern received his first appointment as *Kapellmeister.* This ran from June to September, 1908, in Bad Ischl, the summer residence of Emperor Franz Josef, where the young composer had to put on concerts and operettas for the spa residents. He was bitterly disappointed with his first position as a practical musician. 'This job is absolutely awful', he wrote to his cousin Diez, 'What a great blow would be struck for humanity if one were to do away with all operettas and slapstick farces'. In the same letter, he disclosed his plans for an opera. Schoenberg had shown approval of the beginnings of a setting of Maeterlinck's *Aladie et Palomidas.* Diez proposed to write a libretto and the offer was accepted: 'Away from all that now goes under the name of theatre! To its diametrical opposite!'

During this period Webern produced several important works: songs with piano to texts by Richard Dehmel and Stefan George; the choral work *Entflieht auf leichten Kähnen* (Flee in Speedy Ships); the *Five Movements for String Quartet* (Opus 5), the *Six Pieces for Orchestra* (Opus 6), and the *Four Pieces for Violin and Piano* (Opus 7). He was in frequent contact with Schoenberg, whom he idolized, and with Alban Berg. Of all those belonging to the Schoenberg circle Berg was his closest friend, even though they did not always agree. Berg did not have the same aversion to light music that Webern had; he liked listening to such things as the *Walzertraum* by Oskar Strauss. Generally speaking Berg had a soothing influence on his slightly older friend. In July 1909 he wrote to his fiancée, Helene Nahowski, that Webern had no time for Karl Kraus, whom Berg much admired. Strangely enough Webern was later to set some verses by Kraus to music. The great events for the two men during these years in Vienna were the first performances of Schoenberg's *Second String Quartet* in 1908, given by the Rose Quartet and the soprano, Marie Gutheil-Schoder, and of the songs from Stefan George in January 1910, performed by Etta Werndorff and Martha Winternitz-Dorda.

From spring to autumn 1910 Webern conducted operettas at the municipal theatre of Teplitz-Schönau (now Teplice Lazne) and from October 1910 till April 1911 he worked at the opera in Danzig as second *Kapellmeister* and chorusmaster. Here, in February 1911, he married his cousin, Wilhemine.

Although on one occasion he conducted his *Passacaglia* at a concert given by the theatre orchestra, Webern's job in Danzig left him generally dissatisfied. He lived a withdrawn life, seeing only Dr Heinrich Jalowetz, an old friend from the Schoenberg circle, who was also working at the theatre. In the spring Webern left Danzig to spend the following months in Austria. Shortly after the birth of his first daughter in April of the same year a concert was held in Vienna, devoted to works by Schoenberg's pupils, including himself and Alban Berg.

In the autumn of 1911 Schoenberg moved to Berlin, and Webern followed him in the hope of finding work there. From Zehlendorf, a rural suburb of Berlin, he wrote to Berg that he was overjoyed at being so near his celebrated teacher. In Schoenberg's honour friends and pupils compiled a book that was published by Piper in Munich the following spring. Webern contributed two chapters: one on Schoenberg's music, the other on Schoenberg as a teacher. Both chapters are hymns of praise which testify to the father-son relationship between Schoenberg and Webern. Webern was also involved in a concert at the Choralion Room, where the first performance of his arrangement of part of Schoenberg's *Five Pieces for Orchestra* (Opus 16) for double piano duet was given. The four pianists were Eduard Steuermann, who had been recommended to Schoenberg by Busoni, Louis Grunberg, Louis Closson and Webern himself. But Berlin was unable to hold him. The need to provide for his family forced him to accept another theatre post. After a short visit to Schoenberg in Prague at the end of February, Webern joined his wife in Vienna to sign a contract with the municipal theatre of Stettin (now Szcecin), a position which he held from July 1912 to January of the following year. However, Webern was even unhappier in Stettin than in any of his previous appointments. The root cause of the trouble was probably his inability to adapt himself to the discipline of the theatre routine. During these months in Stettin he composed nothing, though they probably did much to complete his experience and perfect his technique as a conductor. He wrote desperate letters to Berg. Finally he was granted leave of absence, which, as it turned out, was the occasion for a complete severing of his link with the theatre.

Webern left Stettin and took an apartment in Vienna, not far from his friend Alban Berg. Despite financial hardship he found time to compose intensively, and, in this short spell before the outbreak of war in 1914, his own personal style evolved. The highly condensed, aphoristic forms of Opus 6 and Opus 7 found their most convincing expression in 1913 in the *Bagatelles for String Quartet;* the synthesis of orchestral polyphony and sound-painting effects was achieved with considerable success in his *Pieces for Orchestra* (Opus 10).

His Opus 8 began a whole series of songs for one voice and a variety of instruments. They are settings of poems by Rainer Maria Rilke, using those intervals now considered characteristic of Webern, acknowledging no difference between vocal and instrumental writing. Webern had rejected the concept of tonality based on a key-note as early as 1908. Along with Schoenberg and Berg he followed the basic canon of total chromaticism and unresolved dissonance. His Opus 11, the *Pieces for Cello and Piano,* shows extreme condensation and brevity; in later years he was critical of them: 'It is virtually impossible for either performers or listeners to get anything out of them', he wrote to his friend, the musicologist Willi Reich.

Shortly after the outbreak of the war Webern, because of his poor health, volunteered for service with the Red Cross. His application was ignored and he was drafted to a school for officers in 1915, to be finally discharged from active service on 22 December 1916.

Three years previously Alexander von Zemlinsky, principal conductor of the *Neues Deutsches Theater,* had been in touch with Webern in Prague. Now, from 1917 to 1918 and again from August to October 1920, Webern assisted Zemlinsky at the Prague

Opera. However, for all Zemlinksy's good intentions and friendship, Webern was still not happy.

After the end of the war Schoenberg took an apartment in the little town of Mödling near Vienna. Webern followed him there and spent the rest of his days, virtually without a break, in this peaceful, rural province. He took an active part as a performer in the Society for Private Musical Performances, founded by Schoenberg, until the society was dissolved in 1922. It was here that most of his works were rehearsed and performed, sometimes in their original form, sometimes in arrangements. Webern derived the greatest possible satisfaction from his work in the company of kindred spirits, members of the Schoenberg circle, though his mode of existence was modest in the extreme, and he struggled for years against material need.

When his father died in 1919 Webern devoted himself entirely to his family—his wife, a son Peter, and three daughters. The summer months would be spent in the Austrian mountains which Webern loved so dearly. He felt a close affinity to nature, was a keen lover of flowers, and delighted in tracing the connections between plant-life and art forms. He was also interested in religion and would always take with him on journeys, in addition to Goethe's *Faust*, a copy of the Bible; it was said that before going to bed he would kneel and say his prayers.

Gradually his fame spread. Universal Edition in Vienna bought and published his first works, including the *Pieces for Orchestra* (Opus 6)—which had been received with horror at its first performance in Vienna, 1913. The performance of his *Passacaglia*, which he conducted himself at the Festival of German Composers in Düsseldorf in 1921, was a resounding success, and his works were received with ever-growing interest at the Donaueschingen Festival and at Festivals held by the International Society for New Music. In 1924, at the Theatre and Music Exhibition, Webern was awarded the Vienna Music Prize. Shortly before that he had become conductor of the Workers' Choral Union (*Arbeiter-Singverein*) in Vienna, and continued as such until the dissolution of the Austrian Social Democratic Party. His performance of Schoenberg's *Friede auf Erden* for an unaccompanied choir during the Theatre Exhibition in Prague will never be forgotten by those who were present.

In 1927 Webern's long-cherished desire for regular artistic work

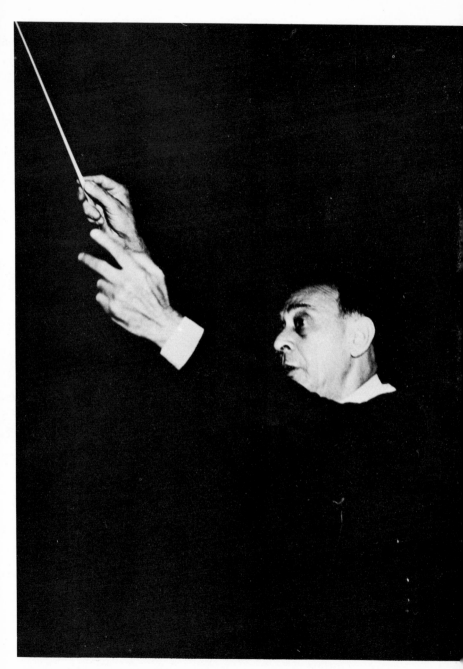

11 Arnold Schoenberg (1874–1951). Through Schoenberg's invention of the tone-row and its three mirror images (retrograde, inverse, inverse-retrograde), the twelve-note melody became a compositional technique. The chaos into which he threw the musical world at the beginning of the century has still not been resolved.

12

12 Anton von Webern (1883–1945) with his cousin, Ernst Diez, who accompanied him on a visit to Bayreuth in 1902.

13 Webern: *Opus 9*, composed in 1913. The highly condensed and aphoristic forms of Webern's preceding works were expanded and fully realized in these *Bagatellen* for string quartet.

13

14 Alban Berg (1885–1936) with Anton von Webern near Vienna in 1912. Berg tried to defend his new ideas within the traditional framework; Webern invented a new framework, which he considered to be its own justification. They were Schoenberg's most celebrated and influential pupils and remained lifelong friends.

15 Josef Matthias Hauer (1883–1959) as portrayed by Schade in 1928. Hauer probably wrote atonal melodies before Schoenberg and his pupils. It was the autumn and winter of 1912–13 that saw the turning-point in Hauer's musical career. As he later wrote, 'at the age of twenty-eight I could celebrate my spiritual rebirth ... One day I was suddenly playing a kind of music hitherto heard only in my dreams.'

and for financial security was at last realized when he was appointed permanent conductor of the Austrian Radio in Vienna. Later, in 1930, he was also appointed Lecturer in Contemporary Music. During these years he gave well-prepared performances of a wide repertoire of classical, romantic and modern works. The strain of work on his none-too-robust physical constitution was often great, especially since he was still composing. At the end of 1928 Webern fell seriously ill and could only resume his conducting after several weeks' convalescence in a spa hotel in Semmering.

By now his fame had spread abroad. He was especially popular in London where he appeared many times after 1929 as a guest conductor. To his delight, both as a composer and as a conductor, a concert was held in the *Kleiner Musikvereinsaal* at Vienna in 1931 devoted entirely to his music. Among the performers were his close friends Rudolf Kolisch and Eduard Steuermann. His reputation as a teacher was also established. From 1918 he had some thirty pupils, including Karl Amadeus Hartmann, Philipp Herschkovitz, Karl Rankl, Erwin Ratz, Willi Reich, Humphrey Searle, Leopold Spinner, Hans Swarowsky, Peter Stadlen, Stefan Wolpe and Ludwig Zenk.

However, at the same time as the outside world was learning to hold his music in ever higher esteem, political events in Germany began to hinder his career. The increasing influence of Fascist politics on art after 1932 drove his works from the concert programmes of Germany. He was also forced to relinquish his posts in Austria one by one. In 1934 the workers' orchestral concerts were stopped, and after the *Anschluss* he was removed from his Radio appointment. Schoenberg's proscription by the Nazis and his subsequent emigration to the United States of America was a bitter blow for Webern, who had always maintained close contact with his teacher and friend; the death of Alban Berg in 1935 was another terrible loss.

Webern had first met the poetess Hildegard Jone and her husband, the sculptor Joseph Humplik, in 1926 and the couple had since become close friends of his. In 1934 Webern wrote two Lieder for voice and piano *Viae Inviae*, to texts by Hildegard Jone and a year later followed them up with three more songs, Opus 25, and the choral work *Das Augenlicht* (Sight) as well as the two cantatas in 1939 and 1941-3. The strange nature philosophy of

Hildegarde Jone's lyrical poetry inspired Webern to compose some of his most sublime music.

Webern's fiftieth birthday in December, 1933, passed almost unnoticed in Germany and Austria. But friends dedicated a special contribution to him in the small journal, *23*, edited by Willi Reich. In 1938 the number of his pupils dwindled rapidly until only a handful were left. On conscientious grounds he turned down the offer of a lectureship at the predominantly Nazi Academy of Music in Vienna. Occasionally he was given work to read or correct for Universal Edition. Works such as the *First Cantata* could only be performed in private and his sixtieth birthday was totally ignored by the whole of Europe.

In the last year of the war the whole of Austria suffered under severe air raids, leaving as sensitive a person as Webern in a state of utter emotional exhaustion. In March, 1945, he heard that his son Peter had been killed. At Easter he and his wife fled to the village of Mittersil in Oberpinzgau, Salzburg, carrying with them only the barest necessities; on 15 September, having just recovered from dysentery and reduced almost to a skeleton through undernourishment, he visited a son-in-law who was in contact with the Americans and was able to offer him a good meal and a cigar. Webern had been a heavy smoker since his youth and he went outside the house to enjoy the cigar in peace, completely unaware of the fact that a curfew had been enforced. He came face to face with an American occupation soldier who promptly shot him.

Together with Berg and Eisler, Webern was the most important representative of the Schoenberg school. Just as he had followed Schoenberg in the discovery of atonal music in 1908 so he followed him in 1924 with his *Folk Texts* (Opus 17), in twelve-note composition. His works up to the *String Trio* (Opus 20) are characterized by their highly condensed forms; they display the talents of a composer with a sensitive ear for melody and for delicate tone-colours requiring the minimum of volume. His introvert style of music was best suited to the lyrical texts of Richard Dehmel, and later to those of Stefan George, Rilke, Georg Trakl and Karl Kraus; and these form the main part of his predominantly vocal output. In later years he chose his texts exclusively from the lyrical poetry of Hildegard Jone.

The most prominent form in Webern's polyphonic music is the canon. His melodies are built on themes of three or four notes with a narow range. The twelve-note rows following the *Concerto for Nine Instruments* (Opus 24), are frequently built from small cells which are presented in three mirror forms. A quasi-spatial element enters his music in that rhythm, tone-colour, and dynamics are integrated with melody and harmony. Webern's devotees in post-war years have read into these facets of his style a break from all tradition. But he himself felt as close an affinity with traditional forms as did his teacher and friend, Schoenberg, whose innovations he sublimated to greater simplicity, transparency and logic. It was the experience of Webern's late music that led the seventy-year-old Igor Stravinsky to modify his own technique and musical ideals radically in the 1950s.

6 Alban Berg

In the autumn of 1904 a tall, handsome young man with an expressive face and features reminiscent of Goethe and Oscar Wilde became a private pupil of Arnold Schoenberg in Vienna. He was Alban Maria Johannes Berg, the son of a wealthy Nuremberg merchant and his Austrian wife, born on 9 February 1885 in Vienna. His mother was a daughter of the court jeweller, Franz Braun, and he had two elder brothers and a younger sister. The Bergs lived in the grand style, loved music and literature, and owned land in Carinthia where they often spent the summer months.

Alban Berg was a highly intelligent child, outstanding at school, though he did not appear to be as musically talented as his brother and sister. It was through them that Alban's interest in music was roused during the important years of adolescence. Around the turn of the century, without any formal training, he began to compose, generally Lieder, in the romantic tradition of Schubert and Wolf.

About this time his father died. This was the end of the family's prosperity though his mother tried to maintain the shop for devotional books and articles near St Stephen's Cathedral in Vienna. Only with assistance from the family could Alban be kept on at school. At the same time as his passion for music developed he grew intensely interested in literature.

Berg's love for such artistic pursuits proved detrimental to his school-work and in 1903 he failed his matriculation examination and had to take it again a year later. His brother Karl had noticed in a newspaper an advertisement for courses in composition given by Schoenberg. Without Alban's knowledge he went to the composer with some Lieder written by his brother. And so it came about that Berg became a pupil of Schoenberg.

In spite of a robust appearance Berg's physical and nervous constitution was anything but stable. In 1902 the funeral of Hugo Wolf, whom he greatly admired, had such a profound effect on him that he fell very ill. From early years and throughout his life he suffered from asthma, and every summer he was afflicted by hay-fever. His failure in the matriculation examination, combined with an unhappy love-affair, led him to attempt suicide in 1903. Throughout his life, however, Berg was to find relief from emotional stress in nature and in composing.

On leaving school, Berg entered the civil service as a junior assistant in the municipal accounts department where he made a very meagre living. But in 1908 he gave up the job to devote himself entirely to music, some inherited money providing his financial security.

In 1949 Schoenberg wrote of the most successful of his former pupils:

> When Alban Berg came to me in 1904 he was a terribly shy young lad, but when I looked through the things he had written I realized immediately that here was real talent. As a result I accepted him as a pupil even though he was not in a position to pay the tuition fees. Later his mother came into a large inheritance and told Alban ... that he could go on to the Conservatory. I was told that he burst into tears and could not be pacified until his mother agreed that he should carry on studying with me.

Like all the young musicians who came into contact with Schoenberg at that time, Berg was fascinated by his ideas. He devoted himself wholeheartedly to Schoenberg's tuition and his quick progress between 1905 to 1908 is reflected in his compositions—his *Seven Early Songs,* as well as the *Twelve Variations for Piano* on an original theme. In Easter 1907 he met and fell in love with Helene Nahowski, who was studying singing. In one of the earliest of the innumerable letters he wrote to her he said: 'Helene, is it really not enough for you that one man, who if not physically and intellectually, at least emotionally—in other words in the world of sensibility—stands very high, should prostrate himself utterly at your feet? Can I not become your all?' These words are characteristic of the demand for totality that is one of Berg's salient features. All or nothing—this was his artistic credo—and it also explains the perfection and minute attention to detail of his mature works, and the excessive self-criticism that so radically curbed the flow of his output.

The circle of Berg's friends was large and varied, though he had little contact with musicians other than those in Schoenberg's class—including Anton von Webern. Among his closest friends were Oskar Kokoschka and the poet, Peter Altenberg; they introduced him to the brilliant journalist and theatre critic, Karl Kraus. Berg was a fervent admirer of Gustav Mahler and was one of the many leading artists and intellectuals to join his guard of honour when he left Vienna in 1907.

Berg had a tendency to idolize people and his admiration was as total as his rejection. But his intellectual integrity conquered all differences of opinion and personal dispute, though for a time, even his relationship with Schoenberg was disrupted by personal conflict. He took a lively interest in the latest movements in painting and literature and attended world premières of plays and operas. In 1905, like many musicans from Vienna, he made the journey to Dresden to hear the first performance of Richard Strauss's *Salome,* after Mahler had unsuccessfully tried to persuade the court authorities to stage the first performance in Austria. In 1908 he grew fascinated by Frank Wedekind's *Frühlings Erwachen* at the Deutsches Volkstheater in Vienna.

To alleviate his attacks of asthma Berg took drugs in ever-increasing quantities; the result was insomnia, which in turn he tried to overcome with sleeping tablets. Personal events always had a disturbing effect on his health and artistic problems often became personal ones. Even his relationship with Schoenberg, whose pupil he remained until 1910, gave rise to a thousand problems, though there were moments of exquisite joy when he listened to performances of Schoenberg's music.

The first three works which Berg himself looked upon as mature and supplied with opus numbers were the *Piano Sonata,* the *Four Songs* to texts by Friedrich Hebbel and Alfred Mombert, and the *String Quartet.* These were written between 1907 and 1910. When the period of tutelage was over a subsequent, even more intensive friendship with Schoenberg began.

The year 1911 was a very eventful one for Berg. On 24 April the Sonata and the Quartet were given their first performances at the Society for Culture and Art; press reviews spoke of 'glimpses of talent. Shortly afterwards he married Helene Nahowski; despite her family's opposition, and all the prophets of gloom, it turned out to be an exceptionally happy marriage.

Berg's profound love for his wife is vividly revealed in the letters he wrote her, daily, whenever they were apart. The early months of their marriage were darkened by only two events—the death of Gustav Mahler, whom Berg held in the very highest esteem and, in the autumn, Schoenberg's second departure for Berlin. Berg took every possible opportunity to visit Schoenberg, generally combining the trip with a visit to Anton von Webern who lived in Germany. Another of his friends, living in Vienna at that time, was the famous architect Adolf Loos. Among his most profound literary experiences of this period were performances of the two plays *Advent* and *Intoxication*, by Strindberg, whom both he and Schoenberg much admired.

Of all Schoenberg's pupils Berg was the one with the highest literary interests. It is hard to find any text that he set to music that is of mediocre literary quality—and they range from such German romantics as Nikolaus Lenau and Theodor Storm to the most modern literature of his time. He chose lyrical texts by Rainer Maria Rilke and the mystic Alfred Mombert, and, in 1912, five of the controversial prose poems by Peter Altenberg. These poems are full of aphoristic observation of everyday things, written by the poet to his friends on picture post-cards. One of these miniature texts reads:

Did you see the wood after the thunderstorm?!?!
All is at peace, glistening and more beautiful than before . . .
Take note, woman; you, too, could do with a thunderstorm!

Berg set these miniatures for high voice and a large orchestra with triple and quadruple wind section, harmonium, celeste, piano, and a variety of percussion instruments and strings. The *Altenberg Songs* were given their first performance in March 1913 in Vienna at a concert promoted under Schoenberg by the Academic Association for Art and Literature. They were the fourth item on the programme, coming after the *Orchestral Pieces* (Opus 6) by Anton von Webern, Schoenberg's *Chamber Symphony,* and *Orchestral Songs* by Alexander von Zemlinsky. The audience was uneasy from the start. The second of Berg's songs, *Thunderstorm,* produced an uproar. The concert had to be abandoned. At the ensuing court case a psychiatrist giving evidence said that music of this nature had a detrimental effect on the listener. It is interesting that a similar uproar greeted Igor Stravinsky's *Rite of Spring* a few weeks later in Paris.

Berg simply carried on. In spring 1913 he produced his *Four Pieces for Clarinet and Piano*; in the summer he was able to show them to Schoenberg in Berlin; but he was not particularly impressed and the two quarrelled. Berg took the quarrel very much to heart, but it stimulated him to work even more intensively. In the course of the next twelve months he produced his *Three Orchestral Pieces* (Opus 6), which he dedicated to Schoenberg on his fortieth birthday with the words: 'To my teacher and friend in boundless gratitude and affection.' All three pieces, but particularly the third, which was completed after the outbreak of the First World War, have a dramatic intensity and truly demonic imaginative power. This highly personal statement makes no concessions and reaches out even beyond the new harmonies and sound effects of Schoenberg's *Erwartung* and the *Five Orchestral Pieces* (Opus 16). This work, with its prophetic anticipation of the impending horrors of war, clearly reveals Berg's capacity for music drama.

While he was working on these pieces Berg saw performances of George Büchner's *Woyzeck*. He immediately resolved to make an opera out of it. His first concern was the dramatic arrangement of the material, which he condensed into three acts of five scenes. In 1915 Berg was called up for military service, and drafted into an officers' training centre. Under the interminable strain of training he fell seriously ill. In May 1916 he was finally transferred to service in an office of the War Ministry in Vienna. Experience as a soldier left an indelible impression on his sensitive person, accustomed to the lifelong protection of his physical and mental comfort. Without these experiences one can hardly imagine how he could have composed some of the scenes in *Wozzeck*.

The work was composed between summer 1917 and the end of 1920; the orchestration took nearly another year. The war years had involved him in many anxieties, concerning not only his own private life but also Schoenberg's, who had also been drafted into service and who was living in virtual poverty.

In September 1917 Berg took part in the opening of Schoenberg's seminar for composition at the progressive grammar school

E

directed by Eugenie Schwarzwald. During these years an intimate friendship developed between Berg, Alma Maria, the widow of Gustav Mahler, and her husband, the poet Franz Werfel. Both of them helped and advised him on *Wozzeck*. Alma Maria was responsible for the piano score of the work and did much to promote Schoenberg's seminar, out of which the Society for Private Musical Performances was formed in 1918. The statutes were drawn up by Berg, who gave untiring support as a performer and administrator until its dissolution in 1922. In connection with the Society he produced his analysis of Schoenberg's *Pelleas und Melisande,* as he had earlier done in 1913, for the *Gurrelieder* and the *Chamber Symphony.*

The collapse of the Austro-Hungarian Empire and Austria's economic plight affected Berg's private life very much. On his family's behalf he had to take over the administration of their mountain farm in Carinthia until it was sold early in 1920. But Berg was full of literary ideas. He wanted to write on Schoenberg and on music, possibly as a critic. For a time he helped edit *Anbruch,* a monthly magazine devoted to modern music and published by Universal Edition. It was not long, however, before he gave this up in order to devote himself entirely to working on *Wozzeck.*

By now Berg's music was beginning to gain attention at festivals of contemporary music. Hermann Scherchen repeatedly conducted his works and suggested to Berg that he should arrange parts of *Wozzeck* for concert performance; Berg conducted the *Three Pieces* in Frankfurt in 1924 with great success, and thus prepared the way for the world première which Erich Kleiber had managed to secure at the State Opera in Berlin.

From 1924 to 1925 Berg worked on the *Chamber Concerto* for piano, violin and thirteen wind instruments, dedicated to Schoenberg on his fiftieth birthday. As a result of the première of *Wozzeck* in December 1925 Berg had become a famous and controversial figure. The conservative press attacked him viciously. The critics used such epithets as 'lunatic' and 'criminal'. It was thought that *Wozzeck* would bring about the end of repertory opera. Other critics prophesied that success which it has since come to enjoy.

In *Wozzeck* Berg has achieved a synthesis of traditional recitative—aria opera and music-drama, of such rigid musical forms as fugue, passacaglia, suite and symphony with aria, song and melody, of tonal, polytonal and atonal devices. *Wozzeck* is one of the most significant landmarks of opera in the twentieth century. In spite of the scandal it caused in Prague in 1926, in spite of repeated attacks in the press, it has established itself internationally.

The *Chamber Concerto,* dedicated to Schoenberg, contains a further exposition of some of the techniques developed in *Wozzeck.* It anticipated the spirit of serialism by twenty-five years. Subtle techniques of variation and polyphony are brought together in a new way; the music is also profoundly personal. The three motto themes are derived from the 'musical' letters in the name of Schoenberg, Anton von Webern and Alban Berg. Much use is also made of mathematical symbolism, a prominent feature of Berg's mysticism. The number of instruments used, fifteen in all, reverts to Schoenberg's *Chamber Symphony,* and the violin and piano parts were written with Rudolf Kolisch and Eduard Steuermann in mind, both friends from the Schoenberg circle. In 1922 Kolisch had founded a string quartet which played modern and classical music, including Berg's Opus 3. Between 1925 and 1926 Berg wrote his *Lyrische Suite* for this ensemble; the first performance took place in Vienna in January 1927, and even in so conservative a town it was enthusiastically received and followed up by nearly one hundred performances by the Kolisch Quartet and other ensembles. In spite of its strict twelve-note construction the six movements are romantic, at times even tenderly lyrical. In variety and refinement of sound they surpass anything previously written for the string quartet. Here Berg's perfectionism is at its highest. The quotation from the opening of *Tristan* in the final movement, the *largo desolato,* is very characteristic.

He was now travelling a good deal to hear performances of his own works and to attend competitions which he was frequently invited to judge. He visited Leningrad, Cambridge and London, taking every possible opportunity to see Schoenberg in Berlin and establishing friendships with many musicians. The material problems of existence had ceased to trouble him; he had bought a small Ford and usually spent the summer with his wife in Carinthia on the Wörther See where he had a week-end house.

As early as 1930 Berg began to feel uneasy about political developments in Germany. As in earlier years he still found time to give tuition to a small, hand-picked circle of pupils. But when the Prussian Academy of Arts elected him to Membership in 1930, he turned down the offer of a post as professor of composition at the Academy of Music in Berlin, where his old friend Franz Schreker was principal. The increasing influence of politics upon German cultural life resulted in a gradual decrease in the performances of modern music, causing Berg great financial hardships. Nevertheless he went on composing. His main project since 1934 had been the opera *Lulu*, the outline of which was completed in 1934, though the instrumentation was not finished until very shortly before his death. The work is derived from Wedekind's two plays *Erdgeist* (Spirit of the Earth) and *Die Büchse der Pandora* (Pandora's Box), which has as its central figure a pan-erotic 'femme fatale'.

His financial position become very difficult when the National Socialists seized power in Germany—and Schoenberg's emigration to America was a great personal loss to him. More and more he sought the quiet of his forest retreat in Carinthia. Erich Kleiber asked him for the text of *Lulu* in March 1934 and, despite all the difficulties, tried to persuade the Berlin State Opera to give it its world première. All that ever came of this bold idea was the performance of three concert movements of a *Lulu Symphony* in November 1934.

In spring, 1935 Berg interrupted work on *Lulu* to complete a violin concerto commissioned by the violinist Louis Krasner. It was to become the *Requiem* for Manon Gropius, the eighteen-year-old daughter of Alma Maria and the architect Walter Gropius, who had died of poliomyelitis. With her death on his mind Berg worked for four months with feverish activity, ending the work on 11 August 1935. The score is a brilliant and overwhelming expression of foreboding of his own death, made all the more effective by the use of an Austrian folk-tune and the chorale *Vor deinen Thron tret' ich hiermit* (With This I Step Before Thy Throne) from the Bach cantata, *O Ewigkeit, du Donnerwort*. Berg did not live to hear its first performance under Scherchen in Barcelona.

At the beginning of September, 1935, Berg developed an abcess on his back, possibly as the result of an insect bite. Surgery seemed to have removed the trouble, but in November, when Berg went to hear the rehearsals for his *Lulu Symphony* in Vienna, he developed a fever and by mid-December he was seriously ill. He died on Christmas Eve, 1935, just one year after his fiftieth birthday had been celebrated by a handful of loyal friends.

His last words, written to his wife, might well be read symbolically: 'I think the weather is changing for the worse'.

7 Josef Matthias Hauer

The composer Josef Matthias Hauer died in Vienna on 22 September 1959. He was seventy-six years old, and forgotten by all save a small, exclusive and somewhat sectarian circle of avid admirers. He had lived a life of great poverty, quiet and isolation.

Hauer was born on 19 March 1883 in Vienna-Neustadt. He was the son of a prison warder, who came from a wine-growing family in the Rhine Palatinate. His father played the zither and gave zither lessons; his son soon became his pupil. Josef was trained as a primary school teacher and also learned to play the organ and piano. After five years' study he left the training college, and in 1902 took up his first teaching post in the village of Krumbach. He soon established his long-standing friendship with the poet and philosopher Ferdinand Ebner. In 1907 he married the eighteen-year-old Leopoldine Hönig, by whom he had three children; one of them, Bruno, became a composer and publisher of popular songs and achieved greater prosperity than his father had ever done.

During his course at the training college Hauer taught himself musical theory and composition, and wrote some church music and a string quartet, which predated his earliest surviving compositions by at least seven years. The first works to survive are pieces for piano or harmonium and songs to texts by Hölderlin and the tragedies of Sophocles, the latter dating from 1911. At about this time there was a group of intellectuals, which used to meet in a cafe in Vienna-Neustadt, to which both Ebner and Hauer, then aged twenty-eight, belonged. In the discussions on aesthetics Hauer soon became one of the main protagonists, and the wholly unconventional ideas which were to influence his tonal language began to take shape. The turning point came during the autumn and winter of 1912-13. As Hauer himself wrote later: 'At the age of twenty-eight I could celebrate my spiritual rebirth. . . . One day I was suddenly playing a kind of music which I had hitherto heard only in my dreams.' His friend Ebner (to whom this 'first symphony', later called *Nomos in seven parts* (Opus 1), is dedicated) said of it: 'Often these horrible dissonances appear to be melodies, not yet unfolded but compressed within a chord. . . . For the moment I cannot help feeling . . . that in this work an embryonic, primeval manifestation of musical creation has taken place.'

The work was performed on two pianos in the small town of St Pölten in 1913; one of the pianists was the Viennese composer and theoretician Rudolfo Reti (who in 1922 became a co-founder of the International Society for Contemporary Music). It was wildly applauded by the audience but the critics' response was negative.

From 1904 Hauer taught at a secondary school in Vienna-Neustadt. At his own wish he took and passed three further state examinations between 1906 and 1909, becoming formally qualified to give lessons in singing, violin and piano. However, his teaching activities still left him sufficient time for composition. In 1913 he wrote the second *Nomos* and the *Apocalyptic Fantasia* (both originally entitled 'Symphony' and written for piano and strings) besides several minor works. In 1914 Hauer composed his first Hölderlin songs, dedicated to Anna Bahr-Mildenburg, including *Hyperions Schicksalslied,* as well as five choral songs taken from the tragedies of Sophocles and a *Kyrie eleison* for piano and strings.

Soon after the outbreak of war Hauer joined the forces but was classified as unfit for active military service and worked in a government office. In 1915 he sent for his family to join him in Vienna, where he lived until his death.

During the war years, in addition to writing a few piano pieces and songs, Hauer formulated his theoretical ideas, publishing and printing them himself in the book *On Tonal Colour* which aroused wide-spread comment. Many of his ideas come from Ebner, but differences of opinion grew out of their work together which led to the complete break-up of their friendship in 1920. The mainspring of their disagreement was a discovery which Hauer made in 1919 and communicated to his friend. This was the 'twelve-note series' which he saw retrospectively as being the central idea behind all his work. Ebner regarded it as the end of music, Hauer as the beginning of a new era.

Hauer was not alone in his theories long. In November 1918 the well-known author and journalist, Hermann Bahr, expressly referred to the book *On Tonal Colour*. Shortly before this, Hauer had met the architect Adolf Loos, an admirer and friend of Arnold Schoenberg. In 1913 Hauer had written to Schoenberg, then living in Berlin, who had advised him to get in touch with Webern, Berg or Karl Linke. In 1917 he visited Schoenberg, his senior by nine years, but reacted to him with anger and dislike. Nevertheless Schoenberg remained kindly disposed towards him, and between 1918 and 1922 six works by Hauer were performed in Schoenberg's Society for Private Musical Performances. In the second edition of Schoenberg's book on harmony he refers to the 'fashionable atonal composers': 'The Viennese composer Josef Hauer should be excluded from what I have said. Even where there are exaggerations, his theories are profound and original; his compositions reveal a creative talent even where they are more like 'examples' than compositions and his attitude commands respect because of its courage and self-sacrifice.' In 1923 the two composers were still corresponding about plans for a school for twelve-note music or a joint textbook, and it was during this discussion that their differing conceptions crystallized clearly: for Schoenberg the twelve-note structures were only 'possibilities'; for Hauer they were 'necessities'. He was and remained a man of radical revaluations. Nevertheless both his *Piano Studies* (Opus 22) in 1923 and his book *Vom Melos zur Panke* (From Song to Drum) 1925 were dedicated to Schoenberg.

Meanwhile Hauer's life had changed. In 1918 he was released from military service and took a teaching post in Vienna-Neustadt. In June 1919 the school authorities retired him on a pension. Those who knew Hauer might well be amazed at the reason given: 'on account of a highly neurasthenic condition'. Hauer was a tall, strong man of peasant build. He was vigorous and demonstrative in conversation and prone to outbursts of rage against both real and imaginary enemies. He had a sense of humour and was as openly pleased by success and encouragement as a child. His face was broad, with a high forehead and he had a squint which sometimes worried those he was speaking to. However, he was the exact opposite of a neurasthenic artist. Amongst those with whom he associated in Vienna—the poet Peter Altenberg, who suffered from a stomach complaint, the Olympian Hermann Bahr and his wife Anna von Mildenburg, the extremely elegant architect Loos, the delicate, almost fragile Karl Kraus—Hauer looked like a lumberjack. Be that as it may, he was now able to devote all his time to music and musical theory.

In his opinion India was the source of the highest rhythmic culture, and China the source of the highest melodic culture. He championed all things Chinese and identified himself with everything that meant order, political wisdom and good sense. Out of the polarity of rhythm and melody he developed a musical universe which, in its simplicity and greatness, allows no comparison with any other modern aesthetic philosophy. In 1922 he wrote: 'A pure melodic line can bear no strong emphasis, no fortissimo and no pianissimo, no presto, furioso or grave.' He proved that tonal music originates in the rhythms of nature: the elements, climate, physiology, emotions, personality and race. He equates the essence of genius with this tonal music. In contrast to this he asserts his concept of man who subdues the rhythm, moulds it into melodic form and thus gives it meaning.

These theories, the crystalline purity of Hauer's music, the figure of this composer living in poverty and voluntary isolation away from the busy musical centres, stirred the imagination of several writers. In 1920 Franz Werfel wrote his tragedy *Spiegelmensch* in which there is a visionary called Schneeman. He embodies the searching, abstract flight from the senses which was then an important feature of German intellectual life. Schneeman is clearly modelled on Hauer. He looks for a professorship in Germany with music and painting as his main subjects and mathematics as a subsidiary subject, and introduces himself to his partner Themal in the following way:

> I am just black and white, all colour I reject,
> And diatonic sounds I think a vile effect.
> It is my task to fight the things I hate
> And to support what's cold and cleanly made.
> Thus do I move from East to West:
> A Chair in Germany would suit me best.

Werfel's novel *Verdi* appeared a few years later, in 1924. As a double antithesis to his two main characters, Verdi and Wagner,

Werfel has created the young composer Matthias Fischbock in whom Hauer's character is easily recognizable as is Hauer's authentic theory in all he says.

The present writer visited Hauer at his home for the first time in 1924. During their long conversations he got to know Hauer both as a musician and as a person with an unusually accurate ear. Hauer was an excellent cello player and could have become a member of the Vienna Philharmonic Orchestra had he wished it. He played some pieces including twelve-note melodies at his grand piano; then he whistled about a dozen of such atonal sequences. The intonation was precise and the notes followed each other astonishingly quickly without any one being repeated before the other eleven had been whistled.

The year 1924 brought Hauer his first visible success outside Austria: the first five Hölderlin songs (Opus 6) and five completely new string quartet movements (Opus 30) were included in the programme of the Donaueschingen Music Festival that summer. But, much to Hauer's regret, the programme also included Schoenberg's *Serenade* and two works by Anton von Webern: the *Bagatelles* for string quartet and the *Songs* (Opus 14).

During the same year Vienna heard its first orchestral work by Hauer, the *First Suite* (Opus 31), written not long before and dedicated to Hauer's patron, the jeweller Erich Köchert. Strictly speaking Hauer considered those instruments with equal temperament, such as piano, harmonium and celeste, as the only legitimate means of expressing his atonal melodies. He had a special attitude towards tone-colour which was linked with his interpretation of intervals. This was explained in several of his writings, especially in the book *Vom Melos zur Pauke*. But even in his textbook on atonal music *On the Essence of Music*, written in 1923, he writes: 'The "spirit" of an instrument lies in any one interval. If, for example, we play a perfect fifth on the piano in the middle register, we are reminded of a trumpet.' And again: 'Even in the imagination an interval already possesses a definite tone-colour with its own pronounced *musical* character.' His main support for this theory is Goethe's 'Theory of colour'.

Even though Hauer preferred the human voice and instruments of equal temperament, he went on writing chamber and orchestral music with different instrumentation, such as the duo for violin and piano (Opus 28) which he dedicated to the violinist Rudolf Kolisch (later to become Schoenberg's brother-in-law) in 1924; he also produced dramatic works including the opera *Salammbô* in 1929, based on Flaubert's novel, and the *Singspiel, Die Schwarze Spinne* (The Black Spider), written in 1932.

During the years between 1923 and 1925 the young composer Hermann Heiss came to Vienna from Darmstadt to study under Hauer. He became a devoted friend and collaborator; the work entitled *Twelve-note Theory, the Study of Tropes* is not only dedicated to him but arose out of their work together. Heiss is almost the only one to have developed Hauer's teaching fruitfully and to have extended it by introducing into it a new application of rhythmic principles.

What then are these 'tropes', the subject of this study? Hauer carried out close investigation into the possibilities of twelve-note sequences. First of all he calculated all the possible combinations and permutations of the twelve tones of equal temperament. The formula, 12!, gives the answer 479,001,600. There are thus hundreds of millions of melodic possibilities. This enormous number was reduced by Hauer to a system of 'constellations' which he called *tropes*. In order to find them one must halve a twelve-note melody, giving two groups of six notes. These six notes are arranged, in each case, in ascending order or put together as a six-note chord. By doing this, it is found that the two halves, each consisting of six notes, are in strict proportion to each other: their intervals are equal. The first of Hauer's tropes is the chromatic scale; the last is the sequence of two whole-tone scales a semitone apart from each other: E flat—F—G—A—B—C sharp; E—F sharp—G sharp—B flat—C—D. Hauer has forty-four of these tropes. Each one has quite specific melodic and harmonic characteristics. He observes that his twelve-tone melodies always move in several, but never more than six tropes. Since tropes in atonal music are comparable to tonality in tonal music, one can say that a melody modulates from one trope into another.

A further important idea may be found in the book *Twelve-tone theory*, the comparison of musical composition with bridge-building. He argues thus:

A structural engineer is mainly concerned with two forms of energy: on the one hand with the weight of the material, on the other with its

strength and structure. With stone bridges, he must concentrate more
on the problem of weight; he must use a large number of strong piers,
because he can only reckon with comparatively small spans. However,
if he uses concrete or even steel, he can achieve far greater spans,
using fewer and more slender piers. The same is true of music. We
find the principle of gravity in a given note with its series of harmonics.
The principle of large spans may also be found in the closed circle of
twelve notes. Both these principles must be respected under all circumstances, yet in an infinite number of variants.

Hauer's conception of music is clearly expressed in these few
sentences. However, it is significant that this protagonist of equal
temperament and atonality speaks of the law of harmonics as one
of the basic elements in music, an idea which is a consistent factor
in his composition. For this reason his purely atonal music always
goes back to concordant groupings of sounds. It moves in a realm
of well-known three and four-note chords, and is therefore com-
prehensible and easy on the ear in spite of its radical construction.

This may help to explain the immediate success of two of Hauer's
works at their performances in Germany: the *Seventh Suite for
Orchestra* (Opus 48) at the Music Festival of the ISCM at Frankfurt
in 1927 and the Hölderlin-cantata *Wandlungen* (Transformations)
at the Baden-Baden Chamber Music Festival in 1928, both under
the direction of Hermann Scherchen. In 1927 Hauer received the
Prize for Art given by the City of Vienna and in 1930 the city
decided to pay an annual honorarium to the composer, who had
hitherto lived in poverty with his family. In the same year, 1930,
Otto Klemperer conducted fragments from the opera *Salambo* at
the Krolloper in Berlin, and the violin concerto was performed at
the Music Festival of the ISCM in Brussels.

Willi Reich, the Viennese music critic who now lives in Zürich,
has described how he visited Hauer in the winter of 1930. 'When
I entered the room, he was sitting in front of a board on which he
demonstrated the forty-four tropes.' Hauer loved graphic demonstrations of this kind. As early as 1919 he had fascinated the Swiss
painter Johannes Itten (later a master at the Bauhaus in Weimar)
by his 'circle of colours', a graphic interpretation of the circle of
fifths. Itten returned the compliment with an abstract painting.
Ferdinand Ebner was a witness to their first meeting, which he has
described in his *Memoirs*: 'Itten came to see Hauer—I was there at
the time—and got him to play his *Apocalyptic Fantasy*, a work

dating from 1913. Full of enthusiasm, Itten declared: "Hauer's compositions are just like my pictures".'

Hauer also invented a new form of musical notation without sharps or flats for his music; it is based on the arrangement of the piano keys. In order to make the flow of the lines clearer he used coloured crayons.

The rise of fascism in Central Europe and the increasing cultural barbarization of the musical life of Germany and Austria proved fateful for Hauer. By 1930 he had achieved a certain security for himself and his work. Many of his compositions were published by Universal Edition and performed in Europe and America. All this changed during the thirties. The cultural policy of the Nazis rejected Hauer's music as degenerate and forbade it to be performed. After the *Anschluss* in 1938 Hauer lost not only his honorarium but also all his royalties. He had to live on a small teaching pension and from then on was supported by a small circle of close friends. Hauer's friendship with the music critic Johann Muschik dates from that time. Muschik has described the group, which Hauer dominated as much at the age of fifty-five as he had done in earlier years:

Anyone who wanted to meet Hauer then, under the Nazis ... had to seek him out . . . in certain cafés which he frequented. The house . . . in which the composer had lived and which had once belonged to him ... had been sold long before. He lived in poverty ... His audience was not very large, yet Hauer, when intoxicated with wine, felt himself a king, a prophet.

Among this circle of friends, Hauer would rage against Wagner, Scriabin, Strauss and Lehar, all of whom he held responsible for chaos and world wars.

He continued to work. After about eighty-nine opus numbers Hauer called the compositions subsequent to 1940 'twelve-note patterns' and left them unnumbered. Many of them he played to his friends. Thus he survived the war.

When the present writer visited Hauer in Vienna in 1955, for the first time in over twenty years, he was living once again in the old house in Josefstadt that had previously belonged to him. A tall old man with white hair and the long beard of a Chinese philosopher, opened the door. He was dressed in a nightshirt, for it was that day of the week which he used to spend in bed, thinking and composing. Immediately, as though they had met only the day before, he began a conversation about modern music, and about Thomas Mann, whom he attacked vehemently. From a leaflet of his own he read these words:

Absolute, cosmic music permits the deepest insight into the way of the world. The notes with their harmonics are suns with their planets. The solar systems 'temper' one another; the tensions between them arrange themselves with compelling necessity to create the harmony of the spheres. Twelve-note patterns perform the functions of the Milky Way, being the energizing and formative centres of organic processes. Absolute music is a link with eternity, it is religion, intellectual reality as opposed to all the different denominations, philosophical systems and political ideologies. Music and mathematics are of one and the same stamp! If they develop away from their origins and from each other, then there arises on the one hand emotional dreariness and musical nonsense, and on the other a sense of contrivance and experimentation. Organically developed, true twelve-note music must be discernable from twelve-note composed humbug and fashionable noise devised for entertainment and edification.

Then he showed the writer piles of compositions and manuscripts which he was to take with him. It wasn't music, he said, music had died long ago. It was a game with mathematics. But if everyone would only learn to read, hear and write it, there would be no more problems. Of these new pieces, hardly anything had been printed; only a few pages had been published by Fortissimo, the firm belonging to his son, who was a composer of popular songs. Everything he showed, mostly piano pieces for four hands and string quartets, began and ended with the chord of the major seventh, that is B flat—D—F—A. 'When you have looked through them, throw them away', said Hauer, 'I write a new one every day.'

The conversation made a deep impression despite its bizarre nature. Hauer had been serious in his rejection of the modern system and had made a lifelong sacrifice of philosophical magnitude to his convictions. Every alliance with the powers of this world was repellent to him. He received his few honours after 1945 almost grudgingly. He accepted graciously the homage of his own small circle but no other.

Hauer's musical output reached almost immeasurable proportions. Of his numerous pieces only a fraction has been published. He often stamped the manuscripts with a kind of visiting card: 'Josef

Matthias Hauer, the discoverer and unfortunately the only connoisseur and creator of twelve-note music (in spite of many poor imitations), which cannot be "composed" as hitherto, but which must be grasped purely intuitively, and studied as the oldest language and the highest form of education.'

8 Franz Schreker

The life story of the composer Franz Schreker would be a good subject for a tragic novel. After a carefree childhood he lost his father early and experienced years of bitter poverty during which his mother could hardly earn enough to provide him and her three other children with the barest necessities. Yet eventually he rose to great heights in the theatre, and was, for a time, a dominating figure in the world of music and musical education. But, after 1930, he was driven more and more into the background by the reactionary policy of the National Socialists, and finally, scorned by successful 'artists' of half his talent, and well nigh forgotten, Schreker died in Berlin in 1934 at the age of only fifty-six.

His father, Ignaz Schreker, was of Austro-Czech Jewish stock; his mother, Eleonore von Klossmann, came from the minor aristocracy of Styria. Ignaz Schreker followed one of those trades, new at the time, on the borderline between art and technology. He was a photographer, achieving the somewhat more exalted position of 'photographic artist', whose services were sought by members of the Imperial Court. He worked in Vienna and in such elegant resorts as Spa in Belgium and Monaco. Franz Schreker was born in Monaco on 23 March 1878 and spent his early childhood there. This home, with its grand clientele and the European high-life which the family glimpsed, must have made a considerable impression on an artistically gifted boy. His musical talent was recognized at an early age and his future profession as a musician decided even then. His musical education included violin, organ and piano and was soon supplemented by practical work of all kinds including duties as church organist and conducting orchestras and choirs. In 1888, after his father's death, his mother took all her children to Vienna.

Troubled years followed during which Franz, as organist of Döblingen parish church, brought home ten gulden a month. He entered the Vienna Conservatory on a scholarship, and from 1897 studied composition under Robert Fuchs.

Until 1900 Franz worked hard to acquire that exhaustive knowledge of strict and free counterpoint which laid the foundations of his later success as a teacher. As early as 1896 one of his compositions for strings and harp received its first performance in London. During his final year at the Conservatory he conducted the student orchestra in a slow symphonic movement; his setting of the 116th Psalm was performed as his composition for graduation in July 1900; soon after, he was awarded a prize for his *Intermezzo for String Orchestra.*

Schreker's opera, *Flammen* (Flames), composed in 1902 and based on the text of a friend, Dora Leen, has the academic style of all his early works. But another work, the text and score of which occupied Schreker for nearly a decade, showed development towards a tonal language of his own. This was the full-length opera *Der ferne Klang* (The Distant Sound) begun in 1901 and finished in 1911. During this decade Schreker's career took a decisive turn for the better. For a short time he worked as assistant conductor at the Vienna Volksoper, and in the same season, 1908, he founded the Philharmonic Choir which soon became famous for its excellent performances, particularly of modern music such as Schoenberg's *Gurrelieder*. It was then that Schreker met the young dancer Grete Wiesenthal, a friend of the poet Hugo von Hofmannsthal; her performance of the ballet written for her, *The Birthday of the Infanta,* based on the story by Oscar Wilde, was a decisive artistic experience for the young musician, who himself conducted the performance. While he was still working on *Der ferne Klang,* Schreker wrote the libretto for a second opera, *Das Spielwerk und die Prinzessin* (The Princess and the Toys).

In 1910 Bruno Walter heard *Der ferne Klang* and was so impressed by it that he recommended it to Felix Weingartner, then operatic director of the Vienna Court Opera. Weingartner accepted it, but he retired as director in 1911 and his successor, Hans Gregor, refused to perform it. However in 1912 the opera had its first performance in Frankfurt.

Schreker had become well-known as a result of his successes as a conductor and composer in Vienna. In 1910 he married the young singer Maria Binder and in 1912 the Academy of Music offered him the post of teacher of composition. He met Alexander von Zemlinsky, the friend and brother-in-law of Arnold Schoenberg, who requested him to write a libretto which he suggested should deal with the tragedy of the ugly individual—as, indeed, did *The Birthday of the Infanta*. Zemlinsky, a brilliant musician, was physically a dwarf of fascinating ugliness. Schreker took up the suggestion, but then set the libretto to music himself. It became one of his most successful operas, *Die Gezeichneten* (The Branded Ones).

Der ferne Klang, whose first performance in Frankfurt was a sensational if controversial occasion, shows a technical mastery and maturity which are astonishing for a first work. It has remarkable dramatic unity in the fusion of libretto, music, setting and plot. This new conception of the 'total work of art' remained a decisive factor in Schreker's creative life. He inclined towards symbolism and impressionism and in literature towards a strange mixture of naturalism, fairy-tale fantasy and a utopia of sexual morals, as is sometimes found in Gerhart Hauptmann and Frank Wedekind and which probably originated out of Hendrik Ibsen and August Strindberg. Nearly all Schreker's themes show men in conflict between the sensual and the spiritual, between instincts and creative discipline, between base temptations and a high ideal.

The female counterparts of his idealized heroes, moving ever forwards towards a greater spirituality, are of quite another stamp. They are voluptuous, melancholy creatures; sweet girls gone to the bad, like Grete in *Der ferne Klang*; prostitutes of middle-class or even aristocratic origin; demonic creatures in need of redemption like Els in *Der Schatzgräber* (The Treasure Seeker), in whose bedroom, furnished with oriental extravagance, the murderer and jewel thief, Albi, pleads in vain for amorous delights. It is part of the exalted style of Schreker's love scenes that the heroines take on the mythical personalities of classical goddesses or biblical demons such as Astarte and Lilith, and are often destroyed by their own lust for love.

In the first years of the Great War, Schreker completed his new opera, *Die Gezeichneten* (The Branded Ones), and wrote the libretto for yet another which was to become his most successful *Der Schatzgräber*. He was now recognized as the creator of an unmistakeably individual style, as a juggler with sound on the borders of tonality, as the creator of a new kind of musical idiom, a new kind of orchestral music with erotic overtones. Despite its apparently indefinite outlines, his music is always solidly constructed. In its subtle contrapuntal technique it is clearly influenced by Schoenberg's teaching.

Alban Berg, who in 1910 to 1911 was working on a piano score of *Der ferne Klang*, was fascinated by the music and predicted its success. Later, in a greeting to Schreker on his fiftieth birthday in 1928, he wrote of his 'memory of that happy time when together we explored new realms' and of the 'consciousness of artistic kinship and feelings of human sympathy'. Schreker introduced new music into the programmes performed by the Philharmonic Choir in 1919-20, and it was through him that Vienna first heard not only works by Mahler and Schoenberg, but also the *Mass of Life* by Frederick Delius, and works by Ernst Křenek, Cyril Scott, Karol Szymanowski and Alexander von Zemlinsky.

Schreker's growing reputation could not be diminished by the failure of his opera *Das Spielwerk und die Prinzessin* which was performed in Frankfurt and Vienna. The libretto was influenced by Gerhart Hauptmann's drama *Und Pippa tanzt*, which Schoenberg and Alban Berg had also thought of setting to music.

Schreker, who had begun his career as a composer of abstract music, later turned almost exclusively to the theatre. Only once was the stream of operatic production broken by the composition of another major work, the *Chamber Symphony* for twenty-three solo instruments, written in 1917.

The opera *Die Gezeichneten* was not performed until 1918 when it was produced by the Frankfurt Opera under the direction of Dr Ludwig Rottenburg. This was only the first of a long series of triumphant successes, which ended in Schreker's dominance of the German operatic stage. Between 1912 and 1932 there must have been about a thousand performances of his operas, and not only in Germany, but also in Austria and Switzerland and even in Leningrad, Prague and Stockholm.

Schreker's fame as a teacher was also spreading. His composition class in Vienna became the centre for young musicians, with many of whom Schreker maintained a friendship in later life. Soon after the war the State Opera in Karlsruhe offered him a post as director, but he turned the offer down. He was, however, attracted by another offer, that of the directorship of the well-known State

College of Music in Berlin. He accepted the appointment in 1920 and remained in it until 1932; he also took over a composition class there.

Some of Schreker's best pupils in Vienna followed him to Berlin; among them Karol Rathaus, Ernst Křenek and Alois Hába. Georg Schünemann, who was co-director with Schreker in 1920, gave this description of the summer entrance examinations:

It was amazing how much the young students who came from Schreker's class were able to do. We set them contrapuntal tests with both strict and free setting, heard one fugue after another for voices or for instruments, gave them themes for modulation and improvisation, ear-tests and tests for musicianship—the students were well versed in all of these. I have been present at many examinations since that time, but never again have I experienced so high a standard. Suddenly the composition classes received a fresh incentive and new vigour. An abundance of talented students surrounded Franz Schreker; indeed it was the highest ambition of many to be accepted into his class. But the examination which Schreker had devised remained a very stiff one; most applicants were rejected and only a few were admitted into his circle of pupils.

According to Ernst Křenek, who studied under Schreker from 1916 to 1921, he educated his students on a basis of self-criticism, originality and hard work.

During his first years in Berlin, Schreker concerned himself primarily with his duties as director and teacher and his creative work inevitably had to take second place. At that time he was working on an opera *Irrelohe* (he had already written the libretto in 1919), as well as an arrangement of his ballet *The Birthday of the Infanta* as an orchestral suite. *Irrelohe* was first performed in Cologne in 1924 under Otto Klemperer, but was less enthusiastically received than the three main works of which *Der Schatzgräber* (after its première in Frankfurt in 1920) enjoyed the greatest popularity.

Berlin was gradually recovering from the consequences of its collapse after the German defeat, and was now developing into one of the great intellectual centres of Europe. Schreker was able to call on such men as the pianist Artur Schnabel, the violinist Carl Flesch and the young cellist Emanuel Feuermann to become teachers at the College. In 1920, Ferruccio Busoni had been summoned from exile in Zurich and appointed teacher of a master class in composition at the Academy of Arts. Erich Kleiber, then a young man, soon brought new ideas to the State Opera, that stronghold of tradition, when he became its Musical Director. After the death of Arthur Nikisch, Wilhelm Furtwängler was to become conductor of the Philharmonic Orchestra.

Busoni died in 1924 and Arnold Schoenberg became his successor. His friendship with Schreker, dating from the time of their early struggles in Vienna before the First World War, now grew even stronger. In the greeting which Schoenberg (the elder by four years) sent to Schreker on his fiftieth birthday he wrote: 'We come from those good old days when those who were unsympathetic to our ideas were recognizable as such by calling us "New-sounders". How can we possibly come to terms with the present when they label us "Romantics"?' Here Schoenberg is alluding to a bitter experience which he shared with Schreker, the enmity of the anti-romantic ascetics.

The ideal of the 'objective' young musicians at that time was embodied in Paul Hindemith. This, however, did not deter Schreker from appointing him to the College as teacher of composition in 1927. Hindemith, incidentally, never joined the 'radicals' in their baiting of Schreker and Schoenberg; in the last ten years of his life he repeatedly gave them his support as a conductor. Nevertheless, around 1930 the success of Schreker's operas began to dwindle. The young musicians, insofar as they were not influenced by political considerations, turned to the classicist imitations of Stravinsky or the intellectual music of Hindemith. The rich tone-colour of Schreker's scores was as alien to them as the erotic psychology of his libretti or the slow-moving iridescence of his harmonic thought. The fact that Schreker's music had suddenly developed to an amazing degree in such later works as *Der singende Teufel* (The Singing Devil) of 1928 or *Der Schmied von Gent* (The Blacksmith of Ghent) seems to have been overlooked. That both these operas were unable to establish themselves in the public mind despite their outstanding premières in Berlin, must have been due to the fact that his poetic gifts were fading. In *Der singende Teufel* Schreker goes back to an archaic style as the basis of his music. The introductory two-part movement for organ shows a pre-tonal technique which fuses with modern harmonies in fourths and fifths achieving a stylistic 'bridge' between these different periods. The former profusion of sound is even further supplanted by a renewal of the spirit of primitive counterpoint. The orchestral texture appears thinner, dominated by the quality of the organ superimposed above the celeste. In this work, Schreker approached the aesthetics of neo-classicism. His style was still more simplified and intensified in *Der Schmied von Gent*. Simple forms, often with a religious basis, such as the pastorale at the entry of Mary with Joseph and the child, the funeral march, or the passacaglia of Count Alba, give the opera its shape. The title of the work is *Grosse Zauberoper* (Grand Fairy-Tale Opera) and it is clearly based on works by the Viennese authors, Raimund and Nestroy.

For Schreker, too, poetry is 'the obedient daughter of music', but in quite a different sense from Mozart's original idea. The whole of Schreker's talent can only be explained in terms of his music. His imagination, intelligence, naivety and sensuousness are of a kind only found amongst musicians. And so any consideration of his creative work must always return to the point of departure: to the analysis of his scores or, to be more exact, to the total sound picture of which the scores and piano arrangements can give only a faint indication.

In 1919 Schreker was asked what he considered to be his idea of music-drama. He answered:

I haven't really got one. I write without a plan. Whatever I think of is there. However, I proceed from the music. My ideas have very little literary quality. Strange spiritual feelings struggle for musical expression. Around these is entwined an external action which spontaneously bears its own musical form and organization in its very origin. With the completion of the libretto, I can already see, in general outline, the musical structure of the work.

Schreker's individual tonal language is treated with great virtuosity in *Die Gezeichneten*. The trills in D major and B flat minor which begin the prelude are the essence of a musical score whose richness of colour depends not only on the differentiation of the traditional string and wind tone but also on a hyper-sensitive and novel use of the glockenspiel, deep bells, harps, xylophone, celeste and piano. This new percussion tone, first introduced in 1910 in Schoenberg's orchestral writing became, after 1950, an integral part of the music of the generation of Pierre Boulez and Hans Werner Henze, and was also of great importance to the development of Alban Berg.

Schreker's music is rooted in the traditions of Austro-Germany, where he grew up and came to maturity. His kinship with Gerhart Hauptmann and Frank Wedekind shows him as belonging to the German naturalist theatre, although the gentle mists of French or Belgian symbolism occasionally pervade his scenes. His musical language shows links with France and Italy; Schreker integrated into his work not only the orchestral media of Debussy and Paul Dukas but also the impassioned singing style of Puccini. Thus Schreker can be seen as an exceptionally European figure in the history of twentieth-century opera.

In his use of harmony Schreker stood at the very edge of tonality, sometimes closer to the bitonal thought of the younger French musicians than to the 'secessionism' of Vienna to which he belonged. In retrospect his bi-tonality has revealed itself as an historically important stage in the development of the new music.

Schreker spent much of the last five years of his life travelling, and bought himself a holiday home at Estoril on the Portuguese Atlantic coast. His last opera *Christophorus* had been accepted by Freiburg for a first performance there in 1932. On hearing this news the Nazi press began to harass Schreker so unmercifully that he withdrew the work. For the same reason he resigned his post as director of the College at the end of 1932. When he returned to Berlin from Estoril in the autumn of 1933 he was told that he had been permanently relieved of his office. On 18 December he suffered a stroke from which he never recovered. The last months of his life were tormented, both for him and his devoted wife. Abused by the German press, expelled from all his posts for being half-Jewish, almost without financial means, his works no longer performed in Germany, he vegetated, mortally ill and often lying in a semi-conscious state.

After the collapse of fascism in Europe Schreker's music never regained its earlier importance. Only *Der ferne Klang* was revived in Germany by radio performances and in a few stage revivals. Nevertheless Schreker had dominated an important era in the musical history of Germany.

9 Ernst Křenek

On 29 January 1927 the Leipzig Opera House caused a sensation by staging the first performance of the jazz opera, *Jonny spielt auf*. The composer was twenty-seven-year-old Ernst Křenek, a Viennese pupil of Franz Schreker. It was his third attempt at opera, and the result of two years' work. The success of the new work was assured, although some critics rejected it in no uncertain terms. 'The art that Schubert extols in song as holy', one of them wrote, '. . . has been debased and prostituted.'

The eponymous hero of the opera is the jazz violinist Jonny, and his caricature is embodied in the virtuoso Daniello. Their opposite number is a composer called Max, an intellectual Eastern European, tortured by inhibitions, who is clearly a self-portrait of Křenek. The action takes place in a social setting modelled on the picture of American materialism and opportunity which was characteristic of the wishful thinking of many young people in Germany after the First World War. Křenek's music was as surprising as the action of the opera, for stylistically its debt to operetta is unmistakable. The composer, who tries here to flatter the ear of the average listener with jazz rhythms and cantilenas in the manner of Puccini, had written in a very different manner at the start of his career.

Born in Vienna on 23 August 1900, Křenek received his first music lessons at the age of six. He was accepted as a very young student at the Vienna State Academy of Music and by the age of sixteen he was studying composition under Franz Schreker. Křenek later wrote about the intellectual climate surrounding Schreker at that period: 'These artists were interested in unusual, often eccentric subjects, not without pathological and morbid implications. Their ideal for a work of art was of something strange, unique and free of obvious, traditional and popular features.' Schreker's teaching comprised a strict study of counterpoint with Bach and Reger as models.

After military service Křenek studied philosophy at the University and in 1920 followed Schreker to Berlin, attending his composition class at the *Hochschule für Musik* until 1923. During this period the early radical works were written: three symphonies, three string quartets, a concerto grosso, numerous piano works, including the big *Toccata* and *Chaconne,* as well as three totally contrasting operas.

Křenek belonged to a circle of young composers that embodied a new stylistic movement during the early twenties. At the second Festival of Chamber Music in Donaueschingen in 1922 Křenek's *Symphonic Music* for nine solo instruments was performed, and two of his string quartets were heard during the festivals of the Society for New Music in Salzburg in 1923 and 1924. He had avoided any obvious use of Schreker's ideas but was already attracted by Schoenberg's atonal musical idiom.

These early works are unconditionally ascetic and unsensuous. Their renunciation of conventional beauty of sound was more radical than that of any other of these young composers. Křenek himself thinks the Second Symphony of 1922 the most important work written during these years. It was first performed in 1923 at a German Musicians' Festival in Kassel. According to Křenek the finale created the impression of an imminent collapse of the hall or some other catastrophe. The emotional and explosive character of this music needed to find a release in drama.

Křenek's first opera *Die Zwingburg* (The Oppressor's Castle), in which Franz Werfel collaborated on the libretto, seems hampered by abstractions. A grotesque comic opera *Der Sprung über den Schatten* (The Leap across the Shadow) followed soon afterwards and this in turn was succeeded by the setting of an expressionist libretto *Orpheus and Eurydike* by the painter and poet Oskar Kokoschka. Its action, like all Křenek's later operas, is motivated by the ideas of freedom and the individual. Křenek was and is a thinking musician who looks at the world and at humanity and history with a critical eye, beyond the limits of his craft. He himself speaks of the two forces behind his creative output: 'Early in my career I was attracted by the idea of pure, uncompromising creation, independent of the fashions of the day, and even explicitly opposed to them.' He then continues: 'At the same time I always felt the temptation to achieve practical results "in this world".'

In Berlin Křenek met many people who influenced him in different ways. Among these were the great pianist Artur Schnabel, the conductor Hermann Scherchen, the pianist, composer and brilliant teacher, Ferruccio Busoni, and Mahler's daughter, the young sculptress Anni Mahler, to whom he was married for a short time.

The Swiss patron of music, Werner Reinhardt, was attracted by Křenek's extraordinary gifts. At Reinhardt's invitation Křenek spent 1924 and 1925 in Switzerland. Here, and in France, he was deeply influenced by different ways of life, and he established contacts with composers such as Darius Milhaud who represented a point of view less esoteric than his own.

On his return to Germany he became assistant to Paul Bekker, the director of the State Theatre in Kassel. For Křenek this return, in the autumn of 1925, was far from agreeable. However he derived much enjoyment from his various activities as conductor, composer of incidental music, collaborator in the writing of programme notes and, above all, from acquaintance with all the mechanical and institutional problems of the theatre. In 1927 he followed Paul Bekker from Kassel to the Opera House in Wiesbaden.

The result of Křenek's contact with a more southern climate and mental attitude and the almost seductive atmosphere of the theatre was *Jonny spielt auf,* composed between 1925 and 1926 with a libretto written by himself. The immediate and continued success of this work gave Křenek financial independence. He left his post in Wiesbaden and, after long deliberation, chose his native Vienna as a permanent home. Since 1924 he had grown less and less loyal to the modern cause, and he now decided to develop the more reflective side of his nature.

In 1926 Křenek gave a lecture in which, with youthful impetuosity, he attacked Schoenberg's twelve-note technique. But the resulting conflict worried Křenek deeply, and after the completion, in 1929, of the Schubertian *Reisetagebuch aus den Österreichischen Alpen* (Travel diary from the Austrian Alps), a song cycle set to his own words, he made peace with various members of the Schoenberg circle. His enthusiastic support of Schoenberg's cause from then on removed the tension, and Alban Berg and Anton von Webern became members of his small, select circle of friends. In addition to the Viennese followers of Schoenberg, the critic and brilliant satirist, Karl Kraus, had a decisive influence on Křenek. Kraus was a man of great moral integrity whose critical prose became the model for Křenek's own literary efforts.

During these years Křenek became a writer of distinction; his published work includes a wide variety of subjects in addition to music. From 1930 he contributed regularly to the cultural review of the *Frankfurter Zeitung*. Among his articles is a series of travel reports that were collected in 1959 in the volume *Gedanken unterwegs* (Thoughts en route) for Křenek was an enthusiastic traveller. While still living in Vienna he visited North Africa in 1929, Spain in 1934, and the United States in 1937.

In 1930 he established personal contact with Karl Kraus, realizing one of his oldest ambitions. He set to music several poems by Kraus, incorporating twelve-note material into a tonal idiom. During this period his output was influenced by his opposition to the increasingly fascist tendencies in the political life of Germany and Austria. Clemens Krauss, the director of the Vienna State Opera, asked him for a dramatic work. Křenek chose a historical subject touching on Austria's fate: *Karl V*. This score, which occupied him from 1930 to 1933, expresses Křenek's final acceptance of the twelve-note technique. In the libretto Křenek united realism with fantasy and developed with daring poetic strength the dramatic innovations of Paul Claudel and Bertolt Brecht.

The Habsburg Emperor Charles V is not only the hero of the drama; he also mirrors the divided loyalties of the intellectual during the transition from the Middle Ages to the Renaissance. Luther, Francis I of France, Sultan Solyman and Pope Clement VII are introduced as his adversaries. The drama develops as a self-justification of the old emperor who is admonished by the voice of God issuing from a picture by Titian. The music uses the spoken word side by side with pure vocal forms, polyphonic choruses and symphonic orchestral material.

Political events prevented the performance of this work in Vienna. Its Catholicism was in opposition to every tenet of National Socialism. The *Anschluss* had not yet taken place but the ruling reactionary political outlook in Austria was opposed to progressive thinking in the arts. By the time the German Opera House in Prague first performed *Karl V* in 1938, Austria had already been occupied by Hitler.

From 1935 to 1937 Křenek was busy lecturing and conducting. In Vienna his many activities included organizing concerts of contemporary chamber music, acting as Austrian delegate to the International Society for Contemporary Music and fulfilling his rôle as president of the Union of Dramatic Authors and Stage Composers. After his second journey to America in 1938 he remained in the United States. He was appointed professor at Vassar College and from 1942 to 1947 at Hamline University. Thereafter he was a visiting professor at several other universities and academies of music. He became a United States citizen in 1945, and settled in Los Angeles two years later.

His teaching in America led to an intensive study of medieval polyphony and of the history of music. He was especially fascinated by the fifteenth and sixteen centuries and by the Flemish composer Jean de Ockeghem in particular. These studies influenced his own compositions, which, after *Lamentatio Jeremiae Prophetae*, used an attractive synthesis of twelve-note techniques and medieval counterpoint. In the United States Křenek has written a great many works in almost every genre: operas, symphonies, chamber music, piano works, motets and sacred and secular choral works, mostly unaccompanied.

Since 1950 he has frequently travelled to Europe for concert and lecture tours. His contact with the younger generation of European composers has been mutually beneficial. He took part in experiments with serial techniques in Darmstadt and with electronic sounds in Cologne. He invented the term 'totally pre-determined music' referring to compositions in which pre-selected series determine all the parameters of sound—pitch, duration, timbre, dynamics and density; Křenek's *Sestina* for soprano, violin, guitar, flute, clarinet, trumpet and percussion is one of the most radical examples of this type of music. His interest in electronic music has its roots in the work he did for Cologne Radio during 1955 and 1956. The most important result of these investigations is *Spiritus Intelligentiae, Sanctus,* a Pentecost oratorio for voices and electronic sounds. While engaged in these experimental compositions Křenek continued to write dramatic works. Between 1940 and 1950 he wrote several smaller operas such as *What Price Confidence, Dark Waters* and the full-length *Tarquin*.

In 1955, after working for several years, he completed a commission by the Hamburg State Opera, *Pallas Athene weint* (Pallas Athene Weeps). Nine years later the same opera-house gave the first performance of Křenek's *Der Goldene Bock* (The Golden Ram). In both operas classic-mythological subjects are allied with contemporary sociological criticism. *Der Goldene Bock* has an element of surrealist fantasy created, in part, by electronic sounds in addition to conventionally produced music. None of these operas achieved the success of the 'youthful sins' as he himself has since felt compelled to describe them or the magnificent dramatic concept of *Karl V*, which is arguably his finest work.

The United States discovered, developed and promoted the teacher in Křenek, and life there has made a citizen of the world of the devout Austrian Catholic. Before his emigration he had married an actress. After many years the marriage ended in divorce in California. Křenek then married a former pupil, a highly gifted composer of Norwegian descent. The American West fulfilled his longing for a life in the sun. He worked with phenomenal facility, often on several works simultaneously, most of them being performed and published in America and Europe. More honours have been bestowed on Křenek than on most other contemporary composers. The catalogue of his works exceeds one hundred opus numbers, and there are, in addition, countless transcriptions and minor works such as incidental music for the stage and films.

Křenek's theoretical and historical works testify to an imposing range of interests. He has published studies on the modal counterpoint of the sixteenth century and on the tonal counterpoint of the eighteenth. He has edited musicological studies at Hamline University and in an important little book *De Rebus Prius Factis* he has investigated the connection between medieval contrapuntal techniques and modern serial methods of composition. The Viennese lectures on New Music of 1936-7 are collected in a book overflowing with ideas and information. His collected essays on music, which were published in 1958 under the ingenious title *Zur Sprache gebracht* (Induced to Speak), contain writings of astonishing profundity of thought and power of expression.

The conflicting elements which Křenek himself has observed in his emotional make-up have led time and again to dialectical struggles. He is endowed with great mental powers of receptivity and, like Mozart, he has studied and successfully exploited a great variety of different stimuli. As a young man he adopted Schoenberg's atonal musical language. Under the twin influences of French thought and a southern climate he became a neo-classicist, while in 1927 he used contemporary American dance forms, only to return to strict twelve-note techniques soon afterwards. In his maturity he has remained equally open to influence.

He has the enviable capacity of being able to pursue any idea to its inevitable conclusion, even *ad absurdum*. None of the young European composers has pursued the new techniques and the aesthetic consequences arising from their use more radically than Křenek. In the fields of total serialization and of aleatoric liberation he consciously stretched these principles to their most extreme possibilities, yet not without close critical analysis of his own technical procedures.

In a television opera *Ausgerechnet und verspielt* (Calculated and Lost), 1962, Křenek's dramatic idea is based on a contest between a game of roulette and a computer. In *Der goldene Bock* the limitations of time and space are disregarded in the spirit of mythological parody. Thus the action takes place simultaneously in the Greece of Jason and Medea and on the elegant Florida beach of Amédé and Sonja, whose names are anagrams of Medea and Jason. The 'Golden Ram' of Greek mythology is carried by aeroplane and motorcar across space and time. This subject has much in common with experiments made by Jean Cocteau's circle in the twenties. Křenek expresses it in music that combines twelve-note and serial techniques with electronic sounds recorded on tape.

Křenek has repeatedly expounded his attitude to electronic music. He is especially attracted by the possibility of fixing musical events permanently during the process of composition. Total freedom in mastering the sound-material leads to a total rigidity of reproduction. Křenek has also thoroughly examined the mathematical and physical foundations of electronic and serial music. Unlike younger composers, he has never allowed himself to be hypnotized by the magic of mathematical procedures to the extent of obscuring the exactness of his terminology. Where he has come across false pseudo-mathematical reasoning in writings about music, he has unequivocally rejected them as charlatanism. He has thus turned out to be an uncomfortable partisan of, and collaborator with certain schools of contemporary music.

This warm-hearted man, bound in friendship to countless important figures of his era, has nevertheless remained a solitary figure. His view of the world was formed by his classical education as much as by his Catholicism and his Austrian origins, and there is an evident dichotomy of his personality.

No episode of his life is more characteristic of Křenek than his relations with the poet Rainer Maria Rilke. He was twenty-four when he met the forty-nine-year-old poet in Switzerland. The two men became friends. In 1925, a year before his death, Rilke, who was usually unenthusiastic about the musical settings of his poetry, wrote a small trilogy *O Lacrimosa* for the young Austrian musician. Křenek, who was then a conductor in Kassel, set the three poems to music and sent them to Rilke. The poet received the songs on his death-bed and in words that reflect his emotion thanked Křenek for a gift for which he himself had provided the original stimulus. The *Lacrimosa* songs are among the most intimate inspirations that Křenek has published. They are pervaded by the same longing and desire for escape from the world which has been expressed in countless poems by Rilke as a last salute to a vanishing European Austria.

10 Paul Hindemith

A small, stocky, well-proportioned man, with friendly blue eyes,
stands in a large group of young people. He is talking to them
about musical inspiration. 'Don't rely on divine inspiration' he says.
'Composing is work. Those who are lazy have no musical ideas.
Get up early, exercise your body, then the spirit will move in you.
Don't think that you are geniuses!' It is Paul Hindemith speaking to his pupils. He talks with a south German accent because he
was born, on 16 November 1895, the son of simple people, in
the small, old town of Hanau.

The family came from Silesia and belonged to the artisan class.
Paul went to elementary school and learned to play the violin.
By the age of thirteen he was a virtuoso, and he soon learned to
earn money by all kinds of music-making. He played for dances,
in light theatre-orchestras, and in cinemas. In 1909 he became a
student at the Hoch Conservatory in Frankfurt and studied
composition with Arnold Mendelssohn and Bernhard Sekles. In 1915
the musical director of the Frankfurt Opera House, Ludwig Rottenburg, engaged the twenty-year-old Hindemith as leader of the
orchestra, and in the same year, the young musician founded a
string quartet with the violinist Licco Amar, and became its viola
player.

From 1917 to 1918 Hindemith served in the army. But soon after
the end of the first world war, his emergence as a composer began
and from then on until 1929 he was an advocate of the most
extreme forms of contemporary music.

In the years between 1919 and 1924, when the German economy
was struggling to recover from total collapse, artistic activity was
confined to literature and the visual arts. There was new music

but it was felt to be an echo of the nineteenth century; it was not new in the exclusive, anti-romantic way of Gottfried Benn's poetry or the paintings of Emil Nolde or Karl Schmidt-Rottluff.

Despite the advances made by the Schoenberg school towards a musical world unfettered by tonality, the rhythmic power of Stravinsky and Bartok was felt to be a truer expression of the times. Many aimed at music that expressed the New Objectivity (*Neue Sachlichkeit*), a musical language that sought to replace Tristan's ecstasies of love by a more muscular approach. Man himself had become subject to mechanical forces, manipulated by the power of technological achievement.

Hindemith's first successes were due to the fact that these ideas were believed to be present in his compositions. And they did undoubtedly form a part of his musical personality, as, for example, his pragmatic manner of dealing with notes, sounds and rhythms. Nevertheless, some of his compositions were critical of their times as well as expressive of them. But Hindemith always worked both as composer and as practical musician, and his prestige as a performer of chamber music counteracted the displeasure these compositions caused.

Hindemith remained a practical and practising musician even after he had won world-wide acclaim. His time was constantly divided between creative and practical music-making. During the mornings he would rehearse with his quartet and in the afternoons would compose in his hotel room or on a train journey; wherever, in fact, he found the opportunity to fill manuscript paper with his slender and accurate musical handwriting. In the evenings there would be concerts. His early fame rested on chamber music, string quartets, song cycles, choral pieces and sonatas, which he helped to perform from 1921 onwards at the festival at Donaueschingen, of which he was one of the prime innovators. From 1923 onwards, his music was performed in Salzburg at the festivals of the International Society for Contemporary Music. Even Richard Strauss, who showed little understanding of Hindemith's generation, acknowledged his talent and the soundness of his craftsmanship.

But for the admirers of his chamber-music and of the early songs after poems by Georg Trakl, Else Lasker-Schüler and Christian Morgenstern, there was a shock in store. Between 1921 and 1923 Hindemith wrote three one-act operas whose libretti, by Oskar Kokoschka, August Stramm and Franz Blei each expressed the spirit of the times in different ways. Each opera deals with a sexual problem. Blei's *Nusch-Nuschi,* with its castration scene and *Tristan* quotation, caused a scandal at its first performance in Stuttgart. These works led to the jazz parodies of the *Piano Suite 1922* and to the *Kammermusik* for small orchestra (Opus 24). Hindemith's title-drawing to the Piano Suite is reminiscent of the drawings of metropolitan life by George Grosz. The ice-cold, sarcastic attitude of the dance movements of this suite is reflected in major works such as the opera *Neues vom Tage* (News of the Day), 1929, with its cabaret character, and it is also echoed in later works.

One of the movements of the *Piano Suite 1922,* the *Nachtstück* (Nocturne), shows an entirely different spirit, no less part of Hindemith's expressive range. It is a dark, gloomy lament, an expression of the emptiness behind the frantic quest for pleasure during the years of inflation in Germany. This movement is related to Hindemith's religious song-cycle *Das Marienleben* (The Life of Mary) which he wrote in 1924. Its severe tragedy is far removed from any romantic pathos. Tragedy is approached objectively, and self-revelation is replaced by the presentation of the factual description of emotion.

After 1924, the year in which Hindemith married Gertrud Rottenberg, religious feeling affected his output more and more. An objective religious belief and awareness of metaphysical truths and the divine principle are important features of his personality; as are irony, the humour of an 'enfant terrible', variety and objectivity.

All his life Hindemith showed an enviable creative facility. No branch of composition was difficult for him. He was capable of composing a movement for string quartet in the dining-car on the way to Donaueschingen and of performing it the same evening. His pupils were always enthusiastic about the ease with which he could solve the most difficult technical problems that might confront them, a gift that Schoenberg also admired. No problem posed by modern music was neglected by him. His compositions for mechanical piano and the music to Oskar Schlemmer's *Triadic Ballet* for a small mechanical organ were performed in Donaueschingen in 1926. A year later the Festival was transferred to Baden-Baden, and several 'Miniature Operas' were performed, a new kind of music drama that was originated by Hindemith. In Hindemith's own *Hin und Zurück,* a crime story by Marcellus

Schiffer, the text and the music are both played backwards when the middle is reached. *Songspiel,* and *Mahagonny* by Bertolt Brecht and Kurt Weill, the fairy-tale *The Princess and the Pea* by Ernst Toch and Darius Milhaud's *opéra minute, L'enlèvement d'Europe* were also given.

During journeys with his quartet across half of Europe Hindemith produced a rich and varied series of works. In 1924 he wrote a dance-pantomime *The Demon,* a piano concerto, a clarinet quintet, two violin sonatas and a duo for flutes, a string quartet, a string trio and the songbook for mixed choir, based on old poems. In 1925 he composed *Serenaden* (a short cantata based on romantic poems), and several chamber concertos (Opus 38), while 1926 was devoted to *Cardillac,* a full-length opera with libretto by Ferdinand Lion, based on the short story *Das Fräulein von Scuderi* by E. T. A. Hoffmann. After the expressionism and eroticism of the earlier short operas, *Cardillac,* with its use of absolute musical forms, often in a paradoxical baroque idiom, is a different kind of protest against the aesthetics of emotive music.

In addition to his various musical and literary activities Hindemith had always taught, and in 1927 Franz Schreker asked him to take charge of a composition class at the Berlin Hochschule für Musik. Here he entered a new world which he found immensely rewarding. One of his first pupils was the Swiss harpsichordist Silvia Kind. She reports:

Hindemith loved to organize hikes in the countryside with his class. Usually he would provide a huge joint for spit-roasting while we pupils had to bring the *Stullen* (large slices of bread and butter) as well as a round or canon composed by each of us for the sing-song. Hindemith was never annoyed by bad work, but he did not forgive me for a long time his failure to teach me a proper handstand or that his team lost a swimming race through me . . . His great passion was the railway. He possessed about nine hundred yards of model railway track and the most sophisticated electric equipment with remote-control points and signals . . . Frau Hindemith told us that Hindemith and his friends would often appear pale and exhausted at two or three in the morning and ask for schnaps, especially if Artur Schnabel, another railway fanatic, was present.

On his teaching methods Silvia Kind relates:

Hindemith considered of basic importance the invention of a well constructed and organic melody in the manner of Gregorian plainsong

and later the addition of an equally well-balanced counter-melody ...
He demanded further that every exercise should be written with specific
instruments in mind.

Hindemith himself was the eternal student. Between 1927 and
1937 (later more in Ankara than in Germany) he read and studied
incessantly. He studied languages, and history and devoted himself
to musicology. He was possessed by a humanistic desire for
knowledge. Yet the same man who perused thick folios in the
State Library and discussed plainsong with Johannes Wolf wrote
in 1929 the cheekily Offenbachian *Neues vom Tage*. He wanted to
play all the musical instruments. He attempted to master the horn
and the trumpet, the oboe and clarinet, and even acquired the
oriental trick of breathing through his nose while playing the flute.
He practised the piano and reputedly sang duets in private with
his wife who was a good soprano.

Hindemith's renunciation of his youthful revolutionary attitudes
led, in 1930, to his collaboration with the poet Gottfried Benn. The
oratorio *Das Unaufhörliche* (The Perpetual), completed in 1931 and
conducted by Otto Klemperer in an unforgettable performance, is
the beginning of a new creative period. Benn's denunciation of
modern man, the 'white race without myths', and his rejection of
materialism and relativism are as bold as his interpretation of history as perpetual decay and renewal. Hindemith's setting is almost
entirely polyphonic. The music follows the 'law of growth' formulated by Benn, and the musical forms develop from thematic
material contained in the first bars. All the stylistic features of the
earlier works, which later appeared to be continuations of older
traditions, are present. Ostinatos, strummed chords, towering
structures of fourths, mixed tonalities, the twin-layered metrical
structures and shifted rhythmic pivots are all present in this music,
as well as the pungent use of brass, the lyrical laments of the wood-
wind and the ruthless grimaces to meet ruthless words in the text.
Hindemith had met Brecht shortly before and written with him
the *Lehrstück* (Didactic Play) for Baden-Baden, a cruel contem-
plation of the truth that man does not help man.

All this happened while Nazism was growing. Hitler considered
Hindemith a degenerate intellectual who was alien to the people—
volksfremd—and a destructive force in German music. He never
forgave him the fact that in the comic opera *Neues vom Tage*, the

101

heroine Laura had to sing an aria sitting in her bath. Hindemith was world-famous when the Nazis came to power. His influence upon the younger generation of composers in all countries was profound. With his compositions for amateur choirs and instrumentalists and for school-children he had bridged the gap of prejudice that separated many people of good will from contemporary music. His *Schulwerk für Instrumental-Zusammenspiel* (School-work for Instrumental Ensemble-playing) in 1928, preceded that of Carl Orff by one year. His *Frau Musica,* based on words by Luther, became as popular with amateurs and music-lovers as the *Canons* for two voices and instruments. Hindemith was enthusiastic when the engineer Friedrich Trautwein introduced his electronic musical instrument, the Trautonium, at the Berlin Hochschule in 1930. In 1931 he wrote a Concertino for it.

The cultural representatives of the extreme political parties vied with each other to gain Hindemith's collaboration. Brecht's attempts to win him over to communism were thwarted by his collaboration with the right-wing Benn in the oratorio *Das Unaufhörliche.* The progressive musicians in a section of the Hitler Youth were equally unsuccessful. Hindemith recognized the necessity for a decision, and he made it by writing the libretto for his opera *Mathis der Maler,* a proud declaration in favour of the autonomy of art. The fate of this work affected both his own life and the cultural policies of Hitler's Reich. In 1933 the Nazis burned books by Jewish and anti-fascist writers in Berlin, as in *Mathis* the Papists burned Protestant writings. Albrecht, the tolerant Archbishop of Mainz, refuses to take part: 'I cannot sin against the spirit!'

At that time Wilhelm Furtwängler was at the head of the Berlin State Opera. He had believed in Hindemith for a long time and was resolved to perform his opera. When this plan was thwarted he performed instead three symphonic fragments from it, the *Symphony: Mathis der Maler,* at a concert by the Berlin Philharmonic Orchestra. It was a resounding success and the majority of the critics were enthusiastic. However the Nazi newspaper, the *Völkischer Beobachter,* protested: 'Furtwängler has committed a regrettable blunder . . . The case of Hindemith does not differ from that of . . . various artists, who for fourteen years have carried the flag of the old system and who are now being foisted upon us as revoluntionary supporters of the state.' Furtwängler answered on

102

Paul Hindemith

25 November 1934, in an article in the *Deutsche Allgemeine Zeitung:* 'What would be the result if unrestricted political denunciation were applied to the arts?' The article produced a storm which resulted in Furtwängler's resignation from all the positions he held and the total prohibition of performances of Hindemith's works.

The music to *Mathis* intensifies the expressive austerity of the *Marienleben*. Gregorian chant and old folk-songs are integrated into a dissonant musical language that employs church modes and classical tonality side by side with an all-prevailing chromaticism, transcending the limitations of tonality in the scene of the temptation of St Anthony, the masterpiece by Matthias Grünewald who is the protagonist of the opera.

Hindemith was still grudgingly allowed to continue teaching. He remained in Berlin, but in 1935 started to organize a conservatory of music in Ankara at the request of Kemal Ataturk, the creator of modern Turkey. He travelled abroad as a soloist and began a systematic review of his teaching experiences. The result was the writing of *Unterweisung in Tonsatz* (The Craft of Musical Composition) in which the chromatic scale is deduced from the first partials of the harmonic series. In accordance with the rules laid down in this work Hindemith later revised early compositions like the *Marienleben* and *Cardillac*. The idea of the tonic as a centre of gravity led to several philosophic hypotheses about the 'Harmony of the World'.

In 1937 Hindemith resigned from his professorship in Berlin and a year later he emigrated to Switzerland. In May 1938 the Zürich opera house gave the four-hour-long first performance of *Mathis der Maler* to an international audience. The enormous success of this performance has since been repeated in many parts of the world.

In 1937 the Elizabeth Sprague-Coolidge Foundation invited Hindemith to take part in the Eighth Festival of Chamber Music at the Library of Congress in Washington. It was his first visit to the United States. He played his *Solo Sonata for Viola* and the *Viola Concerto* based on old German folksong, *Der Schwanendreher*. The success of this American debut and of two further concert tours in 1938 and 1939 led in 1940 to Hindemith's departure from Europe. Yale University offered him a professorship which he held until 1953.

Up to the time of his emigration Hindemith produced an increasing flow of important works, exploring many different directions in his music. He wrote sonatas for almost all orchestral instruments as well as three each for piano and organ, concertos in a neo-baroque spirit, occasional works like the *Funeral Music* for King George V of England, the ballet *Noblissima Visione* for Leonid Massine and the ballet-music *The Four Temperaments,* conceived as a piano concerto in variations. The music Hindemith wrote in America has two outstanding features: an increasing virtuosity in the techniques of composition and orchestration and a greater profundity of polyphony and in the choice of texts for vocal music. The *Symphonic Metamorphoses* of 1943 on themes from Carl Maria von Weber and some of the piano pieces for four hands, also by Weber, are a standard work of orchestral virtuosity. Their immediate appeal comes from a technical mastery of the utmost refinement and subtlety. Almost simultaneously with this entertaining display of great techniques Hindemith wrote another masterly but less immediately accessible work, which shows him, as it were, in his workshop: the *Ludus Tonalis* for piano. Contrapuntal complications like fugue-subjects in inversion make it necessary to ask the eye to help the ear.

The impressive catalogue of works continues with English songs, a melodrama after Mallarmé's *Hérodiade,* two string quartets, a piano concerto, a ballet *Cupid and Psyche* and the *Sinfonia Serena.* For the second time Hindemith wrote an outstanding work under the impact of tragic events, the *Requiem 'When lilacs last in the dooryard bloom'd'* (1946). This setting of Walt Whitman in memory of the dead of the Second World War is a moving oratorio about transience, a pan-religious continuation of *Das Unaufhörliche.* In his vocal music, which is always thoughtful and committed, Hindemith seems to gather the materials from his teaching of the Harmonia Mundi, expressed in different form in his Harvard lectures and in the book *A Composer's World* of 1950.

Paul and Gertrud Hindemith returned to Europe, at first tentatively as guests, and then finally for good. Hindemith made many changes of residence, starting from the humble house belonging to his parents in Hanau, succeeded by the Sachsenhausen tower lent to him in 1924 by the city of Frankfurt, the elegant West End flat of the Berlin years, the wooden house in New Haven, and finally the villa in Blonay on Lake Geneva. The former revolutionary had

16 Ernst Křenek (b. 1900). More honours have been bestowed on Křenek than on most other contemporary composers. He has written over a hundred major works, plus countless transcriptions and minor pieces, such as incidental music for the stage and the cinema.

17 Franz Schreker (1878–1934) was an outstanding teacher as well as a composer. During his term as director of the Berlin Hochschule für Musik, from 1920 to 1933, he trained both Křenek and Alois Hába.

18 The South-German composer Paul Hindemith (1895–1963) resting during a hike through the woods. This astonishingly versatile musician and internationally renowned composer always retained his taste for simple, robust recreation.

19 Paul Hindemith at the end of the first performance of his *Harmonie der Welt* at the Bayrische Staatsoper.

20 Carl Orff (b. 1895) with the conductor Herbert von Karajan during a rehearsal for the first performance of his *Trionfi di Afrodite* in Milan in 1952. This work is subtitled *Concerto Scenico* and ends the cycle of three works which began with *Carmina Burana* (1935–6) and continued with *Catulli Carmina* (1943).

by now been given honorary doctorates by Berlin and other universities, made Professor Ordinarius in Zürich, Knight of the Order *Pour le Mérite,* and holder of the Hamburg Bach Prize and the Sibelius Prize. The practical musician now became a philosopher. The study of St Augustine and Boethius led him to Johannes Kepler and his coordination of planetary motion and harmony. The result was the opera *Die Harmonie der Welt* (The Harmony of the World), a strange work that alternates between tract and vision and is a continuation of the committed attitude of *Mathis.* This drama, ending in a Brucknerian blaze, was followed by a short opera, based on Thornton Wilder's *Long Christmas Dinner,* which ends with an English Christmas carol.

Again and again Hindemith was attracted by practical musicmaking. It was to him a source of energy like the touch of the earth to Antaeus. He conducted more and more and, by working with the best European orchestras, especially in Germany and Switzerland, he achieved, after clumsy beginnings, a considerable technique. He attempted a new type of concert programme foreign to the classic-romantic conformity of the usual concert promoters. He became a champion of Bruckner and Reger and rescued the chamber symphonies of Schoenberg and Schreker from oblivion. He even performed works written in the twelve-note technique which he had rejected in theory. He championed the work of younger contemporaries like Karl Amadeus Hartmann and the Austrian Anton Heiller. Among his finest achievements as conductor of the Berlin Philharmonic are his realizations of medieval and renaissance music, Rondeaux and Ballades by Guillaume Machaut and poly-choral *Symphoniae Sacrae* by Giovanni Gabrieli.

The last years were clouded by failing health. Hindemith suffered from circulatory disorders and a weakened heart. He had to curtail his work and cancel concerts which were important to him. After *The Long Christmas Dinner* he wrote an organ concerto in 1962 which was destined for Anton Heiller. His last completed composition is a mass for unaccompanied mixed choir, an astringent, difficult work that is based on Gregorian motifs treated polyphonically in a dissonant manner, with dramatic outbursts in the *Resurrexit, Sanctus* and *Hosanna.* Hindemith wanted to conduct the first performance at the end of 1963 in Berlin. During the summer he fell ill, consulted a physician in Frankfurt and was

sent to hospital. He died on 28 December in his home town of
Hanau, to which he had instinctively returned.

After 1950 Hindemith rejected with increasing misgivings and
bitterness the revolutionary directions taken by musical composition. Untiringly he proclaimed his belief in the ear as the highest
arbiter in musical matters. He sceptically read the scores and
listened to the recordings of the Darmstadt experiments in serialism and those of Cologne in electronic music. When John Cage produced his sound mixtures and commented on them at the Berlin
Congress Hall in January 1963, Hindemith sat in the audience down-
cast and speechless.

As a musician who had himself experimented in so many forms
he had a sound basis for his opposition to the new developments.
Although among the composers of his era he was typically German
in his solid craftsmanship, he outgrew his provincial and national
limitations and thought on a European scale at a time when many
Germans followed a disastrously nationalistic doctrine. In the
United States he matured further and became aware of the unity
of the musical life of the world.

Hindemith has influenced the cultural life of the twentieth
century immeasurably. He was one of the creators of a musical
language which has made its way into the concert halls and opera
houses of the entire world.

As a personality, a musician and a thinker he grasped and
condensed the ideas of fifteen hundred years of western musical
composition, linking antiquity to the middle ages and the present;
he understood the heights and depths of his era as only very few
creative artists have done.

11 Carl Orff

In the announcement of a forthcoming biography of Carl Orff by
Andreas Liess it is said that Orff is one of the few contemporary
composers who has escaped from the ivory tower of modern music
and gained a wider audience. He is also said to be the brilliant
re-creator of music-drama. However, the question is not one of
modernity or non-modernity, but rather of the function ascribed
to music in Orff's works for the theatre. Its role is completely different from that given to it in the entire body of operatic writing from
Monteverdi to Wagner, even including such extremes as the early
Florentine attempts at opera and the 'reformed operas' of Gluck.

Orff was born in Bavaria in 1895, the same year as Paul Hindemith. He was the son of a Bavarian officer and received a good
education at one of the grammar schools in his home-town of
Munich. He showed an early talent for music, learning first the
piano and later the cello and organ, and composed songs and music
for puppet plays while still at school. Collections of his songs were
printed as early as 1911 and an enormous choral work based on
Nietzsche's *Also sprach Zarathustra* was written at about the same
time. In addition he showed even at this early age a creative
interest in classical languages and natural history.

In 1913 Orff became a student at the Munich Music Academy,
studying composition under such relatively modern teachers as
Anton Beer-Walbrunn and Hermann Zilcher. He soon left the
Academy and from 1915 to 1917 gained practical experience composing and directing music for the Munich *Kammerspiele,* then
among the most modern theatre companies in Germany. In the last
part of the First World War Orff joined the army for a short
period and thereafter became opera director in Manniheim and

Darmstadt. His first attempt at opera, using his own libretto based on a Japanese model, dates from 1913. All his early works are stylistically influenced by Claude Debussy, Strauss, and Hans Pfitzner.

After the war Orff finally returned to Munich in 1919 where he has been living ever since. His circle of friends, who frequently became his pupils later, included Werner Egk and Heinrich Sutermeister, two composers who concerned themselves primarily with the theatre. At the age of twenty-six Orff came strongly under the influence of Heinrich Kaminski who was reviving polyphony, the old concerto grosso and baroque music in general. Orff became his pupil for a year and a vital interest in renaissance and baroque music has remained with him since that time. The works of Claudio Monteverdi in particular were one of the decisive experiences of his artistic career. In 1925 he published a free arrangement of *Orfeo,* in which the dance element was an important and integral part of the performance. Orff had taken an early and enthusiastic interest in the aesthetics of the 'new dance' as developed by Mary Wigmann and Rudolf von Laban. In 1924 he collaborated with the dancer Dorothée Gunther in setting up the Gunther School for Gymnastics, Music and Dancing in Munich. At the same time Orff began his study of non-European music, especially the music of Africa. Out of his practical work with the dancers grew two important and characteristic ideas: the percussion orchestra, played by the dancers themselves, and the *Schulwerk,* a collection of pieces for practical education in music, composed in 1930 in collaboration with Hans Bergese and the dancer Gunild Keetman.

In his early thirties Orff revised his early works, including an oratorio for double choir to texts by Franz Werfel, a series of cantatas to words by Werfel and Bertolt Brecht and a good deal of instrumental music. However, he finally withdrew all these works and started composing the pieces for the stage which soon made him famous. He became conductor of the Munich Bach Society, for whom he produced controversial stage performances of the spurious Bach *St Luke Passion,* and the *Resurrection* by Heinrich Schütz. The blending of modes of presentation in the border-region between opera and oratorio has remained an essential part of his work ever since. It also explains, paradoxically, the subordinated function of music in his own major dramatic works. Orff's disciples, such as Ernst Laaff or Andreas Liess, have repeatedly emphasized that the purely musical parts of his works should not be regarded in isolation. Rather, Orff's work should be understood 'with the intention of using music to weld language and movement into the same unity which existed in the ancient Greek drama'. Similar opinions had also been expressed about Wagner but without his adherents ever suggesting that his music should not be evaluated out of context. And when Orff himself states that he is concerned 'not with musical but with intellectual problems', he clearly shows the rigid boundaries within which he confines his musical statements.

In Orff's own view his collected works begin with the *Carmina Burana*. This work was published in Frankfurt in 1937 and in some strange way both artistic and political motives contributed to its success. Orff was never one of those musicians who were officially encouraged by the Hitler régime; his music, closer to Stravinsky than Wagner, was instinctively felt and welcomed as being in opposition to the prevailing aesthetic canon. The texts for *Carmina Burana* are taken from a thirteenth-century manuscript of the same name which is also Orff's source for the symbolic wheel of fortune in the first scene. The organization of these *Cantiones Profanae* into dramatic scenes is the product of Orff's visual imagination. In 1937 the wheel of fortune was understood to have a political significance since it showed how swiftly circumstances alter. His allegiance to Stravinsky, who was officially considered to be a 'cultural Bolshevik', struck a refreshing note at that time. Furthermore, the Stravinsky originals were too little known for it to be possible to identify the quotations from the *Symphony of Psalms* and the *Noces*. The visual effect, particularly of the comic episodes such as the lament on a roast swan, was unmistakable, and was not at all impaired by the use of primitive musical means such as the rigid emphasis on the tonic and dominant chords of D minor. Indeed, the effect of the music as a whole was no different from and no more independent than a good stage décor, and in fact this was precisely its function. A similar use of music reappears in Orff's later works even though the intellectual content and seriousness of his material may have developed.

Two years after the *Carmina Burana*, *Der Mond* (subtitled *Ein Kleines Welttheater*) was published in Munich, and four years later, shortly before the closure of all theatres during the war, *Die Kluge*, (subtitled *Die Geschichte von dem König und der klugen Frau*) appeared in Frankfurt. Both works made use of fairy-stories, and both reduce opera to a mere series of scenes, songs and dances of a monotonous and harmonically stunted type, in which the music in isolation has no meaning. At the same time the texts contain elements of criticism of various hallowed traditions and feelings which can give pleasure even to a modern, progressively-minded listener. Bertolt Brecht, who heard Walter Felsenstein's production of *Die Kluge* at the Comic Opera in East Berlin in 1948, was so delighted by its theatrical form that for weeks he attended nearly every performance of the work. Even the frequent repetition of parts of the text, which is a characteristic of Orff's style, is effective in this scenic context and does not sound incongruous as it does in other musical forms.

Orff's courage in going back to the basic elements of dramatic and musical art is clearly seen in the *Schulwerk* with its children's orchestra made up of xylophone, large and small tom-toms, small drums, cymbals, recorders, tambourines and other percussion instruments, as well as in the melodies of his dramatic works, which resemble old town cries or the monotony of a barrel-organ. To this extent the different under-currents of Orff's creative development, part pedagogic, part artistic, form a whole.

In 1939 Shakespeare's *A Midsummer Night's Dream* was produced with Orff's music at the Municipal Theatre in Frankfurt. He is not the only composer who has succumbed to the temptation of trying to produce incidental music to replace that by Mendelssohn, his works at that time being forbidden for racial reasons. The instrumental apparatus required was enormous, calling for a large battery of percussion including thunder and wind machines in addition to the traditional instruments. Orff revised the music twice, the last time in 1952 for Gustav Rudolf Sellner's production at the Darmstadt Theatre. It is impossible to free the work from the political odium associated with it, however much the stylistic intent may separate it from the realities of the Nazi era. At the end of the Second World War and shortly after, Orff wrote two plays, both in Bavarian dialect with incidental music, one a tragedy *Die Bernauerin*, requiring a large orchestra in the Wagnerian pattern, the other a satire drama *Astutuli*, using only percussion instruments for eight or nine players.

Orff's work on the Greek tragedies, the focal point of his output, began in 1947. *Antigone,* which was first performed at the Salzburg Festival in 1949, uses Hölderlin's translation of Sophocles. Orff had already considered a musical setting for this play as early as 1940 and had written down the first sketches for it in 1943. The orchestra uses no strings and only a few wind instruments but includes much percussion, as well as pianos, xylophones, glockenspiel and harps. Here the function of the music is entirely subordinate to the drama. It consists of a number of striking sound effects, and the ear soon tires of their constant repetition. Soft glissandos on the xylophones and fortissimo progressions in octaves on the pianos appear frequently, as do chanted repetitions of single phrases in the voice parts. Only the part of Antigone herself, with her three great scenes, has, musically speaking, anything richer to offer. Some parts, such as that of the night watchman using high falsetto notes, are set at the very limits of the vocal range. Orff's attempt to revive Hölderlin's form of Euripidean tragedy for the modern theatre fails because of its vocal setting, which renders the texts indistinct, although the deliberately simple technique obviously intended the opposite effect. However, this mastery of sound-effects brought Orff great success. With the prestige and hieratical structure of Greek tragedy his setting of *Antigone* reaped honours for him such as few other contemporary composers have enjoyed. He was made a member of the Bavarian Academy of Fine Arts and of the West Berlin Academy of Arts. From 1950 to 1960 he directed a master-class in composition at the Munich College of Music. In 1955 he received an honorary Doctorate of Philosophy from Tübingen University and in 1956 he was elected to the order *Pour le Mérite.*

Orff now belonged amongst the most famous and most often performed theatrical composers of the present time. Great singers like Elisabeth Grummer and Christel Goltz, Josef Hermann and Hermann Uhde were interpreting his music-dramas; Karl Böhm and Clemens Kraus, Ferenc Friscay and Joseph Keilberth had given first performances of his works; Rudolf Hartmann, Günther Rennert, Hans Schweikart, Oskar Fritz Schuh, Walter Felsenstein and Gustav Rudolf Sellner had translated his brilliant theatrical ideas into reality.

To the *Carmina Burana* and the stylistically similar *Catulli Carmina* of 1943, Orff now added a third, concluding work: the *Trionfi di Afrodite.* This work was written between 1950 and 1951 and has the subtitle *Concerto Scenico.* It was conducted by

Karajan in his own production at La Scala, Milan. It ends the cycle with a glorification of the Goddess of Love.

The three works together became known as the *Trionfi*. The name, derived from sixteenth-century theatrical terminology, is characteristic of a baroque style combining mythology and 'mechanical' comedy which was just then coming into fashion. Orff had studied all forms of the baroque theatre and had adopted in particular its representational and showy elements for his theatrical experiments. The baroque theatre is the theatre of extravagance, spectacle and surprise, of the greatest splendour in decoration and costume and also of great dramatic and vocal virtuosity. It may well be defined as 'pluralist' theatre in contrast to the relative simplicity and economy which have characterized the 'domestic' theatre since the nineteenth century.

This tendency to pile on scenic effects, to end with an apotheosis and to include deities and mythological beings in his plays is counteracted by a return to original, primitive forms of expression, to the simplest formulations of the text and equally simple movements by the actors. As Orff himself maintained: 'The simpler and the more significant the utterance, the more direct and striking is the effect.' Nevertheless he makes use of a colourful palette of scenic effects, taking his inspiration from the technical achievements of baroque theatre-designers such as Gali-Bibiena, from the 'World Theatre' of the Jesuits and from the extravagant scenery of courtly spectacles in the seventeenth century. The polarity of the two artistic concepts, an over-elaborate splendour on the one hand and primitive folk-entertainment on the other, is decisive for Orff's work as a whole.

His primitiveness is seen, above all, in his attitude to music. Just as in the *Schulwerk* he undertakes the education of small children from the very first stages through the playing of recorders and simple percussion instruments, leading them on to practical musicianship, so also in the ensembles of his theatre orchestra he uses the simplest tone-colours and sound resources in order to achieve striking stage effects. With Orff the ideal of sound is diametrically opposed to what it was in the nineteenth century. The expressive quality of string tone is absent; indeed, strings are often omitted altogether. An important part is played by percussion instruments, the number of which is increased and differentiated even more than v.as the case with Stravinsky. Orff exploits the percussive potential of the piano—again using Stravinsky, the *Noces* for instance, as his model. In this respect Orff's tonality approaches that of modern contemporary music, though in other ways it tends to be retrogressive. His melodic structure is primitive: in so far as it is not a chant around a frequently repeated note, it uses a simple repetition of small phrases which never develop to the extended form of a theme. The phrases of Orff's tunes are also elementary musical forms, that is, groups of four or eight beats. In this he looks back to a period long before classical music, earlier even than the baroque.

Apart from its technically ingenious devices, Orff's dramatic style also shows a tendency towards primitive theatre. As in the old peasant dramas, comic and macabre elements blend together, for instance in the scene with the corpse in *Der Mond*. The often coarse eroticism of Orff's scenes is conveyed by simple sensuous effects like the famous medieval 'bathroom' in *Die Bernauerin* where the stage directions provide for a large long tub in which all the young men and women are seated, bathing, playing and feasting. They sing a chorus which freely describes the agreeable characteristics of the female form:

A head from Bohemia, two soft arms from Brabant, a breast from Poland, from Carinthia two tits standing out like spears, a belly from Austria, soft and fleshy, two dainty little white feet from the Rhine. The cunt for preference from Bavaria and a fat arse from Swabia. An egg – a mouthful! A mass of hair – a handful! A woman – an armful! An arse – a bosomful! A cunt that's never full!

Here as elsewhere in his own texts he likes to go back to medieval or baroque sources, particularly those of his homeland, Bavaria. Culturally Bavaria is quite distinct amongst the German provinces. Here one still encounters forms of folk-dance and folk-song completely different from the traditional folklore of other regions such as Württemberg, Swabia, the Rhineland, Thuringia and Lower Saxony, or even that of northern and eastern provinces. There are certain cultural links with Austria, especially Salzburg and the Tyrol, as well as with Switzerland. One of these is the custom of yodelling, otherwise unknown in Central Europe, which is a type of singing with split chords and a characteristic alternation between a low register and high falsetto notes. Rhythmically, Bavarian folk music is interesting because of the occurrence of

5/8 time and an alternation of 3/4 and 6/8 time similar to that found in the Czech *Furiant* and some Spanish dances. The *Schuhplattler* dance, where a young man dances around a girl, slapping his knees and ankles between leaps, is, in itself, a transition from a simple dance to an erotic pantomime or wooing, a consequence of the Bavarian people's strong sense of the dramatic.

The peasant dramas, which are still a living force in Bavaria and have had much influence even on the Passion Plays at Oberammergau, draw on such dances for some of their representational effects. The special form of a February carnival which goes by the name of *Fasching* in Munich, and which dominates social life more than in most European cities, draws its strength from these popular traditional sources of mime, fancy-dress, acting and eroticism.

For this reason Bavaria has always produced strong dramatic talent, not only actors, singers and producers but also authors like Bertolt Brecht, composers like Richard Strauss and Werner Egk, and a master of sound effects such as Carl Orff. During the baroque period magnificent churches were built in Bavaria and baroque extravagance lives on even in the architectural curio-cabinets of the palaces built by Ludwig II.

To the pluralistic character of Orff's stage works must be added the inclusion of elements from ballet and oratorio. The great dance-scenes of the *Trionfi*, requiring a maximum amount of movement on stage, contrast with the almost complete immobility of the singers in many scenes of his classical plays. In this static quality and the many narrative episodes Orff comes very close to Brecht's concept of 'Epic Theatre'.

Orff found an unexpected confirmation of his dramatic intentions in the productions of Wieland Wagner. In fact the radical renewal of the Bayreuth *Festspiele* is hardly imaginable without Orff's influence. Wieland Wagner also looked back, as it were, to the origins of drama, interpreting his grandfather's work on the basis of those sources which had influenced him, from classicism to Calderòn. From 1951 Orff became a regular visitor to Bayreuth, although his own work based on the notion of the total work of art must be regarded as the very antithesis of Wagner's music. At the time of Orff's involvement with Wagner, the Bavarian authoress Luise Rinser became his second wife. The marriage was dissolved a few years later.

Carl Orff

The *Comoedia de Christi Resurrectione* was written in 1956 as a play for television and was performed on the stage in Stuttgart in 1957. In 1959 *Ödipus der Tyrann,* an adaptation of Sophocles in Hölderlin's translation, was produced by Günther Rennert in Stuttgart. The performance, lasting almost two hours without a break, was a theatrical event of major importance. Here music once again appears in the background as an independent element; it underlines the dramatic tension with an almost oriental type of singing, combined with ground bass and chords played by percussion and wind and plucked instruments. Orff's latest work goes back to another classical source, the *Prometheus* of Aeschylus. Its first performance took place in 1968, once again in the Stuttgart Theatre, this time under the direction of Gustav Rudolf Sellner. It brings to an end the series of classical tragedies which Orff has adapted for the musical theatre. Music as an independent art has gained nothing from his work. But the versatility of its function as a dramatic auxiliary has been studied by him in greater depth than ever before.

12 Vladimir Vogel

Vladimir Vogel was born in Moscow on 29 February 1896. His father, a commercial director of a textile firm, had originally come from Dresden but was married to a Russian. Both parents were keen and active musicians and Vogel consequently grew up in a strongly artistic atmosphere. Even before going to secondary school the boy began to study the piano and made his first attempt at composition, with a work sombrely entitled *Les Morts*. At an equally early age he developed a fascination for the Promethean music of Scriabin.

When war broke out in 1914 the Vogel family was evacuated from Moscow to the town of Burek in the Urals, where a whole colony of Germans spent a relatively peaceful, and at times even culturally stimulating, period of internment. By this time Vogel had reached the age of eighteen and was able to devote himself seriously to musical studies, assisted by P. A. Lamm, who extended his knowledge of instrumentation. His general education was further broadened by an immense amount of reading, both of classical and modern authors, as well as by attending lectures on a variety of cultural subjects.

In 1918 the period of internment was over. Vogel left Russia and moved to Berlin. At first he studied commercial art and then went on to set himself up as a window-dresser. A man of many talents and interests, Vogel sought the company of painters, musicians and architects and visited exhibitions of avant-garde art. Heinz Tiessen, one of the leading figures in modern music in Berlin, supervised his compositions and remained a friend of his for life. Other acquaintances included the physicist Albert Einstein and the conductor Hermann Scherchen.

In 1919 Scherchen began to gather round himself a circle of musicians bent on revolutionizing musical life. Scherchen, a man of the people and an enthusiast for new ideas, organized from scratch a whole network of enterprises in the cause of contemporary music. He conducted a series of unknown works by Schoenberg and introduced Berlin to the works of Stravinsky, Bartok and modern French and Italian composers. In 1920 he published the first edition of the journal *Melos,* which despite being temporarily silenced by the Nazis is still very much alive today.

The year 1920 was decisive for Vogel, for in that year Busoni returned from Zürich. The great pianist, composer and thinker was given charge of a master class for composition at the Prussian Academy of the Arts. Round him, too, a circle was soon formed, differing in many respects from Scherchen's, though it included some of the same people. They formed a modern equivalent of the early baroque *Camerata* in Florence, a cosmopolitan society of painters, writers, and musicians, including Egon Petri and Kurt Weill.

Vogel and four others were admitted to Busoni's master class. A year later Busoni said of the twenty-five-year-old composer, in the journal *Faust*: 'In addition to a native Russian spirit of rebellion against the existing and established order of things, he has a highly sensitive soul and deeply personal reactions'. Busoni instructed his class to set Goethe's poem *Die Bekehrte* to music and praised Vogel's effort as being 'if not technically the most assured, the most interesting . . . a characteristic example of new paths in music, something indicative rather than definitive'. Busoni taught a neo-classical approach to composition that ran counter to that of Schoenberg, whose style he considered to be expressionistic, and whose influence is reflected in some of Vogel's work—the young composer having been introduced to Schoenberg's music by Tiessen.

Vogel was often to be seen at the house of the painter Willy Jaeckel. There he met the artist's niece, Käthe-Katje Sommer, whom he later married. Jaeckel was well known for his portraits and Vogel composed music for strings and percussion to a series of his biblical etchings. In the same year, 1922, Vogel also composed three songs for low speaking voice and piano based on expressionistic poems by August Stramm. These form the germ cells of much of Vogel's output, with the spoken word—as with Schoenberg

Vladimir Vogel

and Honegger—assuming a foremost role in the expression of great musical ideas.

His most important work of this period was, however, purely instrumental—his *Composition for one and two pianos,* written in 1923 and first performed in 1926. This original and extensive work exploits the chromatic atonality, the polyphonic variation technique and the rhythmical micro-structures characteristic of Schoenberg. These elements were totally excluded a year later from the *Sinfonia Fugata* written in memory of Busoni, where the emphasis is on mono-thematicism and formal compositional techniques. In the same year—again almost as a tribute to Busoni—he arranged Beethoven's *Grosse Fuge* for string quartet. In 1926 he produced a short but important piano work, the *Etude Toccata.*

As a result of his success in Berlin Vogel had by now achieved a fair degree of recognition and had been engaged as professor of composition of the Klindworth-Scharwenka Conservatory. This gave him sufficient financial support to be able to give up writing music of a commercial nature.

In addition to one orchestral work, the *Two Etudes,* Vogel now wrote his first large-scale vocal work, *Wagadus Untergang durch die Eitelkeit* (Wagadu's Decline through Vanity). This is an oratorio for narrators, singers and five saxophones. For all the economy of style the music is expressive and romantic. There are moments of powerful lyricism, as in the *Song of the Partridges* for soprano, contralto and chorus. The music also contains visionary moments and highly effective *a cappella* sections reminiscent of the medieval hoquet technique. The work is characterized above all by a sombre suavity. The formal devices used are predominantly canon and fugue, ostinato bass and rhythmic patterns. The first performance was not destined to take place until 1935 when Scherchen performed the work in Brussels. During the war the complete score and parts were lost and Vogel was obliged to reconstruct the work from preliminary drafts that had survived.

In the thirties the threat of fascism loomed ever larger in Germany, and Vogel, along with many of his generation, was forced to take a defensive stand. The last works written by him in Berlin were orchestral works, the *Ritmica Ostinata* and the *Tripartita,* brilliant music deriving from basic rhythmic and intervallic motifs.

Just as Vogel had left Soviet Russia in 1918 in search of freedom he now left Berlin in 1933 to find asylum in Switzerland. His adopted country did not make life easy for artists and despite the hospitality afforded by Scherchen and other newer friends Vogel was constantly on the move, to Strasbourg, Brussels, Paris, returning for short periods to Switzerland between his trips.

Vogel's first wife had died in Berlin before the advent of Hitler. In Zürich he met the poet Aline Valengin who moved with him to Ascona in 1935 and married him, so that Vogel finally attained the right of domicile in Switzerland in 1940. The greatest of the works produced during these years is the monumental and highly personal *Tyl Klaas*. This is an oratorio in two parts, extending over four hours in performance. The texts are by Charles de Costa and the work is a passionate indictment of political and religious persecution. Although the scene is ostensibly set in the time of Charles V it refers unequivocally to the present century, as does Schoenberg's *Ode to Napoleon*. Vogel worked on the massive score from 1938 to 1945.

Shortly before commencing this work Vogel had taken the vital step towards twelve-note technique. Scriabin's chromaticism had influenced him from his early youth and in Schoenberg he saw a continuation of what Scriabin had begun. Busoni had never quite won him over and Vogel had searched continuously for a means of ordering the newly acquired emancipation of musical idiom. In 1935 Alban Berg died, ten years after Vogel had attended the first performance of *Wozzeck* and been much affected by it. He and Berg were in many ways kindred spirits and so in 1936 he wrote a long piano work, *Epitaffio per Alban Berg,* as a tribute to his memory. This was Vogel's first venture in twelve-note music: and the row is based on A, B, G, F, being the initials of the composer and the words *Grab* (grave) and *Friede* (peace). The subsequent violin concerto of 1937 was strictly but discreetly twelve-note in the third and final movement. Ever since, the twelve-note technique has formed an integral part of Vogel's music, extended to embrace new technical and musical possibilities.

In 1943 Part I of *Tyl Klaas* was first performed in Geneva under Ernest Ansermet and attracted much attention as a work of genius as well as a protest against dictatorship and the denial of human liberty. Ansermet also directed the first performance of Part II for Geneva Radio. The virtuoso requirements of Vogel's peculiar *Sprechchor* technique were so demanding that ideally a new choir had to be established to perform the work. One was founded in Zürich in 1950 under Ellen Widmann and this chamber choir for choral speech soon became famous throughout Europe. Vogel's works from the main part of their repertoire.

The composer was now beginning to settle into the Swiss way of life. He and his wife first lived in the mountains and then moved back to Ascona, where he wrote such works as the *Passacaglia for Orchestra* and the *Sept Aspects d'une Série* for orchestra, as well as other smaller works.

By this time Vogel had collected a large number of pupils and held lectures in Basle and Zürich which were attended not only by young musicians but also by architects. His circle of friends included the Alsatian painter and author, Jean Arp, who inspired him to one of his most beautiful works, the *Arpiade* for soprano, speech chorus and five instruments—flute, clarinet, violin, cello and piano (the same group as in Schoenberg's *Pierrot Lunaire*). The first performance of the work at the Festival of the International Society for New Music in Baden-Baden in 1955 was one of the great highlights of the Festival: Boulez's *Marteau sans Maître* was another. Its juxtaposition of bright and sombre, masculine and feminine, staccato and glissando sound effects reveal the surrealist nature of the text. The variety of sound, rhythmic and melodic effects in the music betray the composer's dramatic instinct, a feature of the composer's personality that has been further revealed in his later works, the oratorio *Jona ging doch nach Nineve*, the *Meditazione su Amadeo Modigliani*, and *Flucht* to texts by Robert Walser.

In his late sixties Vogel separated from his second wife in Ascona and married a doctor in Zürich. Since then he has produced a large number of works, including music for a film in collaboration with Arp. Time and time again Vogel has resorted to the spoken word as a musical device in his works. In his *Dramma Oratorio* to texts by Walser the composer has added a written contribution on his theory and aesthetics of composition. He states that beginning with *Wagadu* he evolved a type of oratorio, and, subsequent to the speech-songs to texts by Stramm, developed a vocal style: the results are embodied in the *Flucht*.

The speaking voices are made to fulfil various functions. A freely speaking voice is, for example, the chronicler, whose job is to mediate information and the course of events. In contrast a chorus of speaking voices is used for choral utterances and mass reactions. In polyphonic style it fulfils all descriptive, illustrative functions, whether pertaining to the outside world or the world of collective emotions. The chorus of speaking voices is also often called upon to produce shock effects or continue and extend particular impressions made upon the audience. Consequently dramatic, emotional elements and background are reproduced by the chorus of speaking voices, just as its function is to narrate and demonstrate.

In the spoken choruses and solo sections in his oratorios there is yet another element, reminiscent of the intonations, psalmodic recitations, invocations and metrical narrative of the Byzantine liturgy. In all probability Vogel has unconsciously processed impressions left from early youth and childhood. For all Vogel's emancipation from outmoded ideas and his dedication to new musical ideals and devices he has never lost his respect for what has gone before, even though his revolutionary approach to music makes it look as if he had burnt his boats behind him.

His world is that of the great humanist ideas and the discovery of new forms and means. Of primary importance to him and occupying the main place in his life and works is the idea of human liberty. The St Gallen monk Notker Balbulus, Nelly Sachs, Sophocles—whose *Antigone* he has set for spoken chorus in the Hölderlin translation, Jean Arp, Schiller, Goethe, August Stramm, Charles de Costa and Robert Walser have all inspired and influenced him.

Implicitly or explicitly all their texts deal with freedom and each of them is treated musically in a different but appropriate way. This adaptability also characterizes his teaching method, as reported by his pupils Liebermann and Wildberger. Liebermann has written:

Ascona 1940. In the piazza I met Fritz Wotruba, whom I know from having studied with Scherchen in Vienna. In his unconventional way he dragged me with him to have a pot of tea at Vogel's. The house is not at all bohemian, with just a few superb objects in it – a statue by Arp on the piano. I sat down at the piano ... Vogel soon interrupted me to analyze the piece, to some extent thinking aloud, and all the obstinacy with which I can arm myself disintegrated in the face of his methodical, unpretentious objectivity. Thus began our five years' work together. Twice a week I would turn up with sketches for new pieces

Vladimir Vogel

I had been working on and we would analyze and discuss them. Vogel never attempted to force any particular technique or ideal upon me. Whether a work was tonal, atonal or twelve-note he was interested only in its essence.

And Wildberger confirms this though he came somewhat later to Vogel and the method appears to have changed a little:

Vogel never made analyses the basis of tuition. He would leave the critical study of the 'classics' to me to do on my own at home. Questions of principle were only raised as the result of poorly done exercises. Here Vogel showed himself to have a wide intellectual horizon. He had the knack of linking up what was centuries apart. Often he would mention Busoni and I would feel myself with awe to be part of a distinguished succession of important musicians.

Vogel is an artist with a high degree of self-awareness. He knows his worth and on occasion can make things as difficult for the world around him as it has made things difficult for him. The neglect of his close associates has been known to arouse anger and protest in him—but then these associates have included such giants as Jean Arp, Luigi Dallapiccola, Hermann Scherchen and Ernest Ansermet. Childhood and youth in Russia, experimentation in Germany between the wars, unsettled years in France and Belgium, maturity in Switzerland—these experiences have made him into a European in the broadest sense of the word. The humanity in his music derives from such varied sources as Scriabin, Busoni, Schoenberg and Berg. And this humanity is given his peculiar stamp in the way he has taken the human voice and given it new forms of utterance.

13 Hanns Eisler

Shortly after the end of the First World War a young student at the Vienna Conservatory visited Arnold Schoenberg in Mödling near Vienna. He was small, and his round, bald head was set low on his broad shoulders, his ears stuck out and bright eyes twinkled behind his glasses. The young man wore a grey military tunic; he had finished his war service a few weeks previously. His name was Hanns Eisler and, on this first visit, he supported his claim to be a composer with settings for voice and piano of some Chinese poems and of some nonsense rhymes by Christian Morgenstern. Schoenberg was sufficiently impressed by these songs to admit Eisler to his master-class. Eisler wrote:

I studied counterpoint and composition with him. He is a strict teacher. Schoenberg did not allow his pupils to write 'modern' music: exercises in counterpoint and composition had to be in the classical style. Bach, Beethoven, Mozart, Schubert and Brahms were the great models for one's attempts to learn the craft of composition.

Twice weekly the students of the master-class took the Vienna-Baden electric railway to their teacher in Mödling, who instructed them for three hours by correcting exercises they did at home. Often they had to walk the ten miles from Vienna to Mödling, because there was a shortage of electricity during the aftermath of the war.

The composer's father, Dr Rudolf Eisler, was a native of Austria, but he had spent a great part of his life in Leipzig. He was a writer on philosophy and a follower of the critical realism of Wilhelm Wundt. His main work is a *Dictionary of Philosophy*. He was married to Ida Maria Fischer, the daughter of a Swabian farmer, and they had three children: a daughter, Ruth, and two sons, Gerhard and Hanns. The latter was born on 6 July 1898. All three children later joined the Communist Party. The daughter, Ruth Fischer, eventually became a follower of Trotsky and severed all connections with her brothers.

In 1901 the family moved to Vienna and Hanns was sent to elementary school and later to grammar school. His ready intelligence made him the outstanding pupil in his form throughout his schooling. In 1916, before finishing grammar school, he was called up. But he was considered politically unreliable because he belonged to a group of pacifist pupils, so he was not sent to an officer's training course but ordered to join a Hungarian regiment.

Neither he nor his parents had thought of a musical career, but during his years at elementary school Eisler showed vague musical inclinations which had been apparent even at the age of five. His parents were too poor to buy a piano and to pay for music lessons, but at school he learned to sing by sight: 'Thus I had to acquire musical knowledge by myself and to work out my compositions in my head'. His first attempt was a piano piece for his grandmother's birthday. Songs, incidental music to Gerhart Hauptmann's *Hanneles Himmelfahrt* and two Symphonic Poems soon followed. At the front and in the trenches the soldier Hanns Eisler continued to compose unperturbed. An oratorio based on poems by Li-Tai-Pe was called *Against War*. At the beginning of 1918 he was wounded and sent to a military hospital in Vienna. Here he found other soldiers with similar views and heard of the October Revolution in Russia, of the peace offers made by the Bolsheviks and of the political unrest among the peoples of the Danube Empire. After his recovery Eisler was not sent back to the front, but to a garrison in Pilsen, in what was later to become Czechoslovakia. In October 1918 the Austro-Hungarian Empire was dissolved. Eisler fled from Pilsen and eventually reached his family in Vienna. His resolve to become a musician was by now unshakable. He joined the Vienna Conservatory and studied counterpoint from the *Gradus ad Parnassum* by Johann Joseph Fux, a discipline he found boring. He searched for a teacher he could look up to and found one in Arnold Schoenberg.

Among his friends and colleagues during those early years in Vienna were Jascha Horenstein and Max Deutsch. Eisler had met Horenstein on the football field while still at school. Deutsch was his companion in the pilgrimage to Mödling which he made twice a week during his student years with Schoenberg. They were joined by others, among them Karl Rankl, Josef Rufer and Paul Amadeus Pisk. Together with Deutsch, Eisler earned a modest living as proof-reader for Universal Edition. The great Viennese publishing house printed his first compositions and offered him a permanent contract in 1924.

Concentration upon Schoenberg's teaching absorbed almost all of Eisler's energies during these years. Even political discussions were curtailed though not altogether neglected. Eisler took an active part in the *Verein für musikalische Privataufführungen* (Society for Private Musical Performances) which was directed by Schoenberg and his older pupils. Among other things he arranged Schoenberg's *Orchestral Songs* (Opus 8) for chamber ensemble. His admiration for his great teacher knew no bounds, despite irreconcilable political differences. Jascha Horenstein relates how Eisler, who was then forty-six, turned white when Horenstein contradicted some opinions expressed by Schoenberg during a visit they both paid to their former teacher's home in Los Angeles. On the way home Horenstein asked Eisler how a society organized on socialist lines would effect Schoenberg. Eisler replied:

A wonderful palace will be built for him, made of glass, of course, with great fountains and exotic, many-coloured birds. The old man will sit in this house of glass and design his twelve-note series in huge note-symbols, undisturbed by what is happening in the world at large, while we will build Socialism round the edge of his glass castle. Thus Schoenberg will live to the end of his life like the caliphs in *A thousand and one nights*.

When Eisler began his studies with Schoenberg in 1919 the new technique of 'composition with twelve notes related to one another' was not yet fully developed. Like almost all of Schoenberg's pupils, Eisler took up the style and the technique of those works, which since 1908 had revolutionized the musical language of the West. An avoidance of a tonal centre and the conscious denial of the difference between consonance and dissonance mark Eisler's works of this period, his first with opus numbers: the *Piano Sonata* in three movements, the *Six Songs* after poems by Hans Bethge, Matthias Claudius and Klabund, and the *Four Piano Pieces* (Opus 3).

In 1922 Schoenberg gave his closest friends and pupils the first indication of his new technique of composition with twelve-note rows, and Eduard Steuermann performed the five *Piano Pieces* (Opus 23) and the *Piano Suite* (Opus 25). Eisler missed none of these performances and also heard the *Serenade* (Opus 24) and the *Wind Quintet,* directed in Vienna by Anton von Webern, whom he respected and admired and to whom he dedicated the *Songs* (Opus 2). Webern advised Eisler to try to obtain a position as choral conductor, as he himself had done. As conductor of the *Wiener Arbeiter Singverein* (Vienna Workers' Choral Society) Webern performed Eisler's choral songs in later years.

The *Palmström-Studien* (Opus 5) are Eisler's first attempt at twelve-note technique, but they follow Schoenberg's example in other ways as well. Christian Morgenstern's nonsense words are recited by a speaking voice as *Sprechgesang* in the manner of *Pierrot Lunaire* and are likewise accompanied by flute (doubling piccolo), clarinet, violin (doubling viola) and cello. The note-row begins with A and E flat (in German nomenclature A and Es, Schoenberg's initials). The five pieces, written at the beginning of 1925, are parodistic and anti-bourgeois, most clearly so in the third, 'L'art pour l'art', where the 'flutterings of a frightened sparrow' are convincingly represented by trills of the piccolo, flutter-tonguing by the clarinet and tremolo *sul ponticello* by the violin.

In 1924 the studies with Schoenberg came to an end. Eisler took his leave from the workers' choirs which he conducted, from Universal Edition and from the *Verein für volkstümliche Musik-pflege* (Society for Popular Music-making) where he had taught, and moved to Berlin. There he joined two circles sharing his artistic and political interests which at that time were not yet reconciled. In the home of the pianist Artur Schnabel he met radical young composers like Ernst Křenek, Kurt Weill and Stefan Wolpe. For Schnabel's piano pupils he wrote the second piano sonata (Opus 6) which unites twelve-note technique with that of character-variation in an artistic and pianistically effective manner. The *Duo* for violin and cello and the *Eight Piano Pieces* (Opus 8) which followed still belong to the world of 'bourgeois concert music'. *Zeitungsausschnitte* (Newspaper Clippings) (Opus 11) for soprano and piano, date from the same period. Their novel, caustic tone made the composer famous. Some of the eleven texts anticipate the social criticism of Eisler's socialist vocal music, like

Liebeslied eines Kleinbürgermädchens (Lovesong of a petit-bourgeois girl) with its final words: 'Offers under "Holy Wedlock", care of this paper'.

Alongside his relationships with the musical avant-garde, Eisler cultivated some entirely different friendships. He approached the communist organizations in Berlin and wrote his first political choral songs for workers' choirs, among them *Vorspruch* with its quotation from the *International* and three settings from Heinrich Heine for male-voice choir. He also taught history of music and musical theory at the Marxist Workers' School, which was founded in 1926 in Berlin, and wrote articles both for the communist press and for 'bourgeois' periodicals like *Melos*.

To be a member of both a radical artistic and a radical political group at the same time was a frequent phenomenon until the end of the twenties, and not only in Germany. In Berlin there was a distinct connection between advanced artistic experiments and left-wing political tendencies. This was demonstrated in the theatre of Erwin Piscator, the dramatic work of Bertolt Brecht, the etchings and paintings of George Grosz, Otto Dix, Felix Müller and the music of Heinz Tiessen, Vladimir Vogel and, up to a certain date, Paul Hindemith. The programme of the Donaueschingen Music Festival for 1925, as always under the patronage of Prince Max Egon zu Fürstenberg, contained in addition to music by Hindemith, Ernst Křenek, Alfredo Casella and Igor Stravinsky, the *Six Songs* (Opus 2) by Hanns Eisler.

In 1927 Eisler began to work for films and the stage. He wrote music for one of the experimental films by Walther Ruttman, for Leon Feuchtwanger's play *Kalkutta 4. Mai,* for Piscator's famous production of Walter Mehring's *Kaufmann von Berlin,* Georg Büchner's *Dantons Tod, Die letzten Tage der Menschheit* by Karl Kraus and for plays by Bertolt Brecht. The socialist actor Ernst Busch and the poet Brecht became Eisler's closest friends during those politically clouded late twenties.

Eisler's use of the old form of responses between soloist and choir for works of a political character dates from this period. His style was totally changed: his aim was the invention of tunes so simple that anybody could sing them after a single hearing. All this completely contradicted Schoenberg's teaching and a conflict seemed inevitable. In a conversation with the conductor Alexander von Zemlinsky at the beginning of 1926 Eisler had made some critical remarks about Schoenberg's aesthetic ideas, and about twelve-note music. Schoenberg heard about this and protested in a letter to Eisler. In his reply Eisler tried to justify his views and observed that his fundamentally sceptical attitude towards modern music had nothing to do with his respect and veneration of Schoenberg himself. Giving offence had been far from his mind and he reproached himself bitterly for having apparently done so. Eisler maintained this attitude towards Schoenberg for the rest of his life. Thanks to this the relations between the two again became very cordial, especially during their exile in California.

Eisler's ideas on socialist music found their greatest and most artistically convincing expression in 1930 in the *Lehrstück: 'Die Massnahme'* (Didactic Piece: The Measures Taken). The first performance took place on 13 December of that year in the Philharmonic Hall in Berlin during the late evening. The conductor was Karl Rankl, a friend of Eisler's from Schoenberg's class in Mödling, a fine composer and then first conductor under Otto Klemperer at the Kroll Opera House in Berlin. The performance, given by actors like Helene Weigel (Brecht's wife), Ernst Busch, and Alexander Granach as well as the opera singer Anton Maria Topitz and three workers' choirs, attracted a brilliant audience of artists and intellectuals. The words were by Brecht and contained political quotations, among them Lenin's 'He who makes no mistakes is not clever, but he who makes them and knows how to correct them quickly *is*'.

Eisler set the words for mixed, mostly two-part choir, sometimes unaccompanied, sometimes with three trumpets, two horns, two trombones and percussion. In one passage piano is added to characterize the bourgeois world. The programme-notes contained this explanation:

The *Lehrstück: Die Massnahme* is not a play in the usual sense. It is a performance by a massed choir and four actors. The parts of the players are given to-night to four actors, but they can also be performed in a quite simple manner by four young people, and that is precisely the intention.

Despite its stylistic simplicity Eisler's music is developed mono-thematically from motivic cells, occasionally using imitation (and even strict canon in the choral setting of the Lenin quotation) as well as frequent changes of time-signature, especially in the passages for choral speech. In the fifth of the eight movements, which are preceded by an orchestral prelude, Brecht poses the question: 'What, in fact, is a man?' Here Eisler employs jazz techniques such as the wa-wa mute of the trombone.

Right up to the time of his emigration in 1933 Eisler's output was primarily connected with the theatre, with films and with political 'utility' music. His political choral songs with their characteristic ostinato basses became known and quickly grew popular in the Soviet Union around 1930. Of his film music during the thirties that for Bertolt Brecht's *Kühle Wampe* is doubtless the most important; his stage works include the incidental music to Gorki-Brecht's *Mother*, which he revised later in the United States. The *Little Symphony* (Opus 29), in which strict forms like the passacaglia are used side by side with jazz and parodistic elements, belongs to the last instrumental compositions of this period.

During the years before Hitler's rise to power Eisler's personality developed in many directions. Emigration first took him from Vienna, where he could not find sufficient scope, via Paris and Brussels to Denmark and to his friend Brecht. From London, where he undertook commissions for film and stage music, he was called to New York, but then a concert and lecture-tour brought him back to Europe and the Soviet Union. A further stay with Brecht on the island of Fynen led to the composition of the *Lenin Requiem* and the beginnings of the *German Symphony*. In 1937 Eisler met friends like Ernst Busch and the writer Ludwig Renn in Madrid and wrote battle songs for the Spanish republicans. Finally in 1938 he settled in the United States.

Eisler's attitude to this democratic-capitalist country was ambivalent. He loved it better than was convenient to his political friends, and he hated it sufficiently to arouse American suspicions. What did Eisler bring with him to America? As a personality, he brought a legendary reputation as a revolutionary artist, whose songs were as popular in the Soviet Union as with the workers of the West, and as an artist he had the prestige of being Schoenberg's most important pupil after Berg and Webern and the closest collaborator with Brecht. The style of the political song for the masses had not been developed by Eisler, but was the result of collective efforts by a number of composers under the temporary leadership of Kurt Weill. The 'Song' created by Weill in cooperation with Brecht, such as the *Moritat* in the *Threepenny Opera*, left its

mark on Eisler as it did on many other composers after 1930. However, Eisler carried the process of simplification still further. He
spoke, in the spirit of Brecht, of 'the simple, which is so difficult to
create'. The revision of his musical idiom after 1925 did not however imply a denial of the craftsmanship he had learned from
Schoenberg. Simultaneously with choral music and songs Eisler
continued to write strictly conceived chamber music and orchestral works. Twelve-note technique remained for him an important
artistic means of expression, to be used when the subject-matter
demanded it.

During his first stay in New York during 1938 he had written
music for the film *Four Hundred Millions* by the Dutch director
Joris Ivens. After settling in the United States he wrote more film
music for *Scenes from Childhood* as well as incidental music to the
play *Night Music* by Clifford Odets. Parts of the music for the film
were later incorporated in the *Suite for Septet No. 1* which consists
of variations on American children's songs.

In 1940 the New School for Social Research asked Eisler to
undertake research on film music and this led to the publication of
his book *Composing for the Films* in 1942. While engaged on this
research he continued to write music for films, above all to *Scenes
from Nature,* where elaborate sections in twelve-note idiom are
cast in forms like invention, chorale-prelude, sonata exposition,
étude and scherzo-trio. This material too was later incorporated
by Eisler in a work of absolute music, the *Chamber Symphony,*
which like Schoenberg's example, is scored for fifteen instruments
but (unlike Schoenberg) employs Novachord and electric piano.

In 1941 Eisler wrote incidental music for the play *Medicine
Show* and for the film *The Forgotten Village* based on a novel by
John Steinbeck. Although much of his professional work tied him
to New York he preferred to live in the country, on Clear View
Farm. Greater opportunities for work made him decide to move
to Los Angeles. There he found, besides many other European
friends, Arnold Schoenberg, Bertolt Brecht and Leon Feuchtwanger.

After finishing the book on film music he collaborated with
Brecht on the anti-Nazi film *Hangmen Also Die* and wrote
numerous songs, mostly based on poems by Brecht as well as six
Hölderlin songs and five fragments from Anakreon in Mörike's
translation.

Hollywood was to Eisler a place of extreme ambiguity. He lived, like his friends, especially Brecht, in very comfortable circumstances, at times even in affluence and luxury. Close relations with men like Schoenberg. Thomas Mann, Igor Stravinsky and Charlie Chaplin provided him with intellectual stimulus. On the occasion of Schoenberg's seventieth birthday on 13 September 1944, Eisler was one of the well-wishers with the dedication of his Quintet, *Fourteen Ways of Describing Rain.* The work is written for the ensemble of *Pierrot Lunaire:* flute, clarinet, violin, cello and piano and is based on one of the *Scenes from Nature* of 1940. In 1945 and 1946 Eisler wrote incidental music to Brecht's *Fear and Misery of the Third Reich* and *Galileo Galilei* in collaboration with the author, as well as film music for Cary Grant's *None but the Lonely Heart* and Jean Renoir's *The Spanish Main.*

In September 1947 Eisler, like his brother Gerhard and Bertolt Brecht, was summoned to appear before the Committee for Un-American Activities. He and his wife were sentenced to prison. This led to the formation of a committee for his rehabilitation by men like Chaplin, Thomas Mann, Aaron Copland and Albert Einstein. Stravinsky organized a concert in Eisler's honour. After a petition signed by Pablo Picasso, Henri Matisse, Jean Cocteau, Jean-Louis Barrault, Jean Cassou and many other prominent Frenchmen, Eisler was deported to England. In 1948 he travelled to Prague to attend the Congress of Composers and Musicologists and then to Vienna. A year later in East Berlin he met Brecht, Ernst Busch and the poet Johannes R. Becher, who had been appointed Minister for Culture in the East German Republic. Together with Becher he wrote the national anthem of the German Democratic Republic: 'Risen from ruins and turned towards the future'. In 1950 Eisler settled permanently in East Berlin.

Hanns Eisler thus became an official artist of the German Worker's and Peasant's State. He was fifty-two, much travelled and had braved all the dangers of illegal existence and of political persecution. A small, stout man, hardened by the privations of his youth, an excellent swimmer and passionate walker, he seemed to be physically indestructible. He was a heavy drinker, and a chain-smoker and he had spent countless nights in discussion or in strenuous work at his desk. He had reached his goal. Prizes and honours came flowing in. He was made a member of the German Academy of Arts and put in charge of the master-class in composition. But now a great project occupied his mind. During the summer holidays, which he loved to spend at Ahrenshoop on the Baltic coast, he wrote the libretto of an opera, the score of which he never finished, *Johann Faustus*. He had to take things easily now. On the 13 August 1952, he wrote to Brecht from Ahrenshoop:

Dear Bert, Faustus is fortunately finished (it is being copied and you'll get a copy at once for criticism and suggestions) and it has improved my health further; my blood-pressure is now normal and the heart as well as can be expected.

Thomas Mann was also sent a copy and wrote from Zürich: 'Your approach is very novel, very bold, very original and meets the requirements of music as well as of the theatre in many ways.... The whole work is delightfully challenging....'

Brecht writes about the plot:

Faust, a peasant's son, has gone over to the masters during the peasants' war. His attempts to develop his personality are doomed by this betrayal. His bad conscience forces him to complete his ambitious plans in such a rebellious manner that he thwarts his chances of success with the masters. When at last the oppressors of the peasants afford him recognition, he collapses, sees the truth and makes a confession.

The publication of the libretto of *Johann Faustus* was taken as an insult by the East German communists. Their official paper, *Das Neue Deutschland,* reproached Eisler for pessimism, cosmopolitan opinions and a mode of expression that was alien to the people (*volksfremd*). Eisler was deeply hurt but did not give in. Like Brecht he found himself in the position of the creative artist who is unable to submit to authority in aesthetic matters. Schoenberg had been rejected by the official communist party as bourgeois and decadent. Eisler, in a speech to the German Academy on the occasion of Schoenberg's eightieth birthday, opened with the statement that Schoenberg was one of the greatest composers, not only of the twentieth century, but of all time, and that it was impossible to exclude him from the annals of musical history.

When Walter Goehr conducted Eisler's *German Symphony* at the East Berlin State Opera in 1959, the wide range of styles employed was at once apparent. Eisler had started the work in 1934 but finished it in 1958 only just in time for the first performance. It contains simple choral songs and complex polyphony as well as three purely orchestral movements. Tonal passages are found side by side with free atonality and sections in twelve-note technique.

Several late works by Eisler still await publication. He set certain parts of *Johann Faustus* like *Der Mensch* (Man) and *Faustus Verzweiflung* (Faustus's Despair) in simple recitative accompanied by three- or four-part chords. He wrote thirty-six *chansons* to words by Tucholsky and also worked on settings of Brecht's *Kriegsfibel* (Primer of War).

Eisler died on 7 September 1962, in Berlin. His state funeral was attended by the government of the German Democratic Republic, and the leading representatives of the arts and sciences as well as a great many common people.

14 Kurt Weill

The Jewish communities in German towns and cities enjoyed more music than was permitted by the strict traditions of the old synagogues. When the Jews became an important element in German culture during the nineteenth century, the musical demands on the cantors increased considerably. These cantors were products of the ancient temple liturgy in which the *chazzan* (solo singer) had to fulfil an important task in a modest way. The cantor's reputation and social standing grew in the liberal Jewish community. The rich Jewish congregations in the United States have continued this tradition by engaging outstanding singers at high salaries for their religious services.

On 2 March 1900 a fourth child, a son, was born to the cantor, Albert Weill, in Dessau, and was given the name Kurt. The family had come from south-west Germany and belonged to the old established Jewry that had settled on the banks of the Rhine during the Middle Ages. Albert Weill was a devout man and a good father. When he recognized the musical gifts of his youngest child, he had him taught by good musicians, including Albert Bing, the musical director of the Dessau Opera House, and he probably hoped that his son would follow in his own footsteps.

However, Kurt Weill's ambitions transcended the narrowness of provincial life and the limitations of liturgical music. At eighteen he passed the entrance examination for the Berlin Royal High School for Music, thanks mainly to his solid grounding in music theory and piano technique. He joined the conducting class of Rudolf Krasselt and studied composition with Engelbert Humperdinck, the composer of *Hansel and Gretel*, and counterpoint with Friedrich E. Koch. After only one year as a student he became a

repetiteur at the opera house of his native city, Dessau, where
Hans Knappertsbusch was musical director. In 1920 Weill himself
was appointed musical director of the opera in the small Westphalian town of Lüdenscheid. He did not stay long; he had grown
aware of his real musical gifts and wanted to become a composer.

Berlin was still suffering from the economic and political consequences of the war. Nevertheless, the revolution led to great
ferment in the arts; the artistic élite of the younger generation
in Germany was attracted by the metropolis. Kurt Weill, too, fell
under the spell and returned to Berlin full of hope, but without
any means of support. In 1920 Ferruccio Busoni, the great Italian
musician, had consented to teach composition in a master-
class at the Berlin Academy of Art after five years of voluntary exile in Zürich. Weill went to see him and showed him some
compositions, including the *Symphony in One Movement,* and was
accepted as a member of the class, a high distinction, since Busoni
admitted only five students for any particular session. Weill
remained a favourite pupil until Busoni's death in 1924.

In 1922 Fritz Busch, the great conductor, performed Busoni's
one-act opera *Arlecchino* at the Dresden State Opera House. The
composer came to the first performance accompanied by some of
his pupils. Among them was Weill, who thus met Fritz Busch,
later one of the young composer's first and most important inter-
preters. Busch introduced him to the dramatist Georg Kaiser
and initiated a collaboration which was to last many years.

During his years in Busoni's master-class Weill wrote mostly
chamber music, such as the *String Quartet* (Opus 8) and *Frauen-
tanz* (Dance of the Women), seven medieval poems for soprano
with flute, viola, clarinet, horn and bassoon. This cycle shows affinities to certain works in archaic style by Hindemith. The *Concerto
for Violin and Wind Band* develops a completely different style
and technique. It employs an idiom of dissonant expressionism
influenced by Mahler and attempts to bridge the gap between the
school of Schoenberg and Hindemith. The work was written in
1924, the year of Busoni's death, at the same time as the one-act
opera *Der Protagonist,* Weill's first attempt at a stage-work. The
dramatic impulse permeates parts of the *Violin Concerto,* especially
the slow second movement which consists of three sections:
notturno, cadenza and serenata. The notturno is influenced by
early jazz and German dance-music of the twenties. Melodies and

rhythms in a vulgar, popular idiom are consciously incorporated and a xylophone is given important solos. In the cadenza a trumpet appears as a second soloist. The serenata is neo-classical.

Georg Kaiser was one of the most frequently performed playwrights in Germany between the two World Wars. He was born in 1878 and died in exile in Switzerland in 1945. His tendentious expressionist plays were mathematically constructed. His career was marked in equal measure by sensational successes and by private scandals, the result of his unorthodox way of life. The libretto which he wrote in 1924 for Weill is set in Shakespeare's time. The 'Protagonist', the head of a group of wandering players, jealously murders his sister during a rehearsal because she has fallen in love with a Duke. The curious mixture of theatre, life and crime was to return in Weill's later operas.

The Kaisers lived in Grünheide in the country near Berlin. During the composition of the *Protagonist* Weill lived with them, and met there a young Viennese dancer who was helping in the house while waiting for a job. Her name was Lotte Lenya. She later described this first meeting. Frau Kaiser asked her one Sunday morning to row the boat across the lake to fetch a visitor. At the railway station on the opposite shore she found a small man with thick glasses, looking slightly ridiculous in a blue suit that was too small for him. They fell in love and two years later, on 28 January 1926, Lotte Lenya married Kurt Weill. Two months after that, the *Protagonist* had its first performance at the Dresden State Opera House conducted by Fritz Busch and produced by Joseph Gielen. The success was tumultuous. Some of the critics predicted that Weill would turn out to be the musical dramatist of the future.

The music for this opera displays a fully developed feeling for dramatic essentials such as contrast and the handling of climaxes. The vocal writing, often recitative-like but rising to arias and a brilliant duet, shows that the composer grew up in the house of a singer. He instinctively wrote well for voices and thus overcame the abstractions and esoteric aspects of expressionism which were still present in his music.

To the young musicians of the period opera was a dying and outmoded art-form. The expressionists of the Berlin November group, of which Weill had been a member since 1921, rejected the bathos of sung drama. Weill, together with Křenek, the most immediately successful composer of his generation, was soon convinced that what music expressed was just as important as the purely musical considerations. In 1924 the Vienna Universal Edition had signed a contract with Weill. The yearbook published by the firm in 1926 contains his *Bekenntnis zur Oper* (Belief in Opera). It is an unmistakable reversal of the then current aesthetics of absolute music: 'We had to stand up for our century against a predecessor which we believed to be encumbered by literary concepts, by a materialistic orientation of the arts. Music was again to be the solitary aim of our creative efforts.' Then follows an affirmation of belief in Mozart's *Don Giovanni,* in the recitatives of Bach's *St Matthew Passion,* in Florestan's prison aria in Beethoven's *Fidelio* and in the final duet of Bizet's *Carmen.* Weill is not afraid to mention names that were anathema to the avant-garde of the twenties: Strauss and Puccini. He also mentions his great master Busoni, who had taught him a fervent respect for artistic truth. Between the lines of Weill's avowal a truth is expressed which was only hesitatingly admitted by the young musicians of the period, who were rather like the fox in the fable of the sour grapes.

In the Romanisches Café in Berlin, the meeting-place of writers, painters and musicians from all over the world, Weill met a pale, thin man who had come from Paris. He was Iwan Goll, a native of Alsace, who wrote fantastic expressionistic poetry in two languages. His poem *Der neue Orpheus* was set by Weill as a cantata for soprano, violin and orchestra. It is a modern tale of a large city. Adapted mythological figures meet at night in its streets. Orpheus sees Eurydice in a painted prostitute, loses her and shoots himself in the waiting-room of a railway station. Goll, who liked Weill's music, then wrote the libretto to a ballet-opera for him. The action of *Royal Palace* is set in a hotel by an Italian lake and includes adjuncts of modern life like the aeroplane and the car. The heroine is a rich, spoilt but misunderstood woman who, disgusted with her three lovers and her life of luxury, drowns herself. The inclination to present on the operatic stage the lives of millionaires, and frivolities normally more appropriate to revue or operetta was then general among young composers and their librettists. Different personalities and temperaments like Ernst Křenek, Paul Hindemith and Kurt Weill exemplify this tendency and a reflection of it can even be found in Arnold Schoenberg's comedy *Von Heute auf Morgen.*

The Dresden success of the *Protagonist* had drawn the attention of the leading men in Germany's opera houses towards Weill. Erich Kleiber, musical director of the Berlin State Opera since 1923, had very courageously put on the first performance of Alban Berg's *Wozzeck* in the teeth of unprecedented opposition. He also gave the first performance of Weill's two works with librettos by Iwan Goll on 2 March 1927: first *New Orpheus,* splendidly acted and sung by Delia Reinhardt, and then *Royal Palace.* Both works aroused only sceptical interest but were performed seven times.

In the meantime Weill had collaborated again with Georg Kaiser in a second opera, the comedy *Der Zar lässt sich photographieren* (The Czar has his picture taken). The first performance took place in February 1928 in Leipzig where the conductor Gustav Brecher and the producer Walter Brügmann had energetically attempted to modernize both the repertoire and the standard of performance of opera. The opera fills only half an evening. It is about a Czar who travels incognito to Paris and is asked by the beautiful photographer Angèle to come to her studio for a photographic session. Conspirators want to kill the Czar and fix a gun inside the camera. At the last moment bodyguards arrive and prevent the murder. Weill uses a chorus of old men placed in the orchestra pit to comment on the exciting action. The characters are musically well drawn and the drama runs as smoothly as a well-cut film. The composer had by this time achieved full mastery of the art of musical drama. Nevertheless, his artistic attitude was soon to undergo a radical change.

In 1927 Weill met the poet Bertolt Brecht. In his *Hauspostille* Weill had found five *Mahagonny* poems which he set to music, elaborating more effectively on the tunes in Brecht's printed version. Brecht put these five songs in the framework of a *Songspiel* which had its first performance at the Festival of Chamber Music in Baden-Baden in June 1927. It created a sensation, and not only because of Brecht's production. On the stage was a small curtain attached to an iron rod. Men in workers' overalls carried posters with provocative socialist slogans. Caspar Neher had designed a set of extreme starkness containing nothing but a boxing ring. Lotte Lenya stood in the middle of this ring and sang Weill's music in a hoarse voice with lascivious inflections. At a later date she recalled: 'I shall never forget the uproar which it caused. The audience rose to its feet and shouted approval, booed and whistled, simultaneously. Brecht had given us all little whistles and we simply whistled back at them.' Thus began Lotte Lenya's career as a performer of Brecht-Weill.

Weill was fascinated by Brecht's dramatic and political ideas. Poet and composer worked together on a new full-length version of *Mahagonny* for soloists, chorus and large orchestra which was given the title *Aufstieg und Fall der Stadt Mahagonny* (Rise and Fall of the City of Mahagonny).

At the same time they were occupied with an undertaking which neither of them took entirely seriously. Ernst Josef Aufricht, a rich young theatrical manager, was looking for a modern play with music for his theatre on the Schiffbauerdamm. Brecht took as his model the *Beggar's Opera* of 1728 by John Gay and John Christopher Pepusch and called the result *Dreigroschenoper* (Threepenny Opera). When the present writer visited Weill at the time he said: 'I have a feeling that it could be a real success': and he was proved right. The first performance on 31 August 1928, following feverishly intense rehearsals, brought together some brilliant and outstanding personalities on stage and in the auditorium. Famous actors like Harald Paulsen, Kurt Gerron, Erich Ponto Rosa Valetti, and Lotte Lenya as Pirate Jenny took part; Otto Klemperer, Karl Kraus, Erwin Piscator and Fritz Kortner were among the audience. Drama and music critics shared the task of reporting the event. The tunes by a composer who had been classed (and feared) by theatrical experts as an atonalist at once made an immediate impression and were soon whistled by everybody. The song *Moritat* of Mack the Knife (*Mackie Messer*) has remained an 'evergreen'. Gramophone records, radio and film soon cashed in on the success of this sensational play.

Weill's changed attitude not only to the theatre but to all the arts was due to the logic of Brecht's thinking. He said later: 'Only the consistent use of a pleasing and easily assimilated type of melody made it possible to achieve what the *Dreigroschenoper* succeeded in doing: the creation of a new type of musical theatre.' This implied the simplification of opera through the medium of the stage play. In place of operatic sopranos and tenors with limited acting talents they now used good actors with little singing ability.

Kurt Weill

This determined the style of the music: dissonance, atonal harmony, polyphony and complex rhythms were useless in this context.

There was a noisy first performance of *Rise and Fall of the City of Mahagonny* at the Leipzig Opera House in March 1930. The play deals in three acts with the fate of a city in a legendary primitive America in the throes of a gold rush. This city has been founded by three criminals. One night when it is threatened by a typhoon, the inhabitants shed all their inhibitions. The four 'visions' of the second act illustrate in a rough manner basic human activities, such as gluttony, sex, boxing and drinking. In the third act one of the protagonists, the lumberjack John, is condemned to death because he is left without money. During the final procession the actors carry posters with provocative inscriptions.

The Leipzig audience reacted with an uproar which ruined the end of the performance. Jeers and cheers vied with each other for fifteen minutes; finally the applause triumphed. The political implications of this reception were obvious. The protesters belonged to the right, to a section of the middle class that had already accepted fascist ideas and reacted accordingly.

Berlin proved itself to be less politically contaminated. When *Mahagonny* was performed in the Theater am Kurfürstendamm in 1932 with a cast of actors and singers conducted by Alexander von Zemlinsky, it was a great success.

Weill continued to produce works diligently but somewhat haphazardly. Following up a suggestion by Aufricht, he collaborated with Brecht on *Happy End,* a play in the manner of the *Threepenny Opera* which reached the level of its model only in *Bilbao Song* and *Surabaya Johnny.* He also cultivated the slighter genre of the *Lehrstück* (didactic play), a cantata that combined the stage with the concert hall. His *Lindberghflug* (Lindbergh's flight) and *Jasager* (Yes-man) are similar in subject-matter. In the *Jasager,* an opera for schools which created some ideological confusion, Weill achieved his most successfully integrated musical forms since the finale of the *Threepenny Opera.*

In 1930 Weill parted company with Brecht, who was then passing through one of his most difficult periods. The dramatist was the central figure of a whole series of disagreements and law-suits. He had to defend himself against changes of plagiarism, confessed to 'laxity in questions of intellectual property' and there was a

143

lawsuit concerning the film rights of the *Threepenny Opera*. Weill could not bring Brecht to concede to his demands for musical autonomy.

He wrote his last opera *Die Bürgschaft* (The Surety) in collaboration with the stage designer Caspar Neher. The libretto is vaguely Brechtian and illustrates the motto: 'Man does not change. It is circumstances that change his attitude' and it describes the corruption of the good by war, price increases, starvation and illness. Weill's music is melodically simple in the manner of folksong, rhthmically based on dances and marches and harmonically triadic. Vocal writing and orchestration are brilliant but polyphonic passages like the fugal prelude to the second act are less successful.

Die Bürgschaft was given a perfect first performance at the Berlin Städtische Oper produced by Carl Ebert and conducted by Fritz Stiedry in March 1932. This première, less than a year before Hitler came to power, had evoked violent reactions from the Nazi press long before its opening, and this fact restrained the progressives from openly rejecting the ideologically questionable work. Middle-class audiences enjoyed its lukewarm modernism but Brecht's friends were indignant. Hanns Eisler spoke of '*Avant-Gartenlaube*', a reference to a family journal that was the embodiment of sentimental petit-bourgeois values.

The rough, hard-drinking and whoring Americanism of *Mahagonny* had become domesticated. At this point politics intervened. Weill learned that he and Lotte Lenya were on the Nazi government's black-list. In February 1933 Georg Kaiser's *Silbersee* with incidental music by Weill could still be performed in Leipzig and Magdeburg, but the composer and his wife were by this time in Paris, settling their differences with Brecht at the Café du Dome. A young dancer and choreographer belonging to the Diaghilev circle, Georges Balanchine, asked him to write a ballet. Dance without words was unthinkable to Brecht the activist. He therefore invented a new form: ballet whose action is clarified by monologues and songs. Weill's music, for orchestra including jazz instruments and male voice quartet, is rhythmical, and melodically easily assimilated. It has great formal clarity and is eminently danceable. The first performance in 1933 at the Théâtre des Champs Elysées with Lotte Lenya and the dancer Tillie Losch enjoyed only literary success.

Paris was not able to hold the large number of German intellectuals driven out by Hitler. Brecht soon left for Scandinavia and Eisler followed him. Weill found occasional employment as a composer of incidental music. In his leisure hours he wrote a *Little Symphony*. Secretly he longed for the land of the gold-diggers on the other side of the ocean, of which he and Brecht had dreamed.

In 1935 a project by the poet Franz Werfel and the producer Max Reinhardt came to be realized in New York. *The Eternal Road*, a biblical super-revue, describes the road of the Jewish people. Weill was chosen to provide the music. He accepted the invitation to conduct the first performance and arrived with his wife in New York in 1935. 'We learned English very quickly and never spoke German again', Lotte Lenya declared much later. *The Eternal Road* was a failure, but new commissions followed, the first for incidental music to a left-wing anti-militaristic play *Johnny Johnson* produced by an avant-garde ensemble.

In New York new friends were added to the old ones from Europe. The Weills once again met Brecht, Darius Milhaud, Eisler, Theodor Wiesengrund-Adorno, George Grosz and Erwin Piscator and soon made friends with George Gershwin, Marc Blitzstein and Maxwell Anderson. Anderson, a 'committed' dramatist like Kaiser and Brecht, was looking for music for a Broadway play about New York in the 1880's, *Knickerbocker Holiday*. In 1938 with Weill's music the play was a sensational success. *September Song*, the greatest hit in the score, explains why: Weill had decided to write 'commercial' music. His songs had lost their poisonous bite. Neither *Lady in the Dark*, a psycho-analytical play with operetta interludes, nor *One Touch of Venus*, nor the America opera *Street Scene* nor the American folk opera *Down in the Valley*, written for students, have the sharp attack of the works written with Brecht. Weill's new collaborators, famous playwrights and social critics like Maxwell Anderson and Moss Hart, experienced lyric-writers like Gershwin's brother Ira, could not provide the element of acid which would have counteracted the sentimental and sugary side in Weill's music. Success was dearly bought by loss of quality.

But success enabled the Weills, following *Lady in the Dark* in 1940, to buy a bizarre little country house in New City on the banks of the Hudson. Here Weill wrote his late works like the musical *The Firebrand of Florence*, a failure in which Lotte

K

Lenya had star billing. The last work was a musical tragedy *Lost in the Stars* in which Maxwell Anderson treated racial problems in Africa. In the year of its performance, 1949, the present writer met the Weills again in New York. They drank coffee at Rumpelmayer's, looked at Central Park and talked of the old days in Berlin. Weill was nostalgic and ashamed of it. 'His moods were inclined to be nostalgic and he was reproached with writing cotton candy music that was soft, sentimental and—this was considered worst—refined', Lottle Lenya declared later. During the spring of 1950 Weill was busy in New York with new plans. In the midst of his work on the third of April he died of a heart attack.

Lotte Lenya has since been passionately and untiringly active on behalf of his music. She has supervised the German and American performances of his main works, the *Threepenny Opera* and *Mahagonny:* she has taken part in performances and developed into a great interpreter. In the two marriages she contracted since his death, in 1951 to the journalist George Davis who died in 1957, and in 1960 to the painter Russ Detwiler, Weill's heritage has remained her chief interest in life.

She once spoke of his death in a New York hospital. His last words were in English. She dressed the body in his favourite pullover and a simple pair of working trousers: 'He will be very busy up there and I want him to be comfortable'.

15 Boris Blacher

The list of Boris Blacher's works clearly reflects the age in which he lived and the Europe in which he worked. It opens with a work that has failed to survive the war as have another dozen or so early works, including a symphony, a string quartet, a piano concerto and a concerto for two trumpets and two string orchestras. This Opus 1 was a chamber opera with the exotic title *Habemeajaja*, written in 1929 at the age of twenty-six.

Blacher was born on 6 January 1903, in the Chinese port of Yingkow. His parents were both Baltic Germans, his father a bank director from Reval. His youth was spent in unsettled times in China during which his parents, who were by no means poor, travelled from place to place through Czarist north-east Asia. They were permanently on the move, communicating with the world around them in Chinese, Russian, German and pidgin English.

When he was eleven, war broke out and the Blachers, like all Baltic Germans, suddenly found themselves looked upon as hostile aliens, even though the composer's father was a reserve officer in the Czarist army. The young Boris was sent to the Russian secondary school in Irkutsk. He had already been given his first musical instruction at an Italian convent which he had attended for a time in 1914 when he was forced to leave the German school. Piano and violin were his first instruments, coupled with musical theory and harmony. The instruction included playing opera arias and marches by Donizetti as piano duets; the influence of this is still apparent in Blacher's later works.

In October 1917 Siberia was roused from its winter slumber and Boris experienced the street fighting and the defeat and return of the white army. At that time he was working in the humble capacity of lighting assistant at the municipal theatre in Irkutsk, thereby gaining practical insight into Verdi's *Traviata,* Gounod's *Faust* and the now rarely performed *Dämon* by Anton Rubinstein. In 1919 the Blachers moved to Harbin in Manchuria which was then a clearing-house for tens of thousands of refugees. For the conductor of the town's symphony orchestra, made up of émigrés, Blacher, now in the sixth form at school, wrote out scores of repertoire works available only in piano reductions, including his own orchestration of Puccini's *Tosca.*

Blacher passed the matriculation examination at his second attempt and to his father's dismay decided on an artistic career. After much debate it was decided that he should study architecture at a west European university. In 1922, he sailed with his mother to Marseilles via Shanghai, Ceylon, the Suez Canal and the Mediterranean. They spent three days in Paris before travelling on to Berlin, where Blacher registered as a student of architecture and mathematics at the College of Advanced Technology in Charlottenburg, barely a stone's throw from the Academy of Music.

For a young man arriving from Siberia Berlin was a revelation. In addition to the opera house, which he visited on his first evening there, symphony concerts under Furtwängler, the theatres and the film premières in the various cinemas on the *Kurfürstendamm* all had their fascination for him. Moreover he heard modern music for the first time. Browsing through music shops he found scores of piano and orchestral works by Schoenberg and Stravinsky and played them on the piano in his flat until his neighbours objected.

After two years Blacher made up his mind to give up architecture and study music privately under Friedrich Ernst Koch. On hearing the news his father in Charbin promptly withdrew his monthly allowance and a year later his mother left him in Berlin to return to Reval. Blacher now found himself alone, a twenty-four-year-old music student in an alien capital struggling to recover from economic ruin.

Blacher took any musical job that came his way, from copying scores to writing out parts, proof-reading, arranging music for light-music bands and playing the harmonium in suburban cinemas. In 1926 he collaborated with Winfried Wolf in producing a two-hour orchestral score for a new film on Bismarck. In the same year he left Koch to enrol at the Music Department of the university where the teaching staff included Professor Arnold Schering and Freidrich Blume. Blacher would have taken a doctorate with a thesis on the history of instrumental theory, had not the urge to compose proved stronger.

Of his early works the sole survivors are the *Jazz Coloraturas* for soprano, alto saxaphone and bassoon, written in 1929. These are rhythmic and melodic miniatures with astringent sound effects produced with the utmost economy. Blacher derived naive delight from the syncopations of early jazz and he clearly felt an affinity with it, just as he did with the dance-line scores of Stravinksy which he has never ceased to admire. On the advice of his friend, the composer Rudolf Wagner Regeny, Blacher attended a dancing school in Berlin which provided the primary inspiration for numerous ballet compositions, beginning with a surrealist danceplay later called *Fest im Süden* (Southern Festival). His latest work in this field was his ballet *Tristan,* written in 1965.

In 1933, the year that Hitler came to power, Blacher was still unknown, though the Berlin music publishers Bote und Bocke had published his *Kleine Marschmusik* for orchestra, based on tunes from Italian opera. His works in subsequent years were generally light music and *Gebrauchsmusik,* based on folk music, often gay and brilliant, as in the *Divertimento for Wind Orchestra* (Opus 7).

Early in 1937 his *Fest im Süden* had been successfully performed in Kassel. At the end of the same year Carl Schuricht gave the first performance of his *Concertante Musik* with the Berlin Philharmonic Orchestra. It was so well received by the audience that the whole work was played a second time as an encore. People became aware of him almost overnight and his music began to be performed more and more in and outside Germany. His *Symphony No 1* was first performed by Johannes Schüler at the opera house *Unter den Linden,* the *Concerto da Camera* was first performed by the BBC orchestra in Birmingham under Leslie Howard. The short ballet *Harlekinade* (also known as *Kaleidoskop*) was produced in Krefeld and shortly afterwards at the opera in Berlin. The ballet, based on the *Hamlet* story, was originally created for the company run by Colonel de Basil; the same theme also inspired Blacher to write first a symphonic poem and then, ten years later a ballet score.

The years 1939 to 1940 were important ones for Blacher. In 1938, at one of the Nazi Festivals of German Music (*Reichsmusik-*

tage) in Düsseldorf he had noted definite political hostility to one of his works and decided that it would be a good thing for him to move from Berlin. On the recommendation of Karl Böhm he was appointed to a professorship for composition at the Conservatory in Dresden. But in 1939 his father died, and at about the same time he met a young pianist Gerty Herzog, whom he married in 1945. 'Since then I have had to keep on churning out the odd piano work', was Blacher's typically humorous comment on his marital situation.

The year 1940 was a particularly prolific one for him. Apart from the symphonic poem *Hamlet*—which was given its first performance by the Berlin Philharmonic Orchestra under Carl Schuricht—he also produced two piano sonatinas, a string quartet, a flute sonata, a concerto for strings, and the full opera *Fürstin Tarakanowa*. This was given a triumphal first performance at the Wuppertal Opera in February 1941. It is a combination of elements from *Wozzeck* and *Rosenkavalier* and is characteristic of Blacher's operatic style.

The rhythmic and tonal effects preferred by the composer are most clearly shown in the two piano sonatinas with the apparently arbitrary changes of rhythm which are, in fact, highly organic and structurally integrated. At this important stage in his development Blacher met the composer Gottfried von Einem, who was then *repetiteur* at the State Opera. For a short time he studied composition with Blacher, and the two have remained close friends ever since. In 1942 and 1943 two further major works were completed though not performed until after the war. They are the oratorio based on Dostoyevsky's *Der Grossinquisitor* and the chamber opera *Romeo und Julia,* freely adapted from Shakespeare.

The year 1945 saw Blacher's rise to fame as a composer and as the teacher of a new generation of musicians from all parts of the world. His teaching commitments, which in Dresden were determined by financial expediency, eventually became his main concern, and he taught at the International Institute for Music in Zehlendorf and after 1948 at the State Academy of Music in Berlin, where he still continues to teach, as indeed he still does at courses at Salzburg, Southern England (Dartington) and the United States.

Since the war Blacher has written a large and varied number

of works. Apart from numerous commissions for radio, plays and films he has written many ballets, including *Chiarina, Hamlet, Lysistrata, Mohr von Erzerum* written in 1941 and finally *Tristan* written in 1965. The most important of these have been written in collaboration with the famous choreographer Tatiana Gsovsky. In addition to these ballet scores he has written two chamber operas: *Die Flut* and *Die Nachtschwalbe* a light-hearted ballet-opera about the Hauptmann von Köpenick with the appropriate title of *Preussisches Märchen* (Prussian Fairy-Tale), the one-act opera *Abstrakte Oper Nr 1* to a syllabic text with stereotyped emotional gestures by Werner Egk, and two tragic-fantastic dramas entitled *Rosamunde Floris* and *Zwischenfälle bie einer Notlandung* (Incidents at an Emergency Landing).

Nobody has been more radical in his treatment of opera than Blacher. His operatic figures have nothing in common with the noble heroes and scheming rogues of the traditional stage. His central figures are all outsiders or people who develop strange characteristics as a result of the unusual circumstances in which they find themselves, and consequently are forced to make unexpected decisions. Even the physical characteristics often reflect these eccentricities, as with the elderly married couple in the *Preussisches Märchen* where the father sings soprano and the mother bass. The cobbler in sergeant's uniform is likewise an outsider, as are all his counterparts. The young Rosamunde Floris disrupts her idyllic surroundings and allows love to turn her into a relentless murderess and deceiver—in spite of which she manages to retain the unqualified sympathy of the audience. The last in the series of outsiders is the host, who offers the hospitality of his bright neon-lit house to the passengers of an aircraft that has performed an emergency landing in a primeval forest. He turns them into prisoners of luxury and then, at the end, turns them out to the night and the prowling beasts of the forest.

The musical devices used by Blacher are no less unconventional. His thoroughly modern style is, however, not the product of any particular musical ideology. Such disparate composers as Scriabin and Stravinsky have served as his models but always adapted with virtuosity in the most up-to-date compositional techniques. *Lysistrata*, written in 1950, is partly twelve-note and partly tonal, yet there is no apparent breach of style. In writing the ballet Blacher evolved from the free rhythm of his earlier works, espec-

151

ially the piano sonatinas, a method of systematic change of rhythm based on arithmetic rows which he has called 'variable metres' in his *Klavierornamenten* (Piano Ornaments).

No one who has heard any of his orchestral music could ever confuse it with that of any other composer. He writes with the utmost economy of texture and colour; it is music that has been stripped, in the sense of Satie's *stile dépouillé*, often merely a contour or the beginnings of a contour. It is an economy born of amplitude that has been revised and pared away. Some comparison is possible with the radical limitations of form self-imposed by Schoenberg and Webern around 1910. The difference is that with Blacher the process of radical reduction begins with the melodic lines and chords themselves and not with the length of time required to perform a work. His music has a wiry quality which is far removed from the gentle sighs that emanate from the works of Webern.

This process of reduction occasionally becomes the content of the composition itself. In *Rosamunde Floris* a man jumps to his death. The jump is accompanied by a twelve-note chord which becomes a sort of leitmotiv throughout the opera. It appears several times, either diminished or augmented by the addition or removal of constituent parts of the chord. A similar system obtains for his use of rhythm, producing new forms vertically and horizontally.

The uniqueness of his orchestration likewise derives from the principle of utter and radical economy. The pure, dry colours of traditional orchestral sound are occasionally made to contain new admixtures, as in the jazz combination in *Rosamunde Floris*.

In 1960 Blacher was appointed to teach electronic music at the Technical University of Berlin. Exposure to this new form has had a deep influence on him. In 1962 studies with electronically distorted piano, voice and trombone glissando were performed in the Academy of the Arts and the Congress Hall in Berlin; even at that time space was already being exploited in the distribution of sound via several channels. Electronic music was made a constituent part of the full opera *Zwischenfälle bei einer Notlandung* written in 1966. It says much for his creative genius that he has convincingly managed to overcome the inherent stylistic problems of the work, for the naturalistic science fiction which inspired Heinz von Cramer's libretto is far removed from the composer's stylistic radicalism.

21 Kurt Weill (1900–50) at the piano. He married the Viennese dancer Lotte Lenya in 1926, and two months later his first attempt to write for the stage, a one-act opera called *The Protagonist*, written in 1924, was performed to tumultuous applause at the Dresden State Opera House.

22 Hanns Eisler (1898–1962) began to work for the stage in 1927, writing music for plays by Büchner, Feuchtwanger and Brecht, among others. This photograph, taken in Berlin in 1950, shows him (second from right) with the Socialist actor Ernst Busch (left), the poet and dramatist Bertoldt Brecht and Brecht's actress wife Helene Weigel. Busch and Brecht were Eisler's closest friends during the late twenties, and he and Brecht remained friends while they were in the United States. All three of them met up again in Berlin after Eisler settled there in 1949. Brecht and Weill collaborated separately to produce many well-known works, such as *The Rise and Fall of the City of Mahagonny* and the *Threepenny Opera*.

23 Vladimir Vogel (b. 1896) was of Russo-German parentage and was born and brought up in Russia. He moved to Berlin at the end of the First World War, where he became a pupil of Busoni in 1920. In 1939 he left Germany and travelled for several years before making his permanent home in Switzerland in 1940. This photograph shows him (left) after a performance of *Jona ging doch nach Nineve* in Zurich in 1960.

24 The composers Karl Amadeus Hartmann (1905–63) (left) and Boris Blacher (b. 1903) (centre), photographed with Rolf Liebermann in Donaueschingen in 1953, had been friends since the 'forties. Blacher dedicated one of his piano works in his newly developed 'variable metres' to Hartmann, who later used them in his own work.

25

25 The Swiss composer Frank Martin (b. 1900), with his wife, greeting an acquaintance during a break in rehearsals for one of his works.

26 Othmar Schoeck (1886–1957) was born in German-speaking Switzerland and had close links with German and Austrian music all his life, although he felt very much drawn to southern Europe, especially Italy, which he visited often. One of his closest friends was the poet Hermann Hesse, and he set some of Hesse's lyrical poems to music. This photograph was taken by the author in 1912.

27 A stamp issued in memory of Schoeck.

26

27

28 Arthur Honegger (1892–1955) on the footplate of an LNER express engine. He once said: 'I love railway engines just as other men love horses or women' and his *Mouvement* *Symphonique No. 1* is a portrait of a railway engine. It caused a great stir and is generally performed under the more evocative title *Pacific 231*.

Boris Blacher

In comparison with the amount of music he has written for the stage, his music purely for the concert platform is less significant. It is the lesser forms in vocal and instrumental music that have held the greatest attraction for him. If the short *Concertante Musik* proved to be his first great success in 1937 his orchestral variations written ten years later to a famous theme by Paganini made him world-famous. This brilliant piece, lasting twenty minutes, is a powerful demonstration of orchestral virtuosity in its skilful exploitation of variation techniques and as such can bear comparison with much of Hindemith and with the *Young Person's Guide to the Orchestra* (Variations on a Theme of Purcell) by Benjamin Britten. His skill is perhaps best demonstrated in the seven-part canon he manages to weave into the contrapuntal texture.

Otherwise his orchestral works consist mainly of miniatures, such as the *Orchestral Ornament,* a study in the use of pianissimo, the *Orchestral Fantasia,* dedicated to his friend, the composer Georg Rufer, and the *Music for Cleveland* written for George Szell and the famous Cleveland orchestra. All are written with an individual style, and all have in common the terseness and economy that typify his peculiarly ascetic approach to orchestral composition.

Three piano concertos were written by Blacher for his wife in 1947, 1952 and 1961, and the third one is also written as a set of variations. The theme is taken from Clementi, whose piano works are such a constant source of anxiety to children learning the piano. However, Blacher has sublimated the nightmare element into an atmosphere of complete serenity. The nondescript theme is subjected to all sorts of distortions, so that the work is full of rhythmic, melodic, harmonic and structural surprises.

In German-speaking territory there is a certain prejudice against the light-hearted in art. The thinkers that have instilled the concept of discipline into German aesthetic life seem unprepared to allow the arts the right to provide an antidote to the tragic course followed by history. In so doing they contradict some of the greatest creative geniuses of the past centuries. The question as to the respective greatness of comedy and tragedy need not concern us here. It is, however, an indication of emotional sterility when certain people are prepared to veto categorically a particular form of artistic response. The world was no more innocuous in the days of Aristophanes, Shakespeare and Molière all of whom ridiculed their own society. Lightheartedness is not a sign of irresponsibility.

153

Blacher is well aware of the tragedies of our age and its social problems. This he has amply demonstrated in an outstandingly poignant *Requiem* and in his contribution to *Jewish Chronicle* composed collectively by East and West German musicians. He is fully conscious of the tragic basis of great art. On the other hand we have reason to be grateful to him for showing us that gaiety and intellectuality are not mutually incompatible. Blacher loves serene light-heartedness as a personal as well as an artistic attribute, and it is this that stamps his works with their unique character.

16 Arthur Honegger

I was born in Le Havre on March 10th 1892. My parents were both descended from old Zürich families. My father had settled in this old sea-port and was the director of a firm of coffee importers. Le Havre was not a musical centre, quite the contrary. No regular orchestral concerts were held there, in fact, the only regular musical occasion was a Grand Season of Opera which took place in the local theatre every May. When I began composing, I knew nothing but those pieces my mother had played to me on the piano.

With these words Arthur Honegger began his short autobiography in 1950. Those who knew him will not easily forget the impression of his great, sincere personality. This much-travelled and experienced Swiss composer, German romantic by nature, classicist by education, had something of the unifying and reconciling character of Mittler, the mediator in Goethe's *Elective Affinities*. His deeply-rooted benevolence endeared him to many people. Even when the growing tensions in Europe erected barricades between nations and broke many friendships, he always retained his forgiving objectivity. It was no sign of weakness but rather the proof of a calm and unshakeable strength of character.

Honegger's musical studies began in Le Havre where, as a boy, he learnt the violin and studied harmony. In his parents' home there was always music. His mother played the piano and sang; Arthur composed small operatic fantasias based on *The Magic Flute*, *The Prophet* and *Robert the Devil*. When he left school his father sent him to the Zürich Conservatory, where Friedrich Hegar, the distinguished conductor, teacher and chamber musician, recognized and encouraged his talent. His parent agreed that he should make music his profession. After Zürich Honegger's studies were continued in Paris, and here he settled in 1913 at the age of twenty-one.

Honegger's connections with French culture went very deep; it had formed and educated him, and so it was not by chance that from his earliest youth Paris became his adopted home. Yet not even his membership of the 'Six', or his friendship with Jean Coctea and Darius Milhaud could estrange him from the German idols of his youth, composers who were not, at that time, held in high regard in Paris: Richard Wagner and Johannes Brahms. Honegger was accepted by the Paris Conservatory where he studied counterpoint under André Gedalge, composition under Charles Marie Widor, orchestral conducting under Vincent d'Indy and violin under Lucien Capet.

Just as important as his studies under teachers of such high standing were his meetings with his contemporaries in their classes. During these years Honegger established his oldest and closest friendship with Darius Milhaud, which began in the years 1911-13 when the young Swiss composer was travelling back and forth between Le Havre and Paris for his studies in the capital. Another member of his circle of friends at that time was Georges Auric, who caused quite a stir at the Schola Cantorum with his early talent for composition. During the years before the first world war in Paris, Honegger's life was filled to the brim with practising and composing, playing an active part in literary, artistic and dramatic events as well as with his passionate interest in sport, especially football and rugby. In 1916 he had to serve for a few weeks with the Swiss frontier guards. This experience was enough to give him a lifelong aversion to war and soldiering.

In 1918 Honegger conducted one of his first orchestral works, the *Chant de Nigamon* in the orchestral class of the Conservatory. The years immediately after the war were outstanding in the large number of high quality works he produced, including music of many types, pieces for piano, violin, organ or voice and an increasing amount of orchestral music, first in short forms and later in several movements.

Milhaud had been summoned to Rio de Janeiro in 1917 as attaché, at the same time as the poet Paul Claudel became ambassador to Brazil. Soon after the end of the war he returned to Paris; the old friends met again, and new friends such as François

Poulenc, Roland-Manuel and the poet Jean Cocteau joined their circle. The group of the 'Six' resulted from an essay by the critic Henri Collet, though it was more an accidental creation than one based on a unified ideal. Though Honegger belonged to it he responded least of all to the anti-romantic spirit which the works of his colleagues expressed. He himself names as those musicians who most influenced his development both classicists and romantics: Richard Strauss and Max Reger, Claude Debussy and Gabriel Fauré, Stravinsky, Schoenberg and Milhaud. Throughout his life, his admiration for Wagner was great and he spent many summers at the Bayreuth festival. Nevertheless, this 'romantic' of the twentieth century was a modernist and the bold pace-maker for many avant-garde composers. In the seven small piano pieces of 1919 and 1920 he wrote atonal music in the spirit of the Vienna school of Schoenberg and also polytonal pieces with brutal rhythms reminiscent of Stravinsky.

In the summer of 1921 the fame of a new work spread abroad from a small village in the Swiss canton of Waadt. The work was called *King David* and had been composed under unusual circumstances. The poet René Morax had written a biblical work for the open-air *Théâtre du Jorat* and the summer festival associated with it. At the last moment a composer was sought. Ernest Ansermet and Igor Stravinsky recommended the young Honegger. Offered an orchestra of only fifteen players, he wrote the score in two months. The success of the first performance increased and later grew to a positive triumph when it was performed again in Winterthur. Admittedly, the form of the work had now been changed. Honegger had turned the episodically constructed work into an oratorio which he himself called a *Symphonic Psalm*. The dramatic elements remained in this new version, and the music, although stylistically not uniform, had vigour and a theatrical impulse, and showed an unusual mastery in the construction of polyphonic choral scenes. French and German romantic traits combined with influences from jazz and popular music. Its melodic form made its mark, the alternation of solo voices, choruses and recitatives gripping the listener from beginning to end.

Honegger never lost this ability to fuse together disparate stylistic elements and to subordinate them to his personal style. As a true European he stood between the French love of dance and folk song and the symphonically orientated music of the Germans, with its tendency towards polyphony and complex harmony. Aesthetically speaking, the programme of the 'Six' concerned itself with a movement towards melody and away from chromaticism, with the construction of simple forms and the rejection of romantic sentiment. Honegger was too independent a personality to submit to this creed and the often overexacting demands of Cocteau who led the group. But he shared many qualities with his French friends: in particular, he and Milhaud had in common a liking for polytonality and for virtuoso instrumental writing. Soon after his *King David* he again caused a stir, this time with an orchestral work. This was the portrait of a railway engine, also known as *Mouvement Symphonique No. 1* but which reached most of the world's great concert halls under the title *Pacific 231*. 'I love railway engines just as other men love horses or women', confessed Honegger. The work is a small masterpiece of orchestral descriptive music, magnificent in its rhythmic flow which quite realistically depicts the gradual setting in motion of the engine right up to the attainment of its top speed, strictly symphonic and fugal in structure. A similar descriptive work on a sporting subject was also classified by Honegger as a symphonic movement but without further title; it was written in 1933 as a belated act of homage for the fiftieth anniversary of the Berlin Philharmonic Orchestra and its conductor Wilhelm Furtwängler.

The *Concertino* for piano and orchestra, wholly imbued by the spirit of Paris in the twenties, is one of the most charming works which Honegger ever wrote for the concert platform. It was dedicated in 1924 to the young pianist Andrée Vaurabourg who became Honegger's wife two pears later and who was herself a musician of the first rank and a composer from the circle of Nadia Boulagner. In the slow central movement, Honegger uses a new mode of expression much inspired by Blues music and in the quick finale we find the cheerful mood of *musique syncopée* a sublimated jazz-form embodied in a classicist structure. After their marriage Honegger and his wife went on many concert tours to most European countries, including Russia, the United States and South America, where he acted as conductor and sometimes as piano accompanist to singers and instrumentalists.

Honegger's real domain, however, was the theatre, and he always returned to writing dramatic pieces, operas, melodramas, ballets and scenic cantatas. His first and most important opera,

written during the twenties, is *Antigone,* based on the text of Jean
Cocteau, which was given its first performance in 1927 at the
Théâtre de la Monnaie in Brussels. This work, described by
Cocteau with the now famous formula 'classicism as photo-
graphed from an aircraft', boasts a wholly new form of sung recita-
tive going far beyond Debussy's tentative beginnings in this field.
In one of his conversations with the critic Bernard Gavoty, pub-
lished under the title *Je suis compositeur,* Honegger says:

As far as I am concerned, symphonic works give me a good deal of
trouble; they demand strenuous thought and effort. If, on the other
hand, I can lean on a literary or visual model, the work becomes much
easier. Ideally, I should have liked to write only operas, but that would
have been a waste of effort in an age in which opera is on the point of
disappearing.

On this subject, Honegger foresaw serious difficulties. In an interview he once said:

The threatening shapes of three composers guard the realm of opera:
Wagner, Debussy and Strauss. Trying to avoid Debussy brings one to
Massenet; wishing to avoid Strauss leads one to Puccini, which is
worse. But before turning back – for is not every retreat a defeat? –
why not search for a new gateway?

Indeed, Honegger did both seek and find such new gateways,
from King David, by way of *Antigone, Judith* (in which he once
again collaborated with René Morax), and *Amphion* (where he
joined forces with Paul Valéry), right up to his dramatic, though
no longer operatic masterpiece, *Jeanne au Bûcher,* written in
collaboration with Paul Claudel. This dramatic oratorio, which
was inspired by the dancer and actress Ida Rubinstein, was composed practically bar by bar as Claudel produced the text. The
music is a brilliant pandemonium interspersed with roars of primitive sounds from electronic instruments, sad children's songs, such
as are only found in France, brutal choruses, tragic melodramas
and recitatives. Through the open gateway one catches sight of a
remarkable panorama of musical theatre. The work is neither
drama nor opera, neither ballet nor melodrama. Yet combines
all these forms and devices, Elements from the old mystery plays
and from sung heroic epics fuse with the medieval *chanson de
Geste.* Tragic and grotesque, symbolic and allegorical scenes

alternate. In addition to the actors there are choruses and opera singers. As Honegger says:

> The music of today must change its audience and speak to the masses. That is why it must alter its character and make its impact with directness, simplicity and large gestures. The people are not concerned with technique and precision. All this I tried to embody in my *Jeanne au Bûcher*. I forced myself to make myself comprehensible to the man in the street and at the same time to be of interest to musicians.

In this aim Honegger succeeded. Ever since the concert-hall first performance of the work in Basle in 1938 and the full-scale stage performance in Paris in 1950, *Jeanne au Bücher* has enjoyed world fame. The *Danse Macabre* (*Totentanz*), inspired by Holbein's series of the same name and written in 1938, also in collaboration with Paul Claudel, continues the same line of development. It unhesitatingly follows the idea of dramatic synthesis, combining Holbein's visions with 'collages' of folk song, Bach chorales, Gregorian *dies irae* and atonal harmony.

In his conversations with Gavoty, Honegger also talked about the economic and social position of the musician in the twentieth century. He regards the position of the composer with pessimism. His main demand of the composer was one he had always fulfilled himself—to take account of those conditions under which the work would be performed. He never refused to write high-class light music for radio or incidental music for films. He also produced an operetta *The Adventures of King Pausole*, a small masterpiece of its kind based on a text by Pierre Louys. It was first seen at the *Théâtre des Bouffes Parisiens* in December 1930 and it continued for almost five hundred consecutive performances.

In addition to his dramatic works and the composition of incidental music, which brought him enough to live on, Honegger also wrote many chamber and orchestral works. A string quartet dating from his youth was followed in 1936 by a second and also by a piano quintet, something of a rarity in modern music. Piano pieces such as the *Cahier Romand* or the three sonatas on the name BACH for violin, viola and cello, with or without piano, alternate with suites for wind instruments.

The symphonies include the first in C major, composed in 1930, and reminiscent of Gustav Mahler; the second written in 1942 for trumpet and string orchestra, a kind of compendium of

Honegger's ideas and virtuosity; the third 'liturgical' one of 1946, which reflects the horror and fear of the Second World War but closes with a moving gleam of hope for a world of peace, and may be seen as the climax of his creative work and indeed of twentieth-century music; the fourth, written on commission for Paul Sacher and his Basle chamber orchestra, is a gay work in folk-song style which bears the charming title *Deliciae Basilienses*; the fifth and last is entitled *Di Tre Re,* because all its three movements close with a D repeated three times.

On his sixtieth birthday this cheerful, sociable composer received good wishes from music lovers throughout the world. Sitting in his Paris flat on the Boulevard de Clichy amongst his many valuable books and musical scores and with his famous collection of pipes beside him, he read greetings from Stravinsky, Milhaud and Hindemith, from Cocteau, Claudel and Paul Sacher. But a shadow lay over all his enjoyment. For six years Honegger had been a sick man. 'In 1947 Koussevitzky invited me to Tanglewood for a music festival and this was to be followed by a long tour of Mexico and South America. But shortly after my arrival in New York I had a severe attack of angina pectoris and I owe it solely to the excellent treatment by the American doctors that I am still alive.' Now he was compelled to conserve his strength. His travelling was severely limited and he only just managed to get to Basle where Sacher was conducting *The Harmony of the World* by his friend Hindemith. Honegger's creative powers, however, remained strong. His late works, after a heart attack in 1947, show a concentration such as was not always present in the earlier works. There were still pauses, but hardly any minor works were written apart from the incidental music for drama, radio and film. And even here he wrote such excellent music as that for Albert Camus's *L'État de Siège,* Alfred de Musset's *On ne badine pas avec l'amour* and the *Oedipus* of Sophocles.

In 1951 Honegger completed one further symphonic work, the *Monopartita* for orchestra. His last work was the *Christmas Cantata* of 1952 for baritone solo, children's voices, mixed choirs, organ and orchestra. It shows the growing religious feeling of the composer which had already been foreshadowed by the *Symphonie Liturgique* of 1946.

For the last few years of his life, Honegger left France and returned to his native Switzerland where he had often spent the summer as the guest of Paul and Maya Sacher on their Schoenenberg estate near Basle. The collection of essays which appeared in 1948 under the ironic title *Incantations aux Fossiles* is dedicated to Maya Sacher.

In 1952 Honegger was among the speakers at the *Conférence Internationale des Artistes* which took place in Venice from 22—25 September. His lecture on 'The musician in contemporary society' is a warning both to society and to the composer 'who strives with all his might to produce goods which no one needs'. His conclusions were: that it was necessary to convince the budding composer that he would probably not be able to live from his work; that he should educate young people to become listeners to modern music and enemies of 'sportive virtuosity'; that the taste for novelty that the public showed towards literature, drama and painting should be directed by him towards music.

One of Honegger's last written declarations concerned Wolfgang Amadeus Mozart. It appeared in the *Neue Zürcher Zeitung* of February 1955:

I am always talking of the presence of the miraculous in the sphere of music. By this I mean the expression of that which remains inexplicable in a musical work of art. Why does one sequence of notes seem to us a stroke of genius while another is barely noticed? Yet the mere mention of the name Wolfgang Amadeus Mozart conjures up a different aspect of the miraculous which troubles the spirit. Here is a young man who in only a few years created a body of works which makes his name synonymous with that of music; here is a life that goes some way towards making up for all the mass of stupidity and wickedness which is found in the world. How much gratitude, love, admiration and honour we owe him. He is one of the great benefactors of mankind. They are rare.

There was never around Honegger a nimbus of eccentric genius, but always an aura of great goodness and diligent workmanship. Those who spoke to him during his last years were touched by the cheerfulness of spirit which rose above so much pessimism about cultural matters. He considered the artist as an anachronism in the present age and yet he himself embodied the dignity and importance of the artist today as have few others. He possessed warmth and sincerity both as a man and as a musician. His enormous output is uneven in substance and style, yet in each bar one may feel the strength and nobility of his personality. He died in Paris on 27 November 1955. As Pierre Boulez said at his funeral: 'Thanks be to Honegger for awakening in us the desire for adventure.'

17 Othmar Schoeck

The *Lied* is a romantic art-form. It flourished, above all, in nine-teenth-century Germany and survived it for only a short time. As a vehicle for conciseness of expression it has diverse possibilities of form and content. It can be the utterance of a unique feeling or a single swift experience, but it can also compress into a short space of time a dramatic episode or whole. In each case it is the product of a collaboration between two arts, related in origin but almost hostile in their aims. It would be possible to imagine a song with-out text as a pre-linguistic phenomenon, an animalistic type of singing going beyond the mere expression of bodily experiences, like the song of birds. But the song is essentially music, even if in a few borderline cases the underlying text may achieve greater importance.

In modern times not many composers have made use of the song as their main means of expression. With Strauss and Reger song-writing was undoubtedly a by-product of the main stream of their creativity, which tended towards instrumental forms or sym-phonic opera. For Gustav Mahler alone the song became the focal point of his musical thought; for him even his huge symphonies were the extension and large-scale expansion of songs. Mahler was one of the last composers to give prominence to the song-cycle. In this he goes back to the late-classical and romantic models of Beethoven, Schubert, Schumann and Brahms. Isolated instances of such song-cycles still occur in Austrian and German music, for instance in Arnold Schoenberg's Stefan George songs (Opus 15), and Paul Hindemith's *Marienleben*, based on poems by Rainer Maria Rilke. However, in Othmar Schoeck the modern song found a remarkable champion.

Schoeck came from an artist's family. He was born at Brunnen on 1 September 1886, spent his childhood and schooldays there, and spent much time drawing and painting, with the idea of taking up his father's profession. After leaving school, which he had hated, Schoeck became an art student in nearby Zürich. Not until 1905 did his musical talent become really apparent. He had sung with his elder brothers from an early age, had a fine voice, was skilled in yodelling and had piano lessons from his mother, though he disliked practising. He had also tried his hand at a few small compositions, among them an opera based on Karl May's play *Der Schatz im Silbersee*. But frequently these various artistic works were dropped in favour of other interests including sporting ones. Finally, in Zürich, he decided to audition as a music student. He played a few songs at the Conservatory and was immediately accepted. Amongst his teachers was the same Friedrich Hegar who a few years later discovered the talent of Honegger.

During his student years at the Conservatory which continued until 1907, the young composer met the poet Hermann Hesse, who became a lifelong friend and whose lyrical works are frequently re-created in Schoeck's songs. Hesse was a south German who, early in life, had exchanged the provincial pietism of his homeland for the more liberal intellectual climate of Switzerland. Another important meeting was with Reger to whom Schoeck, then twenty, was introduced by a young singer from Brunnen who was engaged in the Stuttgart State Opera. Schoeck showed him some songs in manuscript. Reger played them through and said they ought to be published immediately. A few months later, when he became Professor of Composition in Leipzig, he wrote to Schoeck urging him to become his pupil, and in April Schoeck moved to Leipzig. There he found time to write a vast number of songs. But his original enthusiasm soon gave way to a more reserved attitude towards his teacher who, in the art of song-writing in particular, proceeded from totally different outlook and ideals.

When Schoeck returned to Switzerland a year later, ten books of his songs had already been published. The Zürich publishers Hug, who brought out the young composer's works, remained his publishers until the end of his life. During the Swiss Composers' Festival in Baden near Zürich in the spring of 1908, some of the main events were performances of songs by Schoeck, the *Ratcliff* overture and the *Serenade* (Opus 1) for small orchestra. At the age of twenty-two Schoeck was already an established composer.

The choice of texts for these early songs foreshadows his later development. The poets chosen belong primarily to the German Romantic movement: Nikolaus Lenau, Ludwig Uhland, Heinrich Heine and Novalis, as well as the Swiss poets Gottfried Keller and Conrad Ferdinand Meyer. Three songs, however, are based on quite different lyrical sources. In 1907 Schoeck set Paul Verlaine's *Mandoline* to music and also texts by Dante and Michelangelo. The previous year the first volume containing four songs by Hermann Hesse had been published and Hesse's poems also form the basis of the collections of 1913, 1914 and 1915, as well as of 1929 and appear again in a choral work *Maschinenschlacht* in 1953.

During those early years a beautiful young violinist called Steffi Geyer was receiving widespread acclaim. Béla Bartók had written a violin concerto for her in 1907 which, however, was neither performed nor published (until after her death) because of a tragic love-affair. Schoeck too fell under the artistic and personal spell of this young violinist after he had heard her in Leipzig. To his delight she engaged him as accompanist on a tour of Switzerland, during which some of his own works were on the programme. But strangely enough it was not until 1954 that Steffi Geyer performed any of Schoeck's works for violin, namely the revised *Violin Sonata in D major* of 1905.

In addition to his composing Schoeck now became active as a performer. He frequently accompanied singers in performances of his songs. In 1909 he became conductor of a male voice choir and in 1911 took over as conductor of the *Lehrergesangsverein* (Teachers' Choral Union) in Zürich. Thus, in the years preceding the Great War, the young, successful composer enjoyed a very busy and full life. He felt the magnetic pull of Italy and he visited the cities and countryside of this country south of his homeland many times, experiencing on these journeys the same feelings that Goethe wrote about in his *Italian Journals* and which, in their own different ways, Richard Wagner and, much later, Hans Werner Henze had shared. For Schoeck, both painter and musician in one, travels to the South counterbalanced the meditative tendency of his Nordic ancestors. On some of these journeys he was accompanied by the poet Hermann Hesse, who was also a painter. Hesse, when an old man, recalled these journeys together as well as

Schoeck's visits to Gaienhofen, in his letter of condolence to Schoeck's widow.

In 1910 Schoeck visited Salzburg for the Summer Festival, and went on to Budapest, but was disappointed not to meet Steffi Geyer there. He overcame his sadness by writing a violin concerto with the Beethoven-like title *Quasi una fantasia*.

In 1911 Schoeck considered writing music for a drama for the first time. He had been much attracted by Goethe's *Singspiel, Erwin und Elmire,* and he wrote several songs, an overture and an interlude for it. The work was not completed until 1916 and in that year was performed at the Zürich Municipal Theatre. Schoeck had already begun to feel the limitations of song-writing. From early days his model had been Hugo Wolf, and the *Serenade for Orchestra* of 1907 often echoes Wolf's *Italian Serenade*. Schoeck's grouping of songs into cycles with unifying action or atmosphere also goes back more to Wolf than Schubert, though the development of the music, leading from the songs to the more symphonic parts of the score, is more characteristic of Schubert. But the work bore no resemblance to those Italian operas which Schoeck so loved, neither those of Mozart on the one hand, nor those of Pietro Mascagni and Puccini on the other. Schoeck developed slowly as a dramatist, with a growing assurance in his mastery of dramatic devices and of extended song forms.

Among the many famous people who sought refuge in Switzerland before the Great War was the pianist Ferruccio Busoni. He set up home in Zürich in 1915 and remained there for over four years. During this time, Schoeck made his acquaintance and became his friend. The ideas of the two men were poles apart: Schoeck as an artist was always seeking for all that was romantic, whereas the classical revolutionary Busoni found this suspect and a good target for his caustic wit. In the autumn of 1916, Schoeck found himself in need of a text for an opera. Busoni, who was exceptionally well-read in all European languages, suggested a comedy by the Danish writer Ludwig Holberg with a Don Quixote-like theme and the pompous Spanish title *Don Ranudo de Colibrados*. The material fascinated Schoeck. The score was finished in 1918 and the first performance took place in Zürich in April of the following year, under the direction of Robert F. Denzler and with the famous baritone, Alfred Jerger, in the cast. The timing was propitious. The warring armies had laid down their arms and the Zürich audience responded with cheers to the gaiety and comedy of the work. Thus to Schoeck's fame as a song-writer was now added success as an operatic composer. But in the spring of 1918 Busoni already had a new suggestion to make. This time it was a strange work of Chinese origin, from an anthology by Martin Buber, with the title *Das Wandbild* (The Mural) and the subtitle *Scene and Pantomime*. Schoeck was so delighted with it that he finished the music within a week. Since its first performance in Halle in 1921 this work, with its strange ghost-story, has not been staged elsewhere. The effect of his next opera, *Venus*, was incomparably greater. It was much acclaimed after its première in Zürich in 1922, though it did not have sufficient dramatic unity to become part of the regular operatic repertoire. The music, in its wholly personal lyricism and sensuousness, revealed for the first time the complete spectrum of Schoeck's musical language. All that is characteristic of the composer in his later song-cycles and operas may be traced back to this score.

As a result of his activities as a choral conductor Schoeck had achieved ever greater importance as an orchestral conductor. In 1917 the city of St Gall appointed him conductor for their symphony concerts. He continued in this post for twenty-seven years, whilst continuing to live in Zürich, and carried out his duties with artistic integrity and considerable success. Meanwhile he was producing a large number of compositions, the focal points of which were small collections of songs and longer song-cycles. In addition he wrote choral works, of which several—such as the *Trommelschläge* (Drumbeats) based on verses by Walt Whitman —were performed under Schoeck's direction by his Teacher's Choir in Zürich. On the other hand he wrote virtually no instrumental music during these years, with the exception of two piano pieces, written in 1919 and 1920, and a second string quartet in 1923.

After the Great War many new ideas crowded in upon Schoeck, who had always been responsive to change. He saw the arts changed and questioned in their fundamentals—particularly in harmony and tonality. The revolutions in Russia and Central Europe greatly affected him and increased his tendency to criticize the 'bourgeois' society to which he himself belonged. That inner restlessness which held him in its grip could no longer be banished by creative work alone, and in June 1923 he went to

Paris, where Arthur Honegger introduced him to many French musicians, including those from the group known as the 'Six'. By now Schoeck had reached his thirties, still a lonely figure despite several passionate love affairs.

During these years of inner turmoil, while he was working on the score of *Venus*, Schoeck wrote his *Elegy*. It is a sequence of songs for baritone and chamber orchestra, based on twenty-four poems by Lenau and Eichendorff. This work, one of Schoeck's most important, lies on the borderline between drama and lyricism. In its desire for an excess of expressiveness, its harmony oversteps the bounds of tonality. It is a kind of ultimate music, wrested from a spirit which could no longer come to terms with the problems of the world.

Out of Schoeck's spiritual and musical crisis was born the opera *Penthesilea*, based on Kleist's play, and written during the years 1924-5. Without setting to music a single extraneous word, but simply by shortening and compressing the text, the composer succeeded in developing new forms in music drama. As his friend and biographer Hans Corrodi has written: 'Schoeck created a new, individual technique for music drama: veritable pillars of chords are spread over the scenes as all-embracing bases of sound ... thus Schoeck achieves a true musical perspective in depth'. In addition to the powerful ensembles and arias the score contains, here and there, musical accompaniments to the spoken word, similar to some romantic models later than Weber and Schumann and also related to melodramatic scenes in works by Schoenberg or Alban Berg. While Schoeck was working on his *Penthesilea*, he met the soprano Hilde Bartscher at a party in Zürich. She became his wife at the end of 1925 and outlived him by many years.

Schoeck's work as composer continued. In 1926 he completed a song-cycle for baritone and orchestra, based on fourteen poems in Gottfried Keller's *Lebendig begraben* (Buried Alive), which in its deeply moving seriousness recalls the earlier *Elegy*. This cycle is considered to be Schoeck's main contribution to the national music of Switzerland. Permeated by the spirit of the countryside so typical of Keller, it ends in deep, transfigured serenity.

The first performance of *Penthesilea* took place at the Dresden State Opera in 1927 and was soon followed by its première in Zürich. Since then, the opera, which was given an enthusiastic reception in Dresden, has never quite disappeared from the operatic repertoire in Germany and Switzerland. Even so totally different a composer as Ernst Křenek has said: 'In *Penthesilea* Schoeck enters the sovereign realm of art which is timeless and where the greatest spirits may meet, purified from all earthly bonds'. This opera, the most important of all Schoeck's dramatic works, brought him great honour.

Schoeck followed his tragic opera with a merry one, based on one of Grimm's fairy-tales *Vom Fischer un syner Fru* (The Fisherman and his Wife) using the version of Philipp Otto Runge. This too was first performed at the Dresden State Opera on 3 October 1930, under Fritz Busch, and met with great success. The Zürich premiere took place one year later. In both cities, however, its success was somewhat diminished by the dramatic weakness of the fairy-tale.

Meanwhile Schoeck's mother and father both died within a short time and Schoeck, who was devoted to his parents, was deeply affected by their loss. For a time all composition ceased, but his creative energy was restored at the French Riviera, where he began to paint his impressions of the southern countryside and composed the E major sonata for violin and piano, soon to be followed by a prelude for orchestra. A further song-cycle, the *Notturno* for baritone and string quartet, was written at about the same time. In 1934 the city of Berne organized a week's festival devoted to Schoeck, at which all his most important works were performed. In the same year he began work on an opera based on the story *Massimilla Doni* by Honoré de Balzac, which he had been considering for some time. The title-role of this opera, which received its first performance in Dresden in 1937 under Karl Böhm, is the finest female character that Schoeck had created. At a time of political upheaval and in a world oppressed by the Hitler régime, the work made a deep impression of strength and purity. The present writer attended the first performance and wrote in the Vienna newspaper *Neue Freie Presse* at the time: 'Schoeck's stage works, although not dramatic in the Wagnerian sense ... are among the most individual contributions to the operatic stage.'

Schoeck had now reached the age of fifty; in Switzerland his birthday was celebrated with special performances of his works. Essays and speeches acclaimed the genius who had created new forms of musical drama out of the song. But Schoeck himself found his fame more tedious than pleasant. Moreover, he suffered **greatly**

171

under the political tension which had arisen as a result of Hitler's fascism. In Germany his works were not officially approved; those musical circles that admired him and succeeded in staging perform-mances of his works such as *Massimilla Doni* which was performed in Dresden, did so on their own responsibility and at some risk. Schoeck himself saw no reason to ban performances on German stages. This in turn led to his estrangement from those circles in Switzerland which were politically more involved. The fact that Hilde Schoeck came from Frankfurt and that her family still lived in Germany did not help matters. By the time war broke out in 1939, tension was very great. During these troubled years, Schoeck wrote more articles on artistic problems than he had previously done. He acknowledged his debt to those comp-osers whom he prized most highly—Bach, Mozart and Schubert. He also composed new song-cycles such as the *Wandsbeker Liederbuch* based on Matthias Claudius (1937) and *Unter Sternen* (1943) based on poems by Gottfried Keller.

The main work of these years, however, was an opera, the last he was able to finish. Again it was Hermann Hesse who suggested the material, a strange story by Eichendorff, *Das Schloss Dürande*, which forms the core of the libretto, written by Hermann Burte. The composition took a long time; the opera, begun in 1937, was not finished until 1941. In between Schoeck undertook several concert tours and also went on holiday to Italy. The Berlin State Opera accepted *Das Schloss Dürande* for its first performance and the Vienna Universal Edition printed the piano reduction prepared by Anton von Webern. The première on 1 April 1943 in the heavily bombed city of Berlin must have had a ghost-like quality about it. Schoeck himself was present and at the end received the enthusias-tic acclaim of the audience. In the final scene the castle, symbol of a world founded on madness, crumbles. The performance under Robert Heger, produced by Wolf Völker and with décor by Emil Praetorius brought together singers such as Maria Cebotari, Martha Fuchs, Peter Anders, Willi Domgraf-Fassbänder and Josef Greindl —a star cast. It had a grotesque sequel. Hermann Goering, Admin-istrative Director of the Prussian State theatres, had not attended the première. He was, however, so outraged on reading the libretto that he sent a furious telegram to the director, Heinz Tietjen, call-ing the performance of such 'filthy rubbish' a scandal.

In Zürich, where the work was performed later in the year with

the baritone Marko Rothmüller in the main part, a large section
of the press condemned it, mainly for political reasons. Schoeck
took all this literally to heart. On 9 March 1944, he was conducting
one of his concerts in St Gall, when, during a Schumann symphony
he suffered a heart attack. His health was broken and he was no
longer able to conduct.

It was months before he was again strong enough to compose
and to play the piano. He wrote a new song-cycle, *Der Sänger,*
using poems by Heinrich Leuthold which Hermann Hesse had
brought to his attention. Ernst Haefliger gave the first performance
in St Gall with Schoeck at the piano. Gradually his mental and
physical equilibrium returned. His last years produced a rich
harvest of music: songs with piano accompaniment based on
poems by C. F. Meyer and Mörike songs with orchestra, choruses,
a horn concerto, a *Festival Hymn* for orchestra and ritornelli and
fughette for piano. Schoeck was still able to go on short concert
tours with his wife, for instance to Baden-Baden in 1951, the year
of his sixty-fifth birthday. But there were continual relapses requiring hospital treatment for his heart condition. He was delighted
with the celebrations for his seventieth birthday and the special
concert under Paul Sacher. Many artists like Maria Stader, Dietrich
Fischer-Dieskau and others performed his songs. In 1956 his health
seemed to be improving. Then came the spring, always a critical
time of the year for Schoeck. On 8 March 1957, almost exactly
thirteen years after his collapse in St Gall, he died quite suddenly
in Zürich. Hermann Hesse, then eighty years old, wrote to Hilde
Schoeck: 'Whenever I thought of Othmar, I hoped so fervently
that I should not have to lose him, one of the dearest of all my
friends. I join with you in sorrow and am thankful for the comfort
that his works are with us and may continue to warm our hearts.'

18 Frank Martin

The artistic event which was to influence Frank Martin's whole life was, according to his own report, a performance of Bach's *St Matthew Passion* that he attended in his native Geneva in 1900 when he was ten years old. He was born on 15 September, 1890, the tenth and last child of a Protestant pastor. The Martin family had French and Dutch roots and had settled in Geneva in 1830. The boy learned to play the piano at an early age and took part in domestic music-making before he went to grammar school. On matriculating he studied mathematics and natural sciences between 1908 and 1910 and then decided on music as a career. He became a pupil of the composer Joseph Lauber, who was himself a truly Swiss product of two civilizations: German as a pupil of Friedrich Hegar and Joseph Rheinberger, and French through Jules Massenet. This spiritual twin nationality of the teacher was transferred to the pupil. Although French was Frank Martin's mother-tongue and he used mostly French texts for his settings, he was equally receptive to the impact of Germany polyphony and later to the disruption of traditional tonality by the second Viennese school. When he was twenty he wrote three orchestral songs for baritone to poems by Leconte de Lisle which were first performed in 1910 at the Festival of Swiss Composers in Vevey.

During the following years Frank Martin wrote chiefly chamber and orchestral music. He became his own teacher and tried to come to terms with a variety of stylistic influences. Strauss and Mahler were the first strong influences, superseded later by Debussy.

In 1918 Frank Martin wrote a cantata *Les Dithyrambes*, to words by his brother Pierre, for solo voices, children's choir, mixed choir and orchestra. Ernest Ansermet, who had recently founded the *Orchestre de la Suisse Romande* in Geneva, saw the score and performed it in Lusanne, and to the end of his life the great conductor remained a champion and friend of Frank Martin. He said about Martin's works: 'Their true value lies in their wealth of spiritual experiences, revealed to us in their entirety'.

In 1916, a period of migration started for the composer. He spent two years in Zürich, followed by a short stay in Rome during 1921. A piano quintet and *Four Sonnets by Ronsard* for mezzo soprano, flute, viola and cello were added to his output during these three years. He returned to Geneva in 1922, and wrote his first theatrical music in the form of incidental music for the two *Oedipus* tragedies by Sophocles, performed by the *Comédie de Genève*. A stay in Paris, in 1925, where his first marriage was dissolved, marks the end of this unsettled period. Subsequently, Frank Martin made his home in Geneva and stayed there for over twenty years. He was largely occupied by practical music-making and founded small instrumental ensembles which led to the formation of the *Societé de musique de chambre de Genève*. As a pianist and harpsichordist, he preferred above all the music of Bach and Debussy.

In 1926 Martin began to take an interest in the rhythmic theories of Emil Jacques-Dalcroze. He studied with him until 1928 and was then employed for ten years as a teacher at the Dalcroze Institute. This new influence produced the three symphonic movements *Rhythmes* in which the piano fulfils particular functions within the orchestra. Ansermet conducted the first performance at the festival of the International Society for New Music in Geneva in April 1929. In the same year Martin wrote incidental music to Shakespeare's *Romeo and Juliet* for choir and five instruments.

In the early thirties a Russian couple founded in Geneva the *Technicum Moderne de Musique,* a music school set up in rivalry to the old Conservatory. Martin was appointed its artistic director and held this post until 1939. During these years he began to study Schoenberg's twelve-note technique and to clarify his attitude to it, trying to reconcile this method of composition with the traditional elements and harmonic procedures of tonal music.

I could never follow the school of Schoenberg into the realms of atonality; I have the same feeling that is produced in me when I

Frank Martin

envisage a building that ignores the forces of gravity, or a world where the vertical and horizontal do not exist and where even a right angle is unknown.

He nevertheless acknowledged that the handling of twelve-note series had acquainted him with a new musical language. In fact the scope of Martin's musical idiom greatly increased after he learned to master the technique of twelve-note composition. His first attempts were made in some incidental music, in a piano concerto and a rhapsody for string quintet which have never been published. The personal style he finally adopted was first established in the chamber oratorio *Le Vin Herbé* for twelve voices, seven strings and piano. The work was first performed in Zürich in 1940. The full-length version was also given there in 1942 and it was staged for the first time in 1948 during the Salzburg Festival. *Le Vin Herbé* is a novel treatment of the legend of Tristan and Isolde. The music avoids Wagnerian bathos and achieves an inwardness that explains the world-wide success of the work. The score is based on variations of a twelve-note series that can be treated triadically. Stylistically it is typical of Martin's refined approach, a heritage of his French descent, in which the influence of Debussy is unmistakable.

In 1939 Martin was appointed professor at the Geneva Conservatory. Until then he had only set French words, but now he was inspired by the poetry of Rainer Maria Rilke to write a new work. As the result of a commission by Paul Sacher, a conductor and generous patron of music in Basle, he wrote *Die Weise von Liebe und Tod des Cornets Christoph Rilke* for contralto and orchestra. Roughly at the same time, 1943, he composed the ballet *Ein Totentanz zu Basel* for strings, symphonic jazz and Basle drum and *Six Monologues* for baritone from Hofmannsthal's *Jedermann*. In addition he met the young Rumanian pianist Dinu Lipatti, who was a fellow professor at the Conservatory and who, before his untimely death, was a great source of inspiration to Martin.

Although he had been brought up in the home of a pastor, Martin had maintained an independent attitude towards religion, and apart from an early setting of the mass he had avoided religious texts. But in 1944 Geneva Radio commissioned him to write a

177

choral work to celebrate the end of the war. Between August and October he interrupted work on the *Petite Symphonie Concertante* for harp, harpsichord, piano and two string orchestras, to write a short oratorio *In Terra Pax* on biblical texts for soprano, two mixed choirs and orchestra. The great oratorio *Golgotha* which Martin wrote between 1945 and 1948 under the impact of etchings by Rembrandt bears a close affinity to its shorter precursor. The text is taken from the Gospels and from the writings of St Augustine. In contrast to the classical oratorios, especially those of Bach with their epic approach, Martin concentrates on the tragic drama of the Passion. The work is in two parts, each one hour long, and written for five soloists, mixed choir, organ and orchestra. The score gives the impression of a modern branch that has been grafted on to the tree of romantic religious music. It is permeated by the monumental catholicism of a Bruckner and at the same time, almost furtively, uses modern means of musical expression. Twelve-note series are employed non-functionally as bases and as sources of motivic and thematic material. Nonetheless a homophonic, chordal style predominates. By the time *Golgotha* received its first performance in Geneva in 1949 Frank Martin had left Switzerland. In 1946 he had moved to the native city of his third wife, Amsterdam. Later he built a house in Naarden near Amsterdam where he still lives. His native country was generous enough not to bear him any grudge for leaving and in 1947 he was given the Swiss Composer's prize.

In 1950 Martin was appointed professor of composition at the Musikhochschule in Cologne, where the most prominent of his pupils was Karlheinz Stockhausen. Martin gave up this post when he reached retirement age in 1955.

Between 1949 and 1952 he wrote several works in concerto form, such as the much performed concerto for seven wind instruments, percussion and string orchestra, the violin concerto and the concerto for harpsichord and small orchestra. The main task of these years was, however, the operatic setting of Shakespeare's *Tempest*.

When Martin read this play he was fascinated not by its suitability as the basis of an opera but as a work of art in its own right. The symphony, written in 1940, and the violin concerto already contained elements of the later opera score, but the unaccompanied choral work *Chansons d'Ariel* is the musical embryo from which the opera finally evolved. In the *Tempest* three worlds confront each other: the humanity of Prospero and the young lovers, the spirit-world surrounding Ariel, and the world of the shipwrecked court, with Stephano, Trinculo and Caliban as grotesque figures. Martin endows these worlds with three different modes of musical expression. The exchanges between Prospero, Miranda and Ferdinand are set in traditional operatic forms. Ariel is a dancer whose words are sung by a choir with instrumental accompaniment. The slave Caliban is characterized by trombones and muted tubas, while the world of the court is expressed by jazz with tenor-saxophone, exotic percussion, piano and pizzicato bass. The vocal writing is based on arioso-declamation. The transparent textures of the orchestral sound create an effect of twilight. Only intermittently is the monotony of over-refined sounds interrupted by more dramatic moments such as Prospero's songs, the short duet of the young lovers and the pavane of the goddesses. The first performance at the Vienna State Opera House, conducted by Ansermet, was a great success for the composer, who was present in the audience. Martin is no dramatist and the opera suffers from elements of epic longeur, but it is fascinating as a beautiful late flowering of impressionism.

While working on *Golgotha* between 1945 and 1948 Martin underwent a profound philosophical and spiritual experience which cannot be explained simply by the religious subject-matter of the work. His thoughts became focussed on the problem of artistic responsibility and he expressed them in an article which appeared in French in *Polyphonie* and in a German translation in the musical periodical *Stimmen.*

What sort of responsibility does the composer feel? Let us confront him with his work before and during the process of composition. Before he starts, he will have to decide what kind of work he is going to create. Sometimes this decision is made for him by a definite commission. Then the instrumental and vocal means employed and the approximate duration will have to be decided. Finally he has to imagine the end product, and this cannot be done with any degree of accuracy. It is a kind of premonition, a movement of the spirit which manifests itself in a hundred different ways before the music takes form: visual, tender or passionate impressions like those sudden feelings of joy or sadness that come upon us for no particular reason.

This premonition can sometimes appear in the shape of a musical form: it seems to the composer that the work will be realised as a fugue, a passacaglia or a symphonic allegro. This first vision is very inconstant. It cannot be expressed because only the finished work will express it. All volition, all the powers of being are concentrated upon a goal that is entirely unknown. One knows it only when it is reached.

And Martin declares further:

The correct and fitting solution is the result of a brainwave in much the same way as it is with the mathematician. The process is similar, but with the artist the solution is determined by the demands of sensibility and beauty, with the mathematician by the demands of intellect.

Since 1955 Martin has devoted himself almost exclusively to the joys of composing. For Paul Sacher and the Basle Chamber Orchestra he wrote the long-promised *Orchestral Studies,* elaborately wrought pieces for strings and fugues and variations. *Psaumes,* a psalm-cantata for children's choir, mixed choir, organ and orchestra, commissioned by Geneva Radio for the quarter-centenary of the University of Geneva, is even more polyphonic.

The main work of this period, however, has been *Mystère de la Nativité,* a long oratorio which occupied the composer from 1957 to 1959. The words are taken from a vast mystery play on the birth of Christ, written by Arnoul Greban in 1425, which comprises more than 34,000 verses in beautiful old French, and is alive with faith, mysticism and medieval fear of God. Martin selected from this play the dramatic contrasts of three separate yet integrated spheres: paradise, earth and hell. A large body of performers is employed: two female and seven male soloists, a small mixed choir for the angels, a big mixed choir, a small male-voice choir for the devils and a large orchestra with triple and quadruple wind, large percussion and two harps.

This meticulous score of consummate craftsmanship is stylistically reminiscent of Martin's earlier religious works, especially *Golgotha,* with the addition of the arioso technique which he had developed in the opera *The Tempest.* It is a musical language of great nobility, dignity and taste, even in the ecstatic cantilenas of Mary and the jubilant choruses of the heavenly hosts which are ravishingly beautiful but never sickly sweet.

Here too Martin writes tonally, but the tonality is expressed in harmony that is free, non-functional and flows into cadences of a novel type. The music is pan-chromatic, schooled by twelve-note discipline without fully submitting to it. The character of the music is determined melodically by a free monophonically invented selection of intervals. All that is allowed to develop in the spheres of sound, rhythm and sparing use of polyphony is secondary to the melodic flow.

The oratorio is in three parts, each with scenes set in different places. Two prologues, one in heaven, the other addressed to the audience, open the action. In hell Lucifer, Satan, Beelzebub and Astaroth confer on the use of men as objects of their designs, until Satan capitulates to the virtue of Jesus. On earth we witness the annunciation, the birth of Christ, the adoration of the shepherds, the plaint and consolation of Simeon and the visit of the three kings. The great action concludes with a chorus of jubilation by the angels.

For the scenes in heaven Martin employs melodies of a Gregorian type, embellished by chords. The songs by Mary, Elizabeth and Anne have operatic features, sublimated here and there by melismatic jubilations. Thus in the scenes in heaven cantilena and arioso are the main means of expression. Hell appears in an entirely different musical picture. Over a four-note ostinato of the timpani, voices are heard in a rhythmically fixed *Sprechstimme* in the manner of Schoenberg's *Pierrot Lunaire.* Dissonant interjections by the brass in bizarre counterpoint lead to a kind of diabolic fugue.

The homophonic orchestral sound seems to be derived from Debussy but occasional flashes remind one of Stravinsky, like the sforzati on leaps of the seventh in contrary motion at the beginning and during the scene with Saint Elizabeth. During the adoration of the Child Jesus, the semiquaver movement of the music gives an echo of the angels' concert in *Mathis der Maler.* Martin also approaches the mature style of Hindemith in his harmonic integration of Gregorian melodic formulae. Free formal structures are prevalent; occasionally they are tightened into fugue, march or shepherds' dance.

The first performance of the *Mystére* took place in the new Salsburg Festspielhaus in August 1960. The producer, Margarethe Wallmann, divided the enormous stage reminiscent of a cinema-scope screen, horizontally and vertically into several compartments. On the highest tier was a brilliantly-lit heaven, like a picture by Jan

Memling, while in the lowest the rulers of hell writhed in flames, at their feet vipers from pictures by Hieronymus Bosch or Matthias Grünewald. On the terrestrial plane the stage (over ninety feet wide) was divided into four houses: the habitations of Joseph and Elizabeth, the stable in Bethlehem and the temple where Simeon receives the child in his arms.

The first performance was full of contradictions, because the work, intended for concert performance, seemed to be coarsened by the extraneous effects of the production. But the evening was a success for Martin. The venerable old man, with a face reminiscent of a yearning prophet, stood, somewhat lost on the overlarge stage, and thanked a fashionable international audience that had misunderstood him. He had written in his essay on responsibility:

Matter is recalcitrant and the hand slower than the spirit but the mind or the creative idea can never impose itself on the execution. It therefore seems to me: if the artist is responsible for that which he seeks, he can only be held responsible to a small extent for what he finds. This gives him a certain innocence with regard to success or failure. This innocence may well give him both the freedom and the right to think and reflect about his work and, in all humility, to share the fruit of these reflections with others.

19 Hans Werner Henze

Germany's regeneration in post war years is most clearly typified in the career of Hans Werner Henze. He was born on 1 July 1926, in the Westphalian town of Gütersloh. His father was a schoolmaster. From his earliest youth the relationship between him and his father appears to have been strained, and increasingly so as he grew older. A much closer relationship existed between him and his mother and in later years with his younger brother, an artist whom Henze supported financially for many years. The tensions that existed between himself and his father grew worse after 1933 —when it became clear that the sensitive and artistically talented child had more time for music than for the political discussions that took place at home.

Henze began composing at the age of twelve without any practical or theoretical tuition. He was motivated by an ever increasing longing for the 'wild, sonorous assonance' which he was to encounter later in life in modern music and which at that time was forbidden in Germany; another influence was the poetry of Georg Trakl.

At the age of sixteen Henze was accepted by the State Music School in Brunswick to study piano and percussion, and he stayed there for two years until he was conscripted, first for non-military service, then as a soldier. A year later he was a prisoner of war, though he was soon released by the British and immediately took up a post as *repetiteur* at the Municipal Theatre in Bielefeld, not far from his home town. At the same time he tried his hand at composing; the inadequacy of his training soon became apparent to him and he found a teacher in Heidelberg who shared many of his interests and for some time taught him composition—

Wolfgang Fortner. With the composer and a circle of his young pupils Henze attended the International Vacation Courses for New Music in Darmstadt in 1946 and subsequent years.

Henze, an able and sensitive writer, has written this account of his early studies:

> To Fortner, whose pupil I became in 1946, I owe a thorough knowledge of early methods of composition – strict harmony and counterpoint and the art of the fugue. At the same time Fortner gave me a comprehensive introduction to the realm of modern music and its inherent problems.

In 1947, while he was still studying under Fortner, Henze experimented with twelve-note tone rows in his violin concerto. A year later René Leibowitz instructed him in the rules of this technique and for a time he studied with Josef Rufer, a pupil of Schoenberg's.

His period of tutelage over, Henze returned to the theatre. He directed the ballet in Constance and in 1950 was appointed to the opera-house in Wiesbaden. His tiny, sombre apartment housed a clavichord and, on the wall, a picture of Kafka, whose short story *The Country Doctor* was adapted by Henze as a radio opera. He did not enjoy his work at the theatre and left in 1951 to work as a freelance composer, living in Berlin, Munich, and Paris. Finally he settled in Italy in 1953, living on the island of Ischia until 1956. He felt very much at home in this agricultural and fishing community—where he became friends with the composer William Walton, Truman Capote, the writer, and the choreographer Frederick Ashton. The closest friendship of all was that between himself and the poet Ingeborg Bachmann, a relationship that has much influenced his life and work. He left Ischia for Naples for a few years and then he settled in Rome where he had a house built in the Alban mountains.

The music he composed before 1947 was generally in a playful vein, clearly influenced by the neo-classicism of Hindemith and Stravinsky. The first symphony shows the initial signs of crisis, followed by a consistent move in the direction of the Schoenberg school. Henze looks upon the short cantata *Apollo and Hyacinth* as the most important work of this period. Shortly afterwards he wrote his second and third symphonies. The second expresses all the sorrows of war and death. It is written from the depths of

KARATA gun Power

USE

68

29 Hans Werner Henze (b. 1926) during rehearsal. He began composing at the age of twelve, but did not have any proper practical or theoretical training until he was accepted at the State Musical School in Brunswick four years later. He never felt happy in his native Germany and finally settled in Italy in 1953, living first on the island of Ischia, then in Naples, and eventually in Rome.

30 Henze's latest opera is *Die Bassariden*, a work taken from Greek mythology, with a libretto by W. H. Auden and Chester Kallman. This photograph shows (left to right) Kallman, Auden and Henze during a rehearsal for the first performance at the Salzburg Festival in August 1966.

30

31 The Bavarian composer Werner Egk (b. 1901) (right) during a rehearsal for his *Die Verlobung von San Domingo*, which was chosen as the opening production for the new National Theatre in Munich in November 1963. Egk had planned this opera thirty years before, but a journey to Central America via Lisbon had reawakened his interest in the subject.

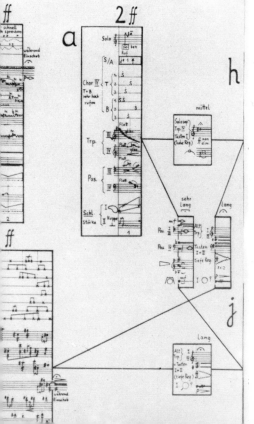

32 Karlheinz Stockhausen (b. 1928) studied in Cologne and attended courses in *musique concrète* and electronic music at the Darmstadt Summer School in 1951. He has been in charge of the electronic studio of the Cologne radio station since 1963.

33 A page from Stockhausen's *Momente*, commissioned by the Cologne broadcasting station and written in 1961 and 1962. The score uses speech as a phonetic musical device.

33

34 A photograph for the family album showing Herr Richard Hartmann with his wife Gertrud and their four sons; Karl Amadeus, the composer (1905–63), is third from the right.

35 Karl Amadeus Hartmann playing with his son Richard in 1939. The outbreak of the Second World War affected him deeply and it was in this year that he wrote a concertino for violin and strings known as *Music for Mourning*.

depression and is full of religious pathos, culminating in the chorale
How brightly shines the morning star in the final movement. The
third is in stark contrast, with its dance-like drive and cult of
sensual beauty—a salient feature in Henze's personality.

Not only did Henze suffer from the memory of the war and death,
but he also intensely disliked the German way of life, and it was
not until he came to Italy that he found a mode of existence with
which he could identify himself. His version of the artistic life transcending a routine bourgeois existence took shape in his opera
Manon Lescaut, after the novel by Abbé Prevost. The libretto differs
considerably from that used by Massenet and Puccini. The central
figure is no longer Manon but her lover, Armand des Grieux. He is
addicted to cocaine, philosophizes on death and becomes an
accomplice to Manon's brother's murder of the elderly Lilaque. In
the final scene, in which Manon is transferred from one jail to
another, dream and reality become one. The music clearly demon-
strates Henze's dramatic talents. Despite its incredible mixture of
styles—coloratura, folk-dances, duo-decaphony, jazz rhythms and
sound effects it is clearly written in his own personal idiom. It is
subtle, sensitive and full of erotic sublimation. Immediately after
he left Germany Henze said:

Two suitcases contained all my belongings – books and scores. My
first evening in Venice was spent sitting still for hours in unknown
squares and corridors in the labyrinth of deserted Venetian alleys. All
that has been is now to be forgotten, everything will be different, the
sun dissolves everything. Crossing through Tuscany, a mighty, spac-
ious vessel of charm and symmetry.

In Italy his music grew brighter, with a new feeling for melody
and intervals. Vision and imagination are now in ascendancy
over calculation and contrivance. Henze rejected the ideals of his
generation. He became—even if at first only unconsciously—the
diametrical opposite of the Darmstadt school with their serial
charts and automatic electronic music-making.

In collaboration with Heinz von Cramer he wrote the opera *King
Stag* after Carlo Gozzi's fable of the king who voluntarily assumes
animal form. This large-scale work, set in fairyland, was given its
controversial première in Berlin in 1956 at the *Städtische Oper*
under Hermann Scherchen. By this time Henze was thirty years
old and had overcome his technical limitations. The sound of the

large orchestra with harpsichord, piano, accordion and guitar as additional colour ingredients is particularly rich and the composer has deliberately fused tonal, atonal and twelve-note textures. The vocal lines are free-ranging and arioso, with the occasional hint of Italian folksong. Henze wrote:

> Whilst waiting for the first act, in spring 1953, my 'Italian experience' began . . . . . I landed in an antique world, at first totally alien to me and uncanny, a landscape from which human lives ceaselessly emerge and return . . . .the miraculous happenings in the legend of King Stag, the idea of metamorphosis, notions of a freedom that goes beyond the bounds of the tolerable, the death of a tyrant, peace; they are all themes that had to be presented without any distortion, without parody and gimmicks.

His 'Italian experience' lies at the heart of this opera, and in like manner Naples is reflected in the *Five Neopolitan Songs*, 1956, that have become famous through their interpretation by Dietrich Fischer-Dieskau.

As musical director in Constance and Wiesbaden Henze had already written a number of short ballets. In 1952 he wrote *The Idiot* after Dostoyvesky's novel of the same name for the choreographer. Tatiana Gsovsky, a commission for the *Berliner Festwochen*. It is scored for fourteen instruments and the texture is extraordinarily light and transparent, though the figures, rhythms and thematic material are substantial by contrast and evoke correspondingly substantial gestures from the dancers and from the speaker/clown, originally played by Klaus Kinski.

After an interval of four years, Henze's next ballet was *Maratona di Danza*, an experimental jazz work with Luchino Visconti. Then came his first full length ballet, *Undine*, a strange score, full of romantic reminiscences with nostalgic orchestral accompaniment. The idea of it sprang from a discussion with Frederick Ashton: the work was given its world première at Covent Garden in 1958, with Margot Fonteyn in the title role, and was subsequently performed by companies all over the world.

During the years in Naples from 1957 to 1961 Henze devoted his attentions to various experiments and sketches in strictly logical music, such as the *Nocturnes and Arias* for soprano, the *Sonata per Archi*, the *Three Dithyrambs* and *Antifone*. The short *Concerto per il Marigny*, conducted by Boulez at one of the concerts of the

Domaine Musicale in Paris and the *Chamber Music 1958* for tenor,
guitar and eight instruments were all composed at about that time.
The next important work was another opera—*The Prince of
Homburg* with a libretto after Kleist's work by Ingeborg
Bachmann.

All that happens is related to the world of Italian opera as it
gathered momentum at the beginning of the nineteenth century and
then dominated the whole century, permeating even Kleist's Berlin (see
also Heine's letter). My interest in this art form was just on the upsurge,
and my need to steep myself in it very acute, when I decided to
engage on the *Prince of Homburg*. Bellini's serene melancholy, Ros-
sini's sparkle and brio, Donizetti's heavy passion, and all of it united
and condensed in Verdi's robust rhythms, his hard orchestral colours
and melodic lines that set one's ears tingling – these were things that
had captivated me for years and were first reflected in *Undine*, but
now sought expression in pure melodrama.

In Henze's score the lyrical element far outweighs the dramatic.
Generally speaking the idiom of *The Prince of Homburg* is less
personal than in *King Stag*. Inspiration and imagination are given
artistic sense. Henze avoids being influenced by the pseudo-
baroque or the Prussian milieu of Kleist's play. Often, especially
in Act I, the opera lacks climax and emotional impetus. The title
role is given less prominence than that of Princess Natalia of
Orange, who is particularly well drawn by the composer. The
production of the première in Hamburg in May 1960 was assigned
to Helmut Käutner, a film producer, whose production of
Honegger's operetta *Le Roi Pausole* had aroused much interest.
It was conducted by Leopold Stokowsky and was a tremendous
success, despite a few shouts of protest that greeted the first performance.

Henze's diary contains the following entries:

Naples, summer 1960: the ancient houses of the Pizzofalcone surrounding my house are being pulled down. First cranes insinuate
themselves in the landscape, then, supported by the noise of bulldozers,
high, trenchant palaces grow between my terrace and the view that
once was there, Posillipo, the fishing harbour at Mergallina, the Sor-
rentine peninsula of Capri, Vesuvius. Work on the *Elegy for Young
Lovers*, on which I had just begun, had to be broken off. In the search
for a suitable place to work undisturbed I decided on Berlin.
Autumn and winter, cool clear air, peace and quiet in Grünewald,

people helping me in my work. Though the Munich Opera was already in rehearsal, Act I and parts of Act II were still being despatched, bit by bit like a subscription scheme, and Act III was nowhere near ready. Despite that the first performance somehow took place at the end of May, 1961, in Schwetzingen.

Of all the texts which Henze has set to music, with the possible exception of the radio opera in absurd style, *The End of a World*, this text to the *Elegy for Young Lovers* by W. H. Auden is the strangest; it has an egocentric and ruthless poetic genius as its central figure: The score requires only six singers, a speaker, and chamber orchestra. As such it is in keeping in its dimensions with the delightful rococo theatre in Schwetzingen, where the Munich Opera company gave the opera's first performance. Percussion instruments such as xylophone, vibraphone, and tubular bells largely determine the light, plaintive atmosphere of the work. Strings and wind instruments are omitted from the score, the piano is pre-recorded and electronic timbres are added.

Apart from Gregor, the main figure, the interest is focused on the semi-insane widow, Hilda Mack, with her mixture of coloratura, cantilene, and *Sprechgesang* in the manner of *Pierrot Lunaire*. Inspired duets and ensembles, and Gregor's tremendous outburst at the end of Act II demonstrate Henze's virtuosity as a vocal composer.

During the period of writing the opera Henze discussed music with students at the Technical University in Berlin. The discussion ranged over rhythm then over serial and totally logically organized music. Henze, was asked if such music was intelligible to the ear. 'I think not' was the answer.—'I don't even think it is intended to be.... Analysis on the written page is all they want ... and the feeling of moral satisfaction that everything is in order on paper.'

Early in the sixties the Mozarteum in Salzburg offered him a master-class in composition. At first he refused, but the idea and responsibility of working with young people appealed to him and he finally accepted. His lessons all take the form of individual tutorials with harmony and traditional counterpoint forming the basis of the tuition. The techniques of modern music are explained 'as a subject like any other subject'.

In summer 1961 Henze discovered the beauty of the Castelli Romani. In Castel Gandolfo, near the summer residence of the Pope, he developed an interest in the life and fate of Giordano

Bruno, a Renaissance philosopher, who was burnt at the stake by the Inquisition. In consequence he wrote the oratorio *Novae de Infinito Laudes*, composed to words by Bruno, for many voices and a great consort of lutes, pianos, harps, cors anglais, trumpets and trombones.

Henze is almost unique amongst contemporary composers in that he continues to write symphonies. The music of *King Stag* was adapted as his *Fourth Symphony* in five movements in 1955. In 1962 he wrote his fifth, for an orchestra without clarinets or bassoons, and with alto flute, viola and harp as solo instruments. To a crowded auditorium in the Congress Hall in Berlin in January 1963 he said:

> For me the forms of the past are, as it were, classical ideals of beauty. They are no longer accessible, yet they are visible at a great distance, giving life to dreamlike memories. The path that leads to them is filled with the immense darkness of the age, the path that leads to them is the hardest and most impossible of ways. But for me it is the only folly worth living for.

The *Fifth Symphony* marks the end of experimentation for the sake of it. Subsequently Henze's works have spoken, not in a contemporary idiom, but one that belongs equally to the past and to the future. In May 1963 he went to the United States for the first time, and was hailed as one of Europe's leading composers. In the summer he collaborated with Alain Resnais in writing music for the film *Muriel*. Smaller works of this period include the cantata *Being Beauteous* for coloratura soprano, four cellos and harp.

The idea that appealed to him most at that time was the creation of a comic opera. A few preliminary attempts had been made in such works as *Das Kleine Wundertheater* (Miraculous Little Theatre), the radio opera *The End of a World*, the clown scenes in *King Stag* and a few fleeting scenes in the *Elegy for Young Lovers*. In all these, however, death, pain, and 'sweet need' were the basic ingredients. *The Young Lord* is an adaptation by Ingeborg Bachmann of the fairy tale by Wilhelm Hauff. In satirical terms reminiscent of Aristophanes, German middle-class provincialism in the nineteenth century is held up to ridicule. The central figure is a disguised chimpanzee who has been introduced into society in a German provincial town and proceeds to set the tone of life there until the discovery of the deception and its chaotic conse-quences. Henze, who had long detested the middle-class, conserva-tive way of life in Germany, took malicious delight in setting the libretto to music. Stravinsky, Verdi and Mozart all have a hand in the style of the work, which is predominantly tonal, with passa-caglias, fugues, sarabandes, minuets and waltzes appearing in Act II. Its première took place in Berlin under Christoph von Dohnànyi and has been performed since then in many opera houses in and outside Germany.

The work represents a rejection of all the composer's previous ideas. Stylistically the clock has been turned back, in the same way it was by Strauss in *Der Rosenkavalier*, Hindemith in *Mathis der Maler* and in the great symphonies of Shostakovich.

A musician like Henze who enjoys company, conversation, travelling and good food cannot thrive in solitude. Teaching went some way to providing the stimulus he needed, but was not enough. Finally he took up conducting again, having had lessons on the technique of conducting fifteen years earlier from Hermann Scherchen in Darmstadt. He also had experience as a ballet conduc-tor in Constance, Wiesbaden and later at Covent Garden. Now he was to conduct a symphony orchestra for the first time. In 1964 he conducted the Berlin Philharmonic in concerts devoted to his own music. This debut, given to a predominantly young audience was a great success. He returned a year later to conduct *Giordano Bruno* and the hyper-complicated orchestral work *Antifone,* the first performance of which had been given by Karajan. He proved himself to be a sound conductor with a good control over the orchestra, and an eloquent advocate of his own music—as has been confirmed by subsequent tours in Japan and the USA. It was at about this time that his contemporary and former friend Pierre Boulez also moved to conducting. Although one would not look upon Henze as Boulez's equal on the rostrum it must be remembered that, for Henze, conducting is only a minute part of his complex musical personality: composing has remained his primary concern.

Even before the first performance of *The Young Lord* the rumour was that Henze was working on a new opera taken from Greek mythology to a libretto prepared by W. H. Auden and Chester Kallman. In 1966 the mythological opera was completed. It is called *The Bassarids* and was given its world-première at the

Salzburg Festival in August of that year by the *Deutsche Oper Berlin*. The main figure is the god Dionysius. Auden and Kallman allow him to range through time and space in the various guises of Lord Byron, of an antique godhead, and of Beau Brummel, complete with monocle. Tiresias, the blind soothsayer, is an Anglican priest, inquisitive about the cult of Dionysius as the *dernier cri* of religion. The riotous crowd prance around in medieval armour and mini-skirts with long dirty hair and shaggy beards. Agave, the daughter of King Cadmus, rips the head off her own son, King Pentheus, an opponent of Dionysius, thinking, in a drunken stupor, that she has killed a young lion, a horrible scene of pseudo-religious sacrificial death.

The four acts of the libretto correspond to those of the opera, divided into the movements of a symphony: sonata, scherzo, adagio, passacaglia. The orchestra produces a wealth of new combinations of familiar orchestral colours, the vocal parts are virtuoso, with chansons, baroque dance, polyphonic choral fugues and an abundance of dissonance. The music is extremely difficult, though unmistakably Henze, with allusions to Rameau, Wagner, Stravinsky, Berg, Schoenberg and Messiaen. A gay intermezzo even shows kinship to Offenbach and Sullivan. In a quartet in the horrific finale we hear sighs reminiscent of Bach in the *St Matthew Passion*.

The *Bassarids*, Henze's most recent opera, was commissioned by the Salzburg Festival. Its baroque romanticism is more akin to the spirit of Hofmansthal than Mozart. The high artistic quality of the work allows it to rise above the mythological horror and the aggressively misogynist nature of the libretto. In the context of German opera it has established Henze as a worthy successor to Richard Strauss.

20 Werner Egk

In 1948 the Bavarian composer Werner Egk wrote on the subject of opera, the art-form to which he owes his major successes: 'Opera like all the arts, seems to be a luxury from a rationalist point of view. It is, however, one of the most purposeful art-forms existing.' He adds that the music-drama's appeal to the senses is a cloak for its tremendous symbolic power. And he maintains with some truth that the magic of opera depends, in a very human and natural way, on union: the union of sounds and words, of drama and music.

An attempt to define the artistic category to which Egk belongs is difficult, for he is not a musician in the same sense as Hindemith, Richard Strauss or Maurice Ravel. His is a composite personality, a complex talent. The stimulus for much of Egk's work springs from a kind of intermediate realm, separating the regions of music, theatre, literature and the visual arts and at the same time forming a link between them. As an author he not only wrote excellent texts for himself, and for colleagues such as Boris Blacher, but he also made imaginative adaptations of works by other dramatists for the operatic stage. Furthermore he wrote articles and essays which give evidence of his lively and creative linguistic skill. At one time he painted, without ever having studied, and the drawings he made in his twenties found favour even with the severest critics. In his knowledge of theatrical matters he is unrivalled and he has been equally successful both as producer and as conductor of his own works.

Egk's father was a schoolmaster in the small Bavarian town of Auchsessheim where Werner was born on 17 May 1901. From 1911 to 1919 he attended St Stephen's School in Augsburg, and here he matriculated. At the same time he was receiving music lessons at the Augsburg Conservatory. Subsequently he studied at Frankfurt and under Carl Orff at Munich. Egk began his work for the theatre with commissions for the *Schaubühne* in the Steiniche-Saal in Munich. While still quite young he married Elisabeth Karl, a violinist, with whom he toured Italy between 1925 and 1927. After returning to Munich in 1927 he worked for a puppet theatre run by Munich artists. A short stay in Berlin in 1928 brought him the commission for a composition for a radio programme and this was the beginning of Egk's work for Munich Radio. After settling there Egk wrote a great deal of music for radio plays between 1930 and 1933, amongst them *Zeit im Funk* and *Einundneunzig Tage* (Ninety-one days) with texts by Robert Seitz.

Apart from his work for radio Egk also wrote music for live performances. When Fritz Buchtger founded the Society for Contemporary Music in Munich Egk was one of the first contributors. A festival was held in the autumn of 1930 during whish works by Ernst Křenek, Carl Orff and Béla Bartók were played and a cantata by Egk, *Trebitsh Lincoln,* received its first performance. In May 1931, working together with Buchgter during another festival, Hermann Scherchen conducted the choral work *Furchtlosigkeit and Wohlwollen* (Fearlessness and Goodwill) for tenor solo, chorus and orchestra, based on Egk's own text.

In 1932 in an experimental school in Munich, Egk taught some twelve-year-old pupils two fables by La Fontaine which they then improvised and acted. Egk took down the children's texts and turned them into two operettas *The Fox and the Raven* and *The Lion and the Mouse.* This practical work, which went further than the contemporaneous experiments of Weill, Hindemith and Brecht, gave Egk an insight into the reactions of unsophisticated listeners and was of inestimable value to him later, in his more serious works.

The radio opera *Columbus* of 1932 was the last commissioned work written for Munich Radio. In the same year the music publishers Schott of Mainz, signed a general contract with him, thus encouraging him to write his first full-length opera *Die Zaubergeige* to text by Ludwig Andersen. The first performance took place in Frankfurt in the spring of 1935. This work, interweaving a plain, medieval-type text with music full of Bavarian folk-tunes, brought Egk his first stage success. The Bavarian folklore character of the music is brought out in the rhythms with their surprising changes of time and 5/8 figures.

Egk, a liberal individualist, watched the spread of Nazism throughout Germany with some scepticism. Since he was considered rather left-wing and a cultural Bolshevik in Munich, a move seemed advisable. In 1936 he accepted the offer of a post as musical director of the Berlin State Opera, for which his next opera *Peer Gynt* was written.

In November 1938 Egk himself conducted the first performance at the State Opera *Unter den Linden*. It was a great success. However, the Nazi press wrote of *Peer Gynt* that it was a plagiarism of the *Threepenny Opera* and undesirable from a national-socialist point of view. In some of its scenes Egk had used jazz elements and his tonality, though never atonal, did not appeal to the nordic ideal held by the political authorities: it resembled some of the examples of 'degenerate music' which had been pilloried a few months earlier at an exhibition in Düsseldorf. The work, for which Tietjen had engaged such great singers as Mathieu Ahlersmeyer and Kate Heidersbach, was in danger of quickly disappearing from the repertoire again. At the third performance, Adolf Hitler arrived. He enjoyed it. He sent for the astonished composer during the interval and assured him he had no further worries about the future of German opera. The submissive Nazi critics had once again to change their views. Nevertheless *Peer Gynt* managed only nine performances and was dropped in 1939, shortly before the beginning of the war.

In spite of the variety of musical styles used in *Peer Gynt,* it shows Egk's unmistakable dramatic talent. Colour in every sense of the word is of prime importance. His individual orchestration has revealed new tone-colours for nearly every instrument. It is based on a soloistic treatment of tone-colours which, even when interwoven, never blend together as they do with Richard Strauss or, differently again, with Debussy and Stravinsky. Egk's orchestral sound has a subtle trace of irony, an almost conspiratorial wink. Yet even the untrained ear is captivated by its sensuous quality. His writing for voices is assured and effective, sometimes rather exposed, but always in such a way that even a provincial company would have no insuperable difficulties to overcome. His sense of strong contrasts is evident, for instance in the libretto for

Peer Gynt which differs considerably from Ibsen's drama. The troll scenes and the erotic episodes are treated with special enjoyment; sometimes the influence of Offenbach's operettas is discernible, while waltzes, gallops and polkas are found side by side with the sweet—almost oversweet—lyricism of music of love and nostalgia.

Egk did not have much time to think about the strange position which he occupied in Hitler's Germany. A new work, a ballet also commissioned by the State Opera, was now waiting to be written. This was an interpretation of the Don Juan theme and it received its first performance in the State Opera in January 1940 under the title *Joan of Zarissa*. For the scenario Egk had used old French and Flemish sources. To the orchestra he added a chorus and also a speaker, who narrates in a prologue Joan's descent from the Trojan Paris, who carried off Helen. Between the individual episodes of highly erotic and dramatic tension the chorus, concealed in the orchestra, sings medieval texts reminiscent of the poetry of Charles d'Orléans. The Berlin performance under Tietjen's direction, with Lizzie Maudrick's choreography and Josef Fennecker's settings achieved a success which went far beyond Germany. In 1942 the Paris Opera produced the work with Serge Lifar's choreography and about the same time the great Czech musician Walclav Talich conducted it at the National Theatre in Prague.

Egk, who made no secret of his liberal views and his love of French ideas, found himself much in sympathy with the intellectuals of countries occupied by the Germans. He formed friendships with Jean Cocteau in Paris and with musicians such as Alois Hába in Prague. He enjoyed a sort of 'fool's freedom' with the Berlin authorities, a freedom which was granted to a few successful artists including the great actor Gustav Grundgens. As Boris Blacher wrote later: 'There were difficulties on all sides. And when I think of my colleague Egk, or Orff, or Fortner—none received any kind of protection from anyone, at best they were tolerated.'

At the turn of the year 1940-1 Egk and his wife returned to Munich. They believed that they would be better able to escape cultural and political intrigues there than in Berlin. But they were wrong. The *Reichsmusikkammer,* an organization to which all practising musicians of whatever kind had to belong (and which enabled the State to control all musical activity), had been under the chairmanship of Richard Strauss from 1933-5. Strauss was forced to resign because of his association with the Jewish writer Stefan Zweig and also because some of his correspondence opened by the Gestapo made him seem politically unreliable. His successor was the old conservative conductor Peter Raabe, who in 1941 invited Egk to take over the composer's section. Egk felt compelled to agree and continued in that office until the end of the Hitler régime. It has to be said in his favour that even here he maintained his liberal attitudes, carrying tolerance to the very furthest point which the authorities would accept. On questions of copyright, which he dealt with from 1937 as a member of the *Confédération Internationale des Sociétés d'Auteurs et Compositeurs,* he toed the Nazi line only when absolutely necessary.

In 1941 the city of Frankfurt signed a contract with Egk to write several larger compositions. The first product of this agreement appeared in January 1942 and was a stage version of the old radio opera *Columbus.* Thereafter Egk was silent until the end of the war, retiring to the solitude of village life in Locham near Munich. Several works kept him busy, among them an opera based on a drama by Calderón which the conductor Clemens Kraus had suggested to him. In May 1944 he wrote to a young German friend:

Circe is not quite complete, it should have been produced in Frankfurt, but there's nothing doing there; on the ruins of Goethe's house is a notice saying: "Do not destroy; irreplaceable cultural heritage". If only such a notice could be put up in letters of fire above this whole earth! Instead, streams of bombs flow through the firmament, and a blood-bath is coming such as there has never been before. Even hope is poisoned.

Circe was the title of the Calderón opera, but it was not performed until four years after the end of the war.

In 1946 Egk was de-nazified by an American court. He had no difficulty in proving his political innocence on all important points of the indictment against him. In 1947 the Baden-Baden radio produced his *Tentation de Saint Antoine* for contralto voice and string quartet, a witty work with erotic punning, based on French poems of the eighteenth century. The director of music of the Baden-Baden radio was Dr Heinrich Strobel, Hindemith's biographer and a francophile like Egk himself. The two had been close friends since 1934. The French authorities in occupation were well disposed towards the composer of *Joan of Zarissa.* Thus it was

197

possible for his next work, a ballet *Abraxas* to be introduced in fragments as an orchestral suite in Baden-Baden. This took place in 1947. In June 1948 the Munich State Opera performed the complete full-length work. It was Egk's first major success after 1945 and also a success for the idea of a 'theatre of the dance' which he had been encouraging ever since *Joan of Zarissa*. Like Stravinsky, Egk was always an enthusiastic champion of the classical dance as against the 'dance of expression' and his ballets show this preference clearly. *Abraxas* is a new version of the *Faust* material, based on Heinrich Heine's interpretation. In addition to the old and the young Faust, the main characters are the paramour Archisposa and the sorceress Bellastriga. Margarete is only of secondary importance. Satan and the child devil Marbuel appear instead of Mephistopheles. The second scene takes place at the Spanish Court of Charles IV, where Archisposa appears as Countess of Parma. Mythological figures, such as Helen, emphasize the fusion of different eras, as Heine had indicated. After a very successful premiere at Munich, conducted by Egk himself, the work was produced at the Berlin State Opera, where it was an ever greater success, repeated by the company more than a hundred times.

During the preparations for the Berlin premiére of *Abraxas* in October, 1949, Egk was offered the directorship of the State College of Music in West Berlin. The post was first offered to Paul Hindemith, who declined. Egk, too, hesitated to take up a position which would be a completely new venture for him. A major contributory factor to his decision to attempt it was the increasing vitality of musical life in Berlin. The City Opera was directed by Heinz Tietjen, formerly superintendent of the State Opera and an old friend of Werner Egk. The Philharmonic Orchestra had returned to its old glory under a young Rumanian conductor Sergiu Celibidache, with Furtwängler as guest conductor. At the head of the new Rias Symphony Orchestra was Ferenc Friscay, also a friend of Egk's and recently appointed by Tietjen as head of opera. And so it was that on 1 January 1950, Egk became Professor of Composition and Director of the College of Music. He moved into a fine house in the Berlin district of Grünewald and until April 1953 conducted the artistic and administrative business of the famous college. At the same time he became President of the German Guild of Composers and chairman of the supervisory board of the German Performing Rights Society, as well as an ordinary member of the Munich and West Berlin Academies. He appeared regularly as conductor with the Munich State Opera.

Out of the *Circe* sketches from the war years in Frankfurt grew two completely different works. The first was a three act opera, simply called *Circe,* which received its first performance at the West Berlin City Opera in December 1948. Egk himself conducted,, Tietjen produced and Fennecker designed the décor and costumes. The Wagnerian tenor Hans Bierer took the part of Ulysses, Josef Greindl appeared as Leoporell and Josef Herrmann as Antistes. The splendid performance itself was a success, but the work was uneven; conventional in many respects, though in others dance-like and colourful, as one would expect of Egk. But the vigour of *Peer Gynt* and the simplicity of *Die Zaubergeige* were lacking.

Exactly ten years later the Frankfurt City Theatre gave the first performance of the comedy *Das Zauberbett* (The Magic Bed), a stage play by Egk but without music. This however, fared no better than the opera based on the same Calderón original. Between these two compositions, Egk was busy with other works; he arranged some dances by Rameau as a *French Suite for Orchestra;* in 1952 he wrote a four movement symphony *Allegria* to be followed by a ballet *Die chinesische Nachtigall* (The Chinese Nightingale) and a *Chanson and Romance* for coloratura soprano and orchestra. But he still loved the operatic stage and he remained true to his principle of using works of literary value as his texts. In stories by the Irish writer W. B. Yeats he found material which he arranged freely in his work *An Irish Legend.* This is a work of fantasy about a Countess Cathleen; it has demons and angels, animals turning into humans and humans into animals, the appearance of Faust, the damned, and indeed many links with the second part of Goethe's *Faust.* In a letter on the *Irish Legend* Egk, who stood apart from the experimental musical development which characterized the compositions of the 1925 generation, wrote:

In the score of the *Irish Legend* an observant critic may find a number of 'modern' stylistic techniques, but these are never used as ends in themselves. If, for example, the art of 'change-ringing' is used in a presto movement in order to resolve a chord, it is done quite intentionally to gain an intellectually organised sparkling sequence of sound as the climax of a dramatic scene. I should just like to quote as further examples the straining tension of polytonal counterpoint, the deliberate changing of complementary chords; the lyrical flow of unusual scales, ... the lively monotony resulting from a systematic analysis of 'indestructible' rhythms by simple displacement of accents; the manipulation of harmonies by the use of certain groups of chords; the flat -B. emphasis of the characteristic chord C-D sharp-F sharp -A-F-A.

This work of great musical and literary complexity reached most of Germany's important stages, was successful in Munich and Vienna, but did not really become a part of the operatic repertoire. Egk, accustomed to thinking in contrasts, began work on an *opera buffa,* using Nicolai Gogol's drama *Revisor* as text. He kept to the original more strictly than usual, but reduced the number of characters to twelve singers and three dancers. Russian dances and songs gave some local colour to the music which goes back to the old type of opera with alternating arias and recitatives. The work was produced in 1956 and its down-to-earth comedy ensured its success.

For a short time Egk had turned his attention to experimental music, stimulated by the meetings of the International Holiday Courses for New Music and by his sojourn in Berlin and his friendship with Boris Blacher, for whom, in 1953, he wrote the text for the *Abstract Opera No. 1* an experiment with 'automatic poetry', using syllables instead of words. The *Irish Legend* reflects the restlessness which his association with the avant-garde had stirred up in him. The opera *Der Revisor* helped Egk to overcome it and he now sought for an incentive of a different kind.

An invitation from an airline came just at the right time. In January 1959 Egk and his wife set out on a journey which took them first to Lisbon and thence to Central America. Egk's colourful diary describes the exotic scenery and people. The Negro and Creole dances fascinated him. The year 1960 saw the performance as one of the most brilliant orchestral works, the *Variations on a Caribbean Theme.* A year later all the great German theatres celebrated Egk's sixtieth birthday with special performances of his operas. In May of the same year the journal *Melos* published fragments of a libretto which Egk had written on a story by Kleist *Die Verlobung in San Domingo,* (The Engagement in San Domingo). The plan for this, originating thirty years earlier, had been brought to life again as a result of Egk's travels in the tropics.

The Munich National Theatre, which had been burned down

during the war, was rebuilt in November 1963; its grand reopening with Wagner's *Die Meistersinger* was followed shortly after by Egk's new opera. It is a later flowering of the naturalistic style with cunningly interwoven exotic elements and is enormously effective in its blending of the themes of racial problems, love and war.

2 1 Karlheinz Stockhausen

The picture of this tall, slender man with an almost military bearing and inquiring eyes has become familiar to us from journals, book-covers and record-sleeves. His features betray intense concentration and something of the 'angry young man' of the post-war years. Karlheinz Stockhausen is the latest addition to the Luigi Nono, Pierre Boulez and Hans Werner Henze generation of composers. His father was a schoolmaster of Rhenish peasant stock and Karlheinz was born in Mödrath near Cologne on 22 August 1928. He lived with his parents in provincial seclusion, attending the elementary school from 1935 to 1942, and then, after the death of his mother in a sanatorium in 1941, spending two years at a boarding school in Zanten. His father was conscripted at the outbreak of the war and never returned. From October 1944 to March 1945 Stockhausen was a medical orderly at the front. When the war was over he worked as a farm labourer near the town of Altenburg.

At the age of six Karlheinz started to play the piano; later, at school in Zanten, he took up the violin and the oboe. The training college to which his school was affiliated engaged him as a pianist with their light music trio and an amateur light opera group employed him as *repetiteur*. He made ends meet by playing the piano and conducting light operas and at the same time he took private lessons in Latin and in 1946 was accepted by the secondary school in Bergisch-Gladbach where he matriculated a year later.

In 1947 he went to the Academy in Cologne, studying piano and training as a music teacher. In addition he studied philosophy, German and music at the University. He passed his final examination with an outstanding dissertation on Bartók's *Sonata for Two*

Pianos and Percussion and was then formally qualified as a secondary school teacher. In 1950, a year after he had qualified, he became a pupil with Frank Martin for composition. For Martin the twenty-two year-old Stockhausen wrote strict fugues, songs, and a violin sonata; he also developed an intense interest in the works of Schoenberg, Stravinsky, and Bartók. In the evenings he earned a living by playing jazz and light music. He even went on tour with a celebrated conjuror by the name of Adrian, improvising for him on the piano the background music to his act.

Almost immediately after leaving the Academy, Stockhausen was appointed to Cologne Radio, where a Studio for Modern Music had been set up, producing late-night programmes of the highest quality. Following the example of the BBC in London some very ambitious musical programmes were broadcast with the collaboration of such modern composers as Hindemith, Schoenberg and Stravinsky. After 1945 this work was continued with even greater intensity. The Music Department appointed composers and musicologists of the modern school, and orchestras and choirs were formed and trained for the performances of modern music. These, in addition to broadcasts, gave public performances, thus becoming an important integral part of Germany's musical life. The considerable financial resources of the stations allowed them to offer generous commissions to composers and increasingly these went to the young generation, in revolt against convention and tradition.

Stockhausen's career owes much to this new situation and to the influence of the radio on public concert life. His work for Cologne Radio meant, if not the total solution, at least considerable relief of his financial problems in a way unknown to earlier generations of artists, who were forced either to give up the struggle or to devote the greater part of their energies to the fight for survival.

Rivalry sprang up between the various stations—with happy consequences for composers, for the desire not to appear reactionary resulted in unprecedented opportunities for the revolutionaries. Even the International Vacation Courses for New Music in Kranichstein Castle, and later in Darmstadt, were supported by the radio.

Stockhausen first attended the Courses in Darmstadt in 1951 and since then many of his works have been performed there. It

204

was in Darmstadt that he first heard the *Four Piano Études* of Oliver Messiaen and became interested in serial composition. In the same year, shortly after passing his final examination, he wrote the first of his pieces that have become decisive in the development of avant garde music in Germany. It was the *Kreuzspiel* for oboe, bass clarinet, piano and three percussion players. The first performance of the work in Darmstadt ended in uproar.

Early in 1952 he moved to Paris, to the Cité Universitaire, to study under Oliver Messiaen at the Conservatory and as a private pupil under Darius Milhaud. He became a closer friend of Pierre Boulez and took an interest in the *Studio for Musique Concrète* organized by Pierre Schaeffer, though he remained unconvinced by it. Indeed he corresponded with Dr Herbert Eimert in Cologne on the problems of electronic music, as his own views diverged more and more from those of Schaeffer.

In the summer of 1952 he returned to Dortmund to experience an uproar over a performance of his *Kreuzspiel* conducted by himself. In Dortmund Stockhausen met a circle of musicians including Giselher Klebe, the musicologists Leo Schrade, Henrich Strobel and the present writer, as well as the pianist Pietro Scarpini and Andor Foldes.

His period in Paris was characterized by the amount of work he did and the number of contacts he made. The *Südwestfunk* (South-West German Radio) in Baden-Baden commissioned his *Game for Orchestra*, a percussion quartet for piano and six timpani, the *Piano Pieces Nos. 1-4*, and his *Points for Orchestra*, the first version of the later *Counterpoints*. Meanwhile Eimert had concluded the preliminary work for an electronic studio at the West German Radio and he appointed Stockhausen in 1953 as one of his permanent staff. Stockhausen consequently left Paris for Cologne.

At the end of May the *Festival of New Music 1953* took place in Cologne. It included five concerts under the patronage of the *Centre de Documentation* in Paris and the North-West German Radio in Cologne. At a morning concert Pierre Schaeffer demonstrated the work of his *Club d'Essai* in *musique concrète*, with which he attempted to establish a new art form through the manipulation of every day sounds. In contrast, Herbert Eimert demonstrated studies in electronic music. The acoustic and technical sides of operations were explained by Werner Meyer-Eppler, a lecturer in the University of Bonn, and a sound engineer, Fritz Enkel.

Three modern German works aroused attention—the *Glissando Symphony* by Giselher Klebe, Henze's chamber opera *The Country Doctor* (Der Landarzt) and Stockhausen's *Counterpoints*. Opinions differed considerably over this last work. The music is unspeakably difficult, exploiting extreme instrumental colours in which that of the piano dominates. It is in the Webern tradition of radical condensation and intensity covering a wealth of simultaneous structures. It adheres to a twelve-note row and to rhythmic and dymnamic series. Hermann Scherchen conducted the work, deviating in performance from time to time from the strict but unrealistic rhythmic demands made by Stockhausen. In so doing he established that the composition can be emancipated from its strict serialism without losing its substance.

Not only was Stockhausen composing, he was also engaged on theoretical writings. In 1952 he wrote on pointalistic music, claiming its derivation from Anton von Webern, 'the most consistent composer of the modern Viennese school'. He speaks of the 'order of a note within itself' and nominates four dimensions—duration, pitch, volume and colour, all of which combine to produce a note. In a slightly later article, *Orientierung,* he commented on Edgar Varèse's *Ionisation,* John Cage's pieces for 'prepared piano', Pierre Schaeffer's *Schallmontagen* (Montages in Sound) and Webern's *Pieces for Violin.*

In 1953 he lectured on Webern at the courses in Darmstadt. His main attention, however, was directed to the work of the Studio in Cologne. He was not satisfied by the limited insight into the technical side of things afforded to him by Schaeffer's *Club d'Essai* in Paris. His concept of music was now much influenced by discussions with Karel Goeyvaerts and Pierre Boulez, and by the Belgian, Henri Pousseur, a new addition to his circle of friends in Cologne. With Herbert Eimert as their *chef d'école* they experimented with the still modest facilities at the Studio.

The first results of these experiments were *Studies I and II* in the summer and autumn 1953. The composer said of the first study:

We went back to the element that is basic to all diversities of sound, to pure frequency, which can be produced electronically and is called 'sinus tone'. All existing sound, every noise, is a mixture of these tones, which we call a spectrum. The character of each spectrum is determined by the number, interval and volume of the sinus tones. They determine the colour of the sound. Consequently, for the first time ever, the possibility was created of writing music in which the tonal colours were *composed* in the real sense of the word – that is by putting together the elements, thereby making the universal structural principles of music applicable also to the proportions of sound.

All these ideas correspond surprisingly with those of the technological theory of music advanced ten years previously by Joseph Schillinger in New York. Schillinger's grasp of physics was not exact enough and Stockhausen, realizing this, turned his attention to the scientific aspects of the problem and put what knowledge he acquired into musical practice. In 1954 he registered as a student of physics at the University of Bonn, attending lectures on phonetics and communications research. In this way he made himself familiar with physics terminology and since that time he has continued to apply his highly personal concept of the subject freely to his music.

Stockhausen notated his *Study II* in accordance with the principle of co-ordinates evolved by Schillinger. Traditional notation was completely incapable of handling the new sound phenomena. Its inaccuracy in questions of dynamics and tonal colour—in fact even of pitch, which now differed from the system of tempered semitones—rendered it useless for the mathematical precision required by serial composers. Because electronic music was to be neither sung nor played but dubbed directly from electronic instruments on to tape, the notation had to fulfil two functions: it had to provide all the data necessary for the technician to produce it and it had to provide the readers with graphic information. Consequently it consists of symbols representing pitch, volume and duration. Later developments have exceeded the bounds even of this system so that a variety of other possibilities have been put forward and applied.

In his early years in the Studio in Cologne Stockhausen championed the rigidity demanded by Eimert in the production of 'pure' electronic music. He rejected all forms of natural sound and noise and therefore the whole idea of *musique concrète*, which he looked upon as a fad of the moment. The circle of musicians in Cologne, which now included such names as Gottfried Michael König,

Mauricio Kagel and Gyorgy Ligeti, looked upon electronic music as a means of performing musical textures on an absolute serial basis. Since Webern was considered the originator of serial music his personality and concept of music were transferred lock, stock and barrel to electronic music. The veneration of Webern typified that particular generation of young musicians, and even the Vacation Courses for New Music in Darmstadt where, in the early 1950's, Boulez and Stockhausen were the leading lights, were largely influenced by Webern.

In February 1953 the journal *Melos* published Stockhausen's analysis of the first movement of Webern's *Concerto for Nine Instruments*. The work of the Studio was revealed in an ever increasing number of articles of a theoretical kind—including writings by kindred composers. Some kind of specialist journal was now felt to be desirable and in 1955 *Die Reihe* (The Row) appeared, edited by Eimert with the assistance of Stockhausen. Its sub-title was *Information on Serial Music*. The second issue was dedicated to the memory of Anton von Webern and opened with a prefatory note by Igor Stravinsky, who was then just beginning to adopt the notions and techniques of the new generation of composers in his own music. The journal was published by Universal Edition in Vienna, who have also published all the works of Stockhausen since 1953.

Since the nineteenth century the music publisher has been a decisive factor in the composer's development. The careers of Richard Strauss, Mahler and later of Schoenberg and his school were closely bound up with large publishing houses. Composers such as Carl Orff and Paul Hindemith were publicised and financially supported by their publishers. Firms such as Schott in Mainz, Durand in Paris, Ricordi in Milan, Boosey and Hawkes in London, Universal Edition in Vienna and more recently Suvini Zerbonis in Milan and Bärenreiter in Kassel have done much for contemporary music. Schott's and Universal Edition in particular have been active in promoting composers working since 1950 in Darmstadt and Cologne. They accepted the technical and financial challenge presented by the new types of scores prepared by Boulez, Luigi Nono, Stockhausen and others. Stockhausen has enjoyed the particular favour of Universal Edition, who did much for his and his friends' cause as the new avant-garde of the post-Schoenberg era. On the two-fold basis of his association with Cologne Radio and Universal Edition in Vienna, Stockhausen was now able to compose with some peace of mind.

In addition to composing and writing he has also worked as a teacher. He has lectured at the courses in Dortmund since 1957, assisted by such composers as Gilbert Amy from France, Sylavano Bussotti from Italy, Friedrich Cerha from Vienna and the Yugo-slavian composer, Milko Kelemen; analysis forms an important part of the courses. In 1958 the American composer John Cage gave demonstrations with the pianist David Tudor in Schloss Heiligen-berg, which were partly concert, partly seminar and partly dadaistic cabaret. Stockhausen's *Piano Piece XI* was one of the works discussed. It is a work whose performance depends largely on chance—or put more accurately on the whim of the pianist who is allowed to put together the nineteen basic particles in a variety of ways. It belongs to the same genre of aleatoric music—music that is left to chance—as the *Third Piano Sonata* of Pierre Boulez. Cage was the initiator of this kind of music, if we choose to ignore minor foretastes of it in Schoenberg's *Jacob's Ladder* (1917) and the out-of-tune piano in Berg's *Wozzeck*.

Stockhausen's main work at this time was his *Groups for Three Orchestras*, which had been given its first performance in Cologne and was repeated a year later in Dortmund. The composer him-self introduced the work, emphasizing the importance of the sound 'parameters', that is of the characteristics which apart from pitch and note-values determine its essence, namely volume and colour. The concept of a parameter had been taken over from Schillinger who in turn had taken it from Einstein. Stockhausen added a fifth parameter, the 'place of the sound' and spoke of the possibility and necessity of spatial composition. In so doing he associated himself—without making it explicit—with Edgar Varèse and his *Deserts* of 1954. For this piece three orchestras are to be set up in different parts of the auditorium. The music, which is dynamically uneven and therefore hard to hear as a unity, heralds a new kind of romanticism with affinities to Schoen-berg, Berg—and even on occasion to Richard Strauss. The work last twenty-five minutes, longer than any previous work by Stockhausen, and was composed between 1955 and 1957.

More or less contemporary are two other works, the *Time Measures* (*Zeitmasse*) and the *Song of the Three Men* (*Gesang der Jünglinge*). In the *Time Measures* the composer investigated

o

different types of musical tempi with examples from a movement for wind quintet. He distinguishes: 1. twelve metronomically measured tempi between MM60 and MM120; 2. as fast as possible; 3. beginning as fast as possible and slowing down to approximately a fourth; 4. opposite of 3; 5. as slow as possible. If this work is not quite able to dispel completely the atmosphere of a workshop experiment, the *Song of the Three Men* certainly does spring from genuine artistic vision. Stockhausen defines the work as electronic music, but in fact it is *musique concrète*.

The work . . . . . derives from the idea of unifying vocal and electronically produced sounds. These were intended to be produced as fast, as slow, as loud and quietly, as intertwined and with intervals as large or as small, and with as much variety in the nuances of colour as the imagination required, freed from the physical limitations of any particular singer . . . . . The vocal sounds are at times intelligible as words, at others they are no more than sound values and between these two extremes there are varying degrees of intelligibility. Isolated syllables and words from the *Song of the Three Men* in the *Burning Fiery Furnace (Benedicite)*. Whenever speech emerges for a moment from the noise of the music it is in praise of God.

The work is written for five groups of loudspeakers which were set up 'spatially' for the first performance in Cologne; it has been recorded but without this spatial effect.

In 1958 Stockhausen went on a concert and lecture tour of thirty-two American and Canadian universities. He came back with ideas that have very much influenced his subsequent development. His compositions over the next two years, the *Cycle for a Percussionist* (a show-piece for Christoph Caskel), the *Check* (Carre) for four orchestras and choirs, first performed in Hamburg Andrzej Markowski, Michael Gielen, Mauricio Kagel and the composer himself, the *Refrain for Three Players* and *Contacts* for electronic sounds, piano and percussion all show a tendency towards dadaism and the cult of the 'happening'. Stockhausen brought his *Refrain* to Berlin in October 1959, for a concert devoted to his works. In this, as in the *Cycle for a Percussionist*, the 'aleatoric' principle, with its rejection of organized form and its dependence on chance, predominates. The programme lasted two hours and included various piano pieces. As a result the element of shock was vastly diminished and the end effect was one of utter boredom—a feature consciously sought after, in fact, by the composer in his *Piano Piece IX* with its hundred repetitions of the same chord.

In 1960, in the New York Theatre The Circle on the Square, John Cage put on a stage performance entitled *Theater Piece 1960*. Those involved in the absurd and often comic happenings under the direction of the composer were David Tudor (piano), Arlene Carmen (contralto), two brass players, and two dancers, Merce Cunningham and Carolyn Brown. Stockhausen's *Originals* of 1961 is virtually a replica of this experiment. The premiére in the *Theater am Dom* in Cologne invoked laughter, protests and frenzied applause. The programme contained the names of the artists (including Tudor, Caskel, and the American painter Mary Bauermeister, who has influenced Stockhausen's life and music) plus the comment:

One thing develops into another; opposites are evened out. Black is a degree of white; scale of greys. Things separated by time and place – persons, actions, events in life (nothing pretends that nothing is intended; everything is composed, everything intended) are compressed into one place, one time: Theatre. I = musical theatre.

Kh Stockhausen.

When Herbert Eimert retired in 1963 Stockhausen took over his post as director of the Studio at Cologne Radio. Differences of opinion had arisen at the Courses in Darmstadt, and the Rhenish School of Music proposed that Stockhausen should continue his work in Cologne. He had already composed a new work for Cologne Radio, his *Moments* for soprano, four choirs and thirteen instruments. The score, written in 1961 and 1962, uses speech as a phonetic musical device.

(It is) .... not a self-contained work with a clear beginning, formal development and end but an equivocal composition of independent events ..... The speaking and singing parts continue what was begun in the *Song of the Three Men* and in the *Check* for four orchestras and choirs – the removal of the duality between vocal and instrumental music, between musical sound and silence, between sound and noise ......

In this work all is left to the whim of a vivid imagination that takes the listener unawares. The real talent of the composer is unmistakable and many parts of the *Moments* are utterly convincing.

Radical, volatile and provocative, Stockhausen has aroused the approval of a rebellious rising generation in many parts of the world. Where it will all lead to is anybody's guess.

22 Karl Amadeus Hartmann

I met Karl Amadeus Hartmann for the first time in 1947. He had come to Berlin from his home in Munich to discuss important problems arising from contemporary music, which he championed like a prophet of old or a modern propagandist. Everything about him was passionate, whether it was his attitude towards artistic matters in which he would allow neither compromise nor frivolity, or his political commitment which, from 1933 on, made him the implacable enemy of all manifestations of National Socialism.

He was born in Munich on 2 August 1905, the second son of an artist. He attended secondary school in Munich until 1922 and became a student at the Academy of Music there a year later. His teacher for theory of music and composition was Josef Haas, a pupil of Reger and a church musician. Hartmann stayed with him until 1927. Then he met Hermann Scherchen, who introduced him to modern music. In an article on Scherchen, as conductor and teacher, he wrote: 'I must confess that in no conservatory or university did I learn anything remotely approaching that which Scherchen taught me. And this is simply because he was working from practical experience and dealing with the human element first.' The meeting took place in Munich in 1927 and an initial pupil-teacher relationship rapidly grew into friendship between the two men.

Hartmann's deliberate political isolation began in 1933 when he was working on his first string quartet. Scherchen encouraged the writing of a concerto for orchestra, which Hartmann performed at a working conference on music and drama, but which he thereafter withdrew. At this time, too, he began work on the opera *Simplicius Simplicissimus* which became known very much later and in a different version. From the time that Hitler seized power Hartmann prohibited the performance of his works in Germany for reasons of political conviction. Together with his wife Elisabeth, whom he had married in 1934, he lived an exemplary life of 'inner emigration', directed solely, without any compromise, towards his creative work and aesthetic development, and this he continued until the collapse of the Nazi regime. Abroad, however, Hartmann's name gradually became known. In 1935 his symphony *Miserae* was performed in Prague at the Festival of the International Society for Contemporary Music. This work, too, he later withdrew and destroyed. According to a contemporary musician Nicholas Slonimsky it was composed in a brooding, introspective mood, within an atonal idiom, but not in the twelve-note system. Atonal but not twelve-note is indeed the formula which may be said to apply to the majority, and the most important of Hartmann's works.

Hartmann's first string quartet was given its first performance at another ISCM Festival, this time in London in 1938. This was five years after its composition, but the quartet had already won an important award, for in 1936 a jury which included Ernest Ansermet, Henri Gagnebin, G. F. Malipiero and Albert Roussel had given it the first prize for chamber music in the Carillon competition.

Through his study of Grimmelshausen's novel *Simplicius Simplicissimus* Hartmann had entered the strange, colourful, tragic and grotesque world of German baroque literature. His cantata *Anno 48—Peace,* based on poems by Andreas Gryphius was written in 1937 and received an award in Vienna, the Emil Hertzka Memorial Prize, (established in 1932 after the death of the notable publisher Emil Hertzka, founder of Universal Edition). This work, like many others written at that time, was later withdrawn by the composer but it was not destroyed.

The outbreak of the Second World War affected Hartmann profoundly. In 1939 he wrote a concertino for violin and strings, known as *Music for Mourning* which was performed at St Gall a year later. His symphony *L'Oeuvre,* which had been performed in Brussels and Liège, was also later withdrawn. The symphony which finally became known as the first was completed in 1940, although begun four years earlier. This 'Attempt at a Requiem', as Hartmann called it, is a work of lamenting protest against National Socialism. Of the five movements, only the third is for orchestra alone and is a theme and variations; the others include an alto voice; The poems— by the American, Walt Whitman—were also used by Paul Hindemith in 1946 in his Requiem *When lilacs last in the dooryard bloom'd.* In Hartmann's symphony, despair, anger and pain permeate all lines and sounds. Dynamic outbursts, moments of silence, also laments by wind or strings fuse together in an asymmetrical form. Not until 1948, eight years after its completion, did the work receive its first performance.

Despite the success of a considerable number of his compositions, Hartmann knew that his ability was limited. Scherchen had introduced him to the shattering experience of the Schoenberg school, but Schoenberg himself was in America, and Alban Berg had died in 1935. So in 1941 Hartmann asked Anton von Webern whether he could become his pupil. Webern lived in complete isolation just outside Vienna in Maria-Enzersdorf. Hartmann met him as he was working in the garden, received a warm welcome, and studied under him for two years. In four letters to his wife Hartmann gave her a detailed report on the instruction he was receiving:

At present Webern has no other pupil and I don't believe anyone is bothering about him at all. This is all the better for me as he devotes the whole afternoon to me and with his concentrated method of working, the amount we get through together is immense. We always work intensively for about three to four hours. Then we discuss this or that composer, and he makes value judgments or puts forward his theories on the future of music.

The subjects of these joint analyses were not only works by Beethoven and Reger but also Hartmann's own works such as his *Simplicius* or his *First Symphony.*

In this he seems to me like a learned scientist who dissects an insect under the microscope, fascinated by the veinage of the wings and the brilliant eye.

At this time Webern was working chiefly on his *Second Cantata* to texts by Hildegard Jone. He made ends meet by working as a proof-reader for the Universal Edition. Teacher and pupil got on well together, though their opinions differed on many subjects. Webern shared Hartmann's admiration for Gustav Mahler and Richard Strauss, but not for Bruckner. Schoenberg was their common idol. Both were deeply hurt that both he and his work should have been defamed by the Fascist powers in Austria and replaced by a mass of militant mediocrity. However, Hartmann was the more consistent in his anti-Fascist attitude.

It was my doing that the conversation frequently returned to politics. He was of the opinion that for the sake of good order *any* ruling body must be respected and the government under which one lived should be recognised at any price.... His lack of ill-feeling towards those who opposed him seems to me incomprehensible.

Hartmann's political commitment found no response in his teacher. In spite of this, indeed perhaps just because of this, Hartmann wrote a symphonic overture during that time, under the title *China at War*. It is a work of dramatic expression and is his first use of the twelve-tone series. Of greater importance and more characteristic of Hartmann is the great adagio-movement for orchestra which he called his *Symphony No. 2* and which he composed partly while a pupil of Webern and partly in 1946. The final work on his second string quartet was done after the collapse of the Nazi regime.

Now Hartmann came out of his voluntary isolation and with burning enthusiasm, turned his attention to administration jobs. By the autumn of 1945 he had already founded the series of concerts 'Musica Viva' in his home town of Munich, which, until his death in 1963, remained the most important of its kind. The State of Bavaria and Munich Radio subsidized this organization so generously that every year saw the performance of a large number of contemporary works. With incessant activity and untiring imagination Hartmann gave these concerts not only their high standard but also a many-sidedness which was a model of its kind. The programme planning showed how far he was removed from any dogma or cliquishness, and how much indeed, he was an individualist. Just as a performance of *Der Freischütz* in Munich in his early youth made him remain faithful to the Romantic composer Carl Maria von Weber, and as, in the twenties, he digested stimuli of all kinds ('I readily combined Futurism, Dada, Jazz and others in a series of compositions'), so now his connection with Schoenberg and Webern did not stand in the way of his admiration for Béla Bartók or Igor Stravinsky. And he established a personal relationship with the Russian composer whose middle and late works often found a place in the programmes of 'Musica Viva' when he came to Munich on Hartmann's invitation.

At the International Holiday Courses for Contemporary Music in Darmstadt, Hartmann was one of the first, in 1947, to champion works by Schoenberg, Berg and Webern, in contrast to the prevailing neo-classicist attitude of the young German composers. His own chamber music and the overture *China at War* were among the most discussed works of contemporary German music in Darmstadt—Kranichstein. In 1947 he wrote the *Fourth Symphony* for string orchestra only, a year later (that is, in reverse order) the *Third Symphony*. Both have three movements with a fast movement between two slow ones. Both are rooted, as Hartmann says of his *Third Symphony* written for large orchestra, 'in the spiritual landscape of Alban Berg'.

The year 1948 saw a series of important performances of Hartmann's works. At the Frankfurt Week of Contemporary Music under the direction of Winfried Zilling, a pupil of Schoenberg's, the *First Symphony* was performed for the first time. Hans Werner Henze, who knew Hartmann from Darmstadt days, was extraordinarily moved by it. 'My admiration for the music of Hartmann dates from that time, and its spirituality, its spontaneous unbroken directness, its honesty and straightforwardness all seemed to me important and significant.' The *Fourth Symphony* was also performed in Munich. Finally the Opera *Simplicius Simplicissimus* took place in Cologne in 1949 with great success, which was repeated and four years later in Berlin, during the Autumn Festival. The composition of this opera goes back to the time of Hartmann's close friendship with Scherchen. As Hartmann wrote: 'In 1934 I married Elisabeth. Our first journey together took us to Churwalden in the Engadine where we met Scherchen. At that time Scherchen and I were working on the scenario of *Simplicius Simplicissimus.*' The characters and dialogues in the sequence of six episodes are taken from Grimmelshausen's novel, but both formally and in content the libretto is closer to Bertolt Brecht. The scene is the Thirty Years' War. The despised peasantry is personified in the figure of the boy Simplicius. Murder, rape and intemperance are seen on the stage: the boy is driven by fear of an unknown force; he meets the dying hermit, who befriends and teaches him and with childish innocence he reveals the truth of their situation to the nobles and their courtesans before they die at the hands of the peasants.

Hartmann interweaves the music to this story with chorales, peasant songs and baroque ornaments. Symphonic introductions and interludes display the expressive counterpoint so characteristic of him. The first peasant song, accompanied by percussion, muted trumpet and trombone, is truly magnificent; the antithesis of the true Lord's Prayer with its caricature is dramatically exciting. The influences of both Stravinsky and Alban Berg fuse together in the score, which has a chamber music character but possesses a passionate, personal note. 'If one holds a mirror up to the world so that it sees its horrible face, it may yet turn back from its evil ways. Despite all the political storm-clouds, I still believe in a better future: this is the meaning of the final apotheosis of my *Simplicius*.' The work, dedicated to Carl Orff, was performed at the Mannheim National Theatre in 1957 in a slightly revised version which must be regarded as the final one.

The honours and successes continued. In 1950 the Bavarian Academy of Fine Arts awarded Hartmann its prize for Art. At that time his second and third symphonies had not yet been performed. The Bavarian Radio then played the third, while Hans Rosbaud conducted the great adagio of the second at the Donaueschingen Music Festival. In July, the Twenty-Fourth Festival of the International Society for Contemporary Music took place in Brussels. Apart from experimental pieces by Karel Goeyvaerts and René Leibowitz, it was Hartmann's Fourth Symphony, written for strings alone, which made the strongest impression. Here, going beyond Bruckner, Mahler, Schoenberg and Berg, Hartmann had found a glowing, expressive style which makes an immediate impact; the performance, under the Belgian conductor Franz André, was a notable one.

Now the depression under which Hartmann suffered passed for a time. He wrote his *Symphony Concertante*, numbered the fifth, whose four movements, played without a break, combine baroque forms with classical symphonic structure. The score leaves out horns and high strings. Its slow movement entitled *Melodie* takes the homage to Stravinsky as far as an almost exact quotation from its beginning of the *Rite of Spring*. The Concerto for piano, wind and percussion, written three years later has the same happy mood. It was first performed at the Donaueschingen Music Festival in

October 1953, conducted by Rosbaud, with Maria Bergmann as soloist; there is a new rhythmic approach in it; it was the first time that Hartmann had used the 'variable metres', that is, mathematically arranged forms of time changes, which had been developed by Boris Blacher in 1950. Blacher and Hartmann had been friends since the forties and Blacher had dedicated one of his piano works in 'variable metres' to him. The outside movements of Hartmann's piano concerto are sets of variations which he blends with these rhythmic figures in an unusually skilful way. Between 1951 to 1953, and these two gayer works, Hartmann wrote his *Sixth Symphony* for large orchestra, commissioned by the Bavarian Radio. This new symphony returns to the pathos of the earlier works. The first movement with its tremendous outbursts of wrath is as characteristic of Hartmann's style as the structure of the ensuing presto, with three fugues of which the second and third are variations of the first.

In 1954 Hartmann received the Schoenberg medal and, in 1955, he became a member of the West Berlin Academy of Arts, an honour which came in time for his sixtieth birthday. Finally, the Gryphius cantata (now bearing the simplified title *Laments*) was sung, eighteen years after its composition, on the island of Mainau near Constance. As Hartmann's own contribution to his sixtieth year he composed a concerto for viola with piano, accompanied by wind and percussion, commissioned by the Frankfurt Radio and dedicated to the great English viola player, William Primrose.

In addition to all his organizing activities for 'Musica Viva' in Munich, Hartmann also became President of the German section of the ISCM in 1953, an honorary post which was his due as one of the most active members of the society. The following years were mainly taken up with the symphonic writing. Between 1951 and 1958 Hartmann wrote his *Seventh Symphony* in two movements for large orchestra, which had been commissioned by the Koussevitzky Foundation in Boston. Luigi Dallapiccola, who had for a long time been an admirer of Hartmann, both as man and as composer, wrote about it:

When I heard the *Seventh Symphony* for the first time it seemed to me that in the finale (scherzo virtuoso) we were a long way off from that has so often been defined as 'automatic music'. Indeed, it seemed to me that despite all appearances, this music was not at all 'automatic' but that, on the contrary, during the course of short episodes, Hartmann would sometimes develop a dialectic as strange as anything I have ever come across in recent times . . . . .

The *Eighth Symphony,* written between 1960 and 1962, commissioned by the Cologne Radio is, like the Seventh, a work of almost superhuman emotion. And just as the second part of the Seventh consisted of an adagio presto and the scherzo virtuoso mentioned by Dallapiccola, so here in the Eighth, after an introductory *Cantilena,* it is entitled *Dithyrambe* and consists of scherzo and fugue.

Hartmann's themes always have a monumental quality, tend towards massive structures, build themselves up beside and above each other like rock formations. Harmonically they grow out of a strongly extended tonality which leads to atonal and polytonal forms. Their counterpoints and tone colours are painted with bold strokes, their extensive melodies often form polyphonic patterns difficult to unravel. Twelve-note figures and variables metres only appear episodically. At its strongest moments, Hartmann's music is the subjective expression of a temperament inclined to sudden passions.

In 1962 Hartmann became seriously ill. In 1963, though weak, he wrote a *Gesangsszene* based on words by Jean Giraudoux. He died on 5 December of that year.

23   Béla Bartók

Béla Bartók was born on 25 March 1881, in the village of Nagy-Szentmiklos on the Hungarian-Yugoslavian-Rumanian border, known today as Sânnicolaul-Mare. His father, the principal of an agricultural college, was an extremely musical person, a keen pianist and cellist, the founder of an amateur orchestra, and a composer. He died when Béla was only seven. The composer's mother was hardly less musical: she gave her son piano lessons from a very early age. On the death of her husband she took work as school-mistress in Nagy-Szöllös where her nine-year old son wrote piano pieces and appeared in public as an infant prodigy. The family moved to Bistritz in Transylvania and from there to Bratislava in 1893. The current capital of Slovakia was in those days part of Hungary and its German-Hungarian-Slovakian culture generated an advanced musical life of its own.

Apart from attending secondary school Béla continued to take lessons in piano and theory from Laszlo Erkel till the age of fifteen. He played in chamber music, went to concerts and the opera and by the time he left school he had studied 'the musical repertoire from Bach to Brahms relatively deeply, though Wagner only as far as *Tannhäuser*' Bartók's models at this early stage were Brahms and Dohnányi's *Piano Quintet,* (Opus 1). The latter was only four years older than Bartók and it was he who advised him to study at the Academy in Budapest. During his first four years at the Academy Bartók was most influenced by Wagner and Liszt, but composition took second place to the piano which he studied under Stephen Thoman. In fact Bartók's own appointment at the Academy in 1907 was as professor of piano.

At the age of twenty-one Bartók heard the first performance

in Budapest of Richard Strauss' *Also sprach Zarathustra,* which had been written some six years earlier. The effect upon him was enormous. He began studying Strauss's works and took up composing again. His *Symphonic Tone Poem* caused an uproar in Budapest but was performed again under Hans Richter in Manchester in 1904. The awakening of Hungarian nationalism was strongly reflected in his own music and in that of Zoltán Kodály.

Bartók read avidly Kodály's first collection of folksongs in 1905, and the two composers became close friends. In 1906 Bartók himself began recording folk music in the summer vacations and for ten years undertook extensive travels together with Kodály, journeys which resulted in the joint publication of their research in 1917.

Bartók was virtually predestined by his linguistic talent to perform folklore research of this kind, involving as it did most of the Balkan countries and later the Near East. At the Academy he learned English; in 1906 he learned Slovak on his own initiative and, for a recital tour with the violinist Franz von Vecsey, he taught himself Spanish. In 1908 he learned Rumanian, in 1912 Russian, in 1913 Arabic and in 1938 Turkish. In 1905 he entered for the Rubinstein Prize in Paris with a performance of his *Rhapsody for Piano and Orchestra though* without success. For that event he taught himself French.

Despite his lack of success in the competition Bartók did not regret going to Paris. He grew very fond of the atmosphere of the city, its museums, its gaiety and its women. He felt strongly his own contrasting solitude and wrote to his mother: 'I am looking and searching for my ideal partner, but in vain, I fear. . . . I have almost grown used to the idea that I will never be other than alone.'

In consequence his friendship with Kodály grew deeper, as did his relationship with Franz von Vecsey whom he accompanied in recitals in Berlin, Madrid and Manchester. About this time Kodály showed him music by Debussy. This was the second musical revelation in his life and in works written about 1908 Debussy's use of harmony, sonorities and atmosphere are recognizable in Bartók's music. The first of the six string quartets reveals a disregard for tonality and profuse chromaticism. In the same year the *Bagatelles* for piano were written with bitonal passages, and the whole-tone scale used as a harmonic and melodic device.

Béla Bartók

In 1909 Bartók's solitude ended when he married Marie Ziegler. In the fourteen years until their divorce, in 1923, he wrote a profusion of piano works, some large, some small, but all in the highly personal style he now evolved. These include the *Sept Esquisses,* (Opus 9), *Quatre Neniés,* the *Allegro Barbaro,* the *Sonatina,* the *Suite* (Opus 14), *Three Studies,* (Opus 18), and *Improvizations on Hungarian Songs.* All of them, however, are secondary works compared with the stage works written between 1911 and 1919, in the years leading up to the war, and during the war itself and the Revolution.

Bartók's only opera, *Bluebeard's Castle,* derives from a period of great artistic unrest in Budapest. Performances of works by Schoenberg and Stravinsky had met with mixed reception. Bartók wrote:

As the battle was reaching its climax a group of young musicians, including myself and Kodály, tried to found a 'New Hungarian Music Society' with the aim of organising our own concert orchestra to perform modern and ultra-modern music in a worthy manner.

It proved a failure and Bartók withdrew from the organization. *Bluebeard's Castle* was not performed until seven years after it was written.

One of the avante-garde among Hungarian writers, Béla Balasz, transformed the traditional story into a modern psychological drama, steeped in symbolism and brought up to date by a sense of collective guilt to which the audience is made to subscribe. The seven doors which the Duke opens for his latest wife, Judith, conceal the rooms which everyone uses to hide his most intimate secret. Judith wishes to see behind them all and pays for her curiosity with death. The work was pushed aside for years on the grounds that it was unperformable, but the first performance of this one-hour opera met with an enthusiastic reception. Kodály wrote:

Bartók has tried to retain in the recitatives the natural music of speech; in the more stylised parts of the opera he has tried to follow the spirit of the folksong and in the process has evolved a new style ... It is a work of irresistible suggestive vigour ..... The seven gates give rise to as many musical scenes, each imbued with profound emotion.

Bartók's own writings give a clear indication of his debt to

Hungarian, Rumanian, Bulgarian and South Slavonic folk elements. Subsequent research has only confirmed what Bartók was first to recognize. The tunes of these folksongs and dances derive from times before the establishment of modern major-minor tonality. He himself wrote: 'The most varied of key changes, Dorian, Phrygian, Mixolydian, and Aeolian are found here in full force, but we also come across scales of oriental nature (with augmented second) and even a sort of pentatonic scale.' The old five note scale without semi-tones is especially characteristic of Chinese music and old Gaelic ballads. It represents a stage of development before the seven note scale, and its charm is comparable to that of primitive painting and sculpture.

Bartók was quick to recapture its spirit in his own melodies though not by any process of direct imitation but rather by distilling its essence to establish an unmistakably national idiom. Art music derived in this way from folkloristic elements is possible in very few western countries; in modern music, apart from that of Bartók, we find it only in Manuel de Falla in Spain, Janáček in Czechoslovakia and in Stravinsky before 1919.

Bartók stands out among such folkloristic composers because the national idiom he evolved is made to embrace a variety of modern—notably expressionistic—techniques. In terms of dissonance, the disruption of melodic contours and the outrageous sound effects he achieves, Bartók is hardly less radical than Schöenberg and his followers. With him, however, freedom of tonality is not the result of an absolute concept of chromaticism. It is rather that the different keys are so intermingled as to produce a 'promiscuous' tonality and the effect of this bitonality and polytonality is not far removed from that achieved by atonal music.

Before *Bluebeard's Castle* had been performed Bartók wrote his first ballet score, *The Wooden Prince*. It was composed between 1914-16 and published in Budapest in May 1917. The material is an adaptation by Béla Balsasz of a Hungarian fairy-tale and combines the world of the supernatural with a love story. For all its many beautiful moments this is the least convincing of all Bartók's dramatic scores. Incomparably greater is the one-act pantomime, *The Miraculous Mandarin*. Composed in 1918-19, its eroticism has been a constant source of protest. It is about a mandarin who is attacked by murderers while visiting a prostitute. His sexual desire is so great that he pursues his aim irrespective of stab wounds and strangulation until the girl finally acquiesces to his desires and he dies in her embrace. The difficulties of staging this work are clearly enormous and even in revolutionary Hungary no one dared to perform it. It was finally performed by the Cologne Opera under Eugen Szenkar on 28 November 1926, but after its first performance Konrad Adenauer, then the Lord Mayor of Cologne, ordered its removal from the programme. Since then the work has established itself in the international repertoire, but only in a later, less extreme version. The work has proved more popular as a concert piece, with its immense vigour of rhythm and sonority. The music is characterized by its expressionism and feverish unrest, both reflecting the nature of the text.

It is no mere chance that Bartók felt moved to compose works involving dance. Dance was an important part of his earlier works, in the *Piano Pieces for Children* of 1909, the *Rumanian Dances*, 1910, and in the relentless motorial rhythm of the *Allegro Barbaro* of 1911, as well as in the *Sonatina* and the *Suite*. When he went on his recording expeditions he was fascinated by the dances the peasants would perform in their old traditional costumes. In his early years Bartók loved wearing the laced and embroidered tunic coats that were worn in Budapest for special events, theatre premières and State receptions.

In researching into folklore he discovered not only idiosyncracies of melody and tonality but also of Balkan rhythmic forms. It became clear to him that these peasant dances of southern Europe were rhythmically far more interesting than the rhythms encountered in Western classical and romantic music. This was nothing new: Russian folk researchers had discovered this at the end of the nineteenth century and from this source Stravinsky derived the complex rhythmic structure of the *Rite of Spring* and the *Soldier's Tale*. Bartók went about the matter with his characteristically systematic approach. His musical idiom evolved slowly and organically until 1918. Looking back on the period that followed, Bartók said: 'From about 1918 to 1924 my work became more radical and more homophonic.' To this period belong the three *Studies for Piano* which require great virtuosity of the executant, The third is rhythmically unprecedented with the following, apparently arbitrary juxtaposition of measures: 2/4, 3/4, 5/4, 4/8, 6/8, 9/16, 10/16, 11/16, and 15/16.

This kind of flexible metre became an integral part of Bartók's style. At a time when Stravinsky had exhausted his folkloristic ideals and was devoting himself to a more sedate neo-classicism Bartók was discovering more and more of the vitality of folk dancing especially in Bulgarian music and in the music of those Balkan states that had come under Turkish influence. Western Europeans brought up on classical music find certain rhythms irregular and try to make sense of them as syncopations. In reality they can only be properly appreciated when one has learned to think of the music in other terms than the accustomed triple and common times, so that metres such as 5/8 or 7/8 can be heard and felt in their own right.

In Bartók's music rhythmic invention is not confined to his dance scores. It formed an important part of both the *Sonatas for Violin and Piano,* written in 1921 and 1922. The first performances were given in London by the woman violinist Jelly d'Aranyi with the composer playing the piano. They were also performed with great success at the festivals held in Salzburg by the International Society for New Music. Not all the critics were positive in their reaction, however. Ernest Newman, writing in the *Sunday Times,* said: 'The bulk of the Bartók *Violin Sonata* seemed to me the last word (for the present) in ugliness and incoherence. It was as if two people were improvising against each other.'

Nineteen hundred and twenty-two saw Bartók's discovery throughout Europe as a brilliant pianist, especially as an interpreter of his own works. He gave recitals of his own music in Paris, under the auspices of the *Revue Musicale* as well as in England and Germany. His style was not one of empty virtuosity: he played with a firm touch, relentlessly precise rhythmically, eliciting from the piano a particularly strong tonal colour. Recital tours and international fame made life in Budapest seem monotonous and in 1923 a marital crisis developed. He separated from his wife to marry a young pupil of his, Ditta Pasztory.

In the same year the combined town of Buda and Pest celebrated the fiftieth anniversary of their union. Bartók was commissioned to write an orchestral work, which materialized as the climax of his 'more radical and more homophonic period', the *Dance Suite.* The striking feature of this brilliant work is the successful fusion of nationalistic harmony and rhythm with the most modern compositional techniques. Simple triadic harmonies mingle with layers of fourths: simple, predictable rhythmic forms alternate with highly complex rhythmic structures. The thematic material is largely derived from folk elements but filled out by more sophisticated subject matter. The main theme is basically pentatonic, but with sliding notes between the thirds. Bartók was not content with an unconnected succession of movements—all six are inter-related thematically and harmonically in the manner of a symphony. The first performance in Budapest on 19 November by the Philharmonic Society under Ernst von Dohnányi was a resounding success.

Ditta Pasztory became not only Bartók's marital but also his artistic partner. The pair appeared together throughout Europe as a piano duo. Strangely enough Bartók wrote no major works for two pianos, though he did arrange a lot of solo piano music for piano duet; Paul Sacher, a conductor in Basle, commissioned a work for two pianos from him in 1937. The start of a new marriage coincided with a new period of creativity. In 1926 he wrote the first of his three piano concertos, performed in Frankfurt in 1927 under Furtwängler, with the composer as soloist. Later in life Bartók said that 'beginning in 1926 my work became more contrapuntal and on the whole more simple'. The third and fourth string quartets written in 1927 and 1928 bear witness to this more polyphonic approach. It was in these two years that he visited America, making a triumphal debut with his early *Rhapsody,* played in the Carnegie Hall with the Philharmonic Orchestra under Wilhelm Mengelberg.

A similar success came a year later when he played his *Piano Concerto No. 1* with the Cincinnati Orchestra under Fritz Reiner. The tour took him from coast to coast and Bartók especially enjoyed the Californian West. In January 1928 he wrote to his mother in Budapest, from the train taking him from Portland to Denver:

I arrived in San Francisco at eight in the evening and went off straight to the Chinese Theatre. This was the most interesting thing I have as yet seen over here. I stayed on till midnight . . . . . God alone knows how long a theatre performance of this kind is going to last.

He also enjoyed the hospitality shown to him by the people he met —and new, exotic foods, especially avocado pears, were glowingly described.

The catalogue of his works was growing ever more extensive

and varied. In 1930 he wrote the *Cantata Profana*, based on fairy-tales and legends. A year later he wrote his *Second Piano Concerto* with its characteristic tone clusters and in 1935 his *Fifth String Quartet,* with its third movement *Scherzo alla bulgarese* in 9/8 time, built up of 4 plus 2 plus 3 quavers.

Bartók was greatly disturbed by the political disorders in Central Europe. He had been a confirmed anti-fascist since 1924 and in 1933 he stopped performing in Germany and later in Austria, before deciding to leave Europe altogether when Hungary came under the threat of National Socialism. Despite all this he still found the energy and concentration to write, composing the *Music for Strings, Percussion and Celesta* in 1936. The first of the three movements is in the form of a fan fugue, the chromatic theme of which borders on being twelve-note. The final rondo, with its striking rhythms, sonorities and harmonic writing is one of his finest achievements.

About this time he completed the *Microcosmos* on which he had been working since 1926. It is a collection of one hundred and fifty-three piano pieces in six volumes, embracing the full range of musical and technical complexity, from pieces of utter simplicity to the final *Six Dances in Bulgarian Rhythm,* that require not only considerable digital dexterity but also the greatest rhythmic precision. The first fifty-five pieces are dedicated to his son, Peter.

Immediately following *Microcosmos* came the *Sonata for Two Pianos and Percussion,,* later re-arranged for two pianos, percussion and orchestra. The first performance took place in Basle on 16 January 1938, with Bartók and his wife as the soloists.

When the present writer visited him in 1938 manuscripts were strewn all over his table. He explained that they were of a violin concerto, written for the Hungarian violinist, Zoltán Szekely. He then produced the manuscripts of his two *Contrasts* which were performed shortly afterwards in New York with Josef Szigeti and Benny Goodwin.

In summer 1939 Bartók and his wife were the guests of Paul Sacher at his home near Basle; Sacher commissioned Bartók to write a divertimento for string orchestra. On completion of the *Sixth String Quartet* Bartók left Budapest and, like many other Europeans at that time, was granted asylum in the USA. He was awarded an Honorary Doctorate at Columbia and gave numerous joint recitals with his wife. His financial position, however, was very precarious. In 1943 he was commissioned by Sergei Kussevit-sky to write a concerto for orchestra for the Boston Symphony Orchestra. This work in five movements, including the scurrilous intermezzo, has firmly established itself in the international concert repertoire.

Columbia appointed him to a teaching fellowship in folk music, but he derived little satisfaction from the work. His health began to deteriorate in 1945. He managed to finish his *Third Piano Concerto* and the rough drafts of a viola concerto before being admitted to a New York hospital where he died of leukaemia on 26 September 1945, at the age of sixty-four. He died in utter poverty, the cost of his funeral being borne by the American Performing Rights Society.

Bartók was a man and artist with the highest standards of integrity. He refused to make any concessions of an artistic or political nature. His music acts as a bridge between folk tradition and the twentieth century and has made an indelible impression upon the evolution of rhythm and tonality.

24 Zoltán Kodály

Ever since the two young composers Béla Bartók and Zoltán Kodály journeyed round Hungarian villages together in 1905, taking down traditional folk-music on wax cylinders, they have been regarded as inseparable and forced into a kind of over-simplified intellectual affinity as with Goethe and Schiller, or seen as joint representatives of an aesthetic philosophy like Debussy and Ravel. In every case, simplifying formulae of such a kind have blurred and distorted the picture.

Of course Kodály was influenced by the national characteristics of his Hungarian homeland, just as was Bartók, his senior by one year. Both musicians realized in their youth, with the shock of sudden discovery, that such ancient elements as music, dance and language can perform a re-vitalizing function if explored to their very roots. However, Kodály was more concerned with language and song, Bartók with the instrumental dance. This is the basic difference between them.

Zoltán Kodály was born in Kecskemét on 16 December 1882, an almost exact contemporary of Anton von Webern. He attended schools in small Hungarian towns such as Szob, Galanta and Nagy Szombat. At the age of sixteen he wrote an overture which was performed by the school orchestra. After completing his school examinations in 1900 he went to Budapest, where he took a double course of studies, both at the University and at the Academy of Music. He studied composition under Hans Koessler, and in 1906 he was awarded the degree of Doctor of Philosophy for a thesis on verse-structure in Hungarian folk-song. Then he travelled to Berlin and Paris where Romain Rolland showed considerable interest in the young musician.

He met Béla Bartók in 1905 and the two men soon found a common interest in the folk-lore of their homeland. They set out on their first journey together to many Hungarian villages, and brought back a wealth of recordings.

In 1907 Kodály was appointed as teacher of harmony and composition at the Academy of Music in Budapest. From the start he succeeded in combining his activities as composer, scholar and teacher and continued to do so until the end of his life. In the illuminating conversations between the octogenarian Kodály and Lutz Besch in Budapest and Kecskemét in 1964, Kodály maintained: 'If you think about it, everyone functions on several levels. Just think of Schumann and his dual nature. . . . The things I was interested in never lay very far apart. I have no hobby which is fundamentally different from my main occupation.' His professional activities certainly influenced his private life, for Emma Schlesinger-Sandor whom he married in 1910 was his former pupil. In that same year, 1910, two concerts of chamber music were given in Budapest on 17 and 19 March, of which one was devoted entirely to the music of Bartók, the other to Kodály. His works were also performed in Paris and Zürich. In 1910 he went on a research trip to Transylvania and returned with a number of old Hungarian songs.

As a composer Kodály first achieved success with a string quartet which was soon followed by the much played first cello sonata. At the International Congress of Musicians in Rome in 1911 he met composers from other countries, many of whom became his friends. In the company of his wife and his friend Béla Bartók he undertook a second trip to Transylvania in 1912. In the same year the Academy of Music promoted him to a full professorship.

He was very busy during the years immediately before the outbreak of the Great War and the war years themselves. He continued his research trips from 1914 to 1916, especially to the Bukovina region, where he discovered very old sources of Hungarian folksongs. He wrote several scholarly articles on his finds, one, for instance, on old Christmas songs and another on the pentatonic scale. As a composer Kodály now turned increasingly to vocal music, which became the major part of his creative writing. Several songs with piano and choruses for men's voices show the influence of his researches into folk-lore on his own musical idiom. At the

36

36 and 37 Bela Bartòk, the Hungarian composer (1881–1945), concentrated on studying the piano, rather than on composition, up to the age of twenty-one, which was when he heard the first performance in Budapest of Strauss's interpretation of Nietzsche's *Also sprach Zarathustra*. The effect on him was enormous and he began to devote himself to composing. The photograph of Bartók with his sister Elza was taken in 1904, at the time when he began composing the early piano pieces in the illustration, which date from the period 1903–8.

In 1905 Bartók read Kodály's first collection of folksongs, and the two composers soon became good friends. From 1906 for the next ten years they spent every summer together, travelling and recording and collecting folk music. In 1917 they published the results of their research into folk music in the Balkan countries and the Near East.

37

38

39

40

38 Zoltán Kodály and Bela Bartòk at Kodály's home in Budapest.
39 Bartòk and Kodály collecting folk music together in 1908.
40 Bartòk in front of a nomad tent in Anatolia. Bartók was an extraordinarily good linguist and spoke English, Slovak, Spanish, Rumanian, Russian, Arabic, Turkish and French, as well as his native Hungarian.
41 Kodály and his wife with Bartòk in Budapest about 1910.

41

44

42

KODÁLY ZOLTÁN
ARCKÉPE (1882-1967)
5 Ft MAGYAR POSTA

43

42 Zoltán Kodály (1882–1967) with his first child. Kodály's encyclopaedic knowledge of Hungarian folk song and its relationship to the melodies of other tribes and peoples had a strong influence on his work. He and Bartók were the first modern composers to use the traditional pentatonic scale as it had survived in the folk songs of the Balkans.

43 Kodály with his second wife on the eve of his eightieth birthday in December 1962. When his first wife died in 1958 he complied with her wish that he should marry a girl sixty years younger than himself, Sarolta Peczely.

44 A stamp issued by the Hungarian government in memory of Kodály. Apart from his compositions, Kodály left behind him a great legacy in the form of a new method of musical education based on the sol-fa system and the pentatonic scale. He had achieved astonishing results with this method and had also succeeded in introducing daily singing lessons into hundreds of schools in Hungary. He once said: 'Musical education must begin not only nine months before the birth of a child, but even before that of its mother.'

45 Leoš Janáček (1854–1928) with his wife Zdeňka, a photograph taken in 1881, the year of their wedding. Like Bartók and Kodály, Janáček was passionately interested in folk music, and he made a special study of birdsong and the rhythms of human speech.

46 A page from the score of Janáček's *Katya Kabanova*.

47 Leoš Janáček at the age of seventy. Two years later he won a great triumph with a concert in London and it was during this visit that he made a speech which included the following statement of his belief in the value of folk music: 'Folk song is a unity: it is the expression of men who know only the culture of God, not an alien, inflicted culture ... Folk-song binds together all mankind in *one* spirit, *one* happiness, *one* salvation.'

same time he composed chamber music, especially works including the cello, but also piano pieces and a second string quartet. From 1917 Kodály also worked as a music critic, first for a literary journal and then for the important daily newspaper *Pesti Naplo.*

The collapse of the central european powers in 1918 and the subsequent social revolution had particularly dramatic consequences in Hungary. The Soviet republic was proclaimed in 1919 and the new authorities appointed Kodály as acting director of the Academy. The composer, who was progressive and nationalistic but not much interested in politics, little realized in what deep conflicts this appointment would involve him. After the collapse of the proletarian dictatorship which had been established in March with Béla Kun at its head, there was a period of great confusion in which many political denunciations were made as the result of the sudden shock of revolution. Kodály was suspended, along with many other men in public life, and accused of being a collaborator. Béla Bartók's behaviour, as always in such situations, was exemplary, and in a letter of 3 February 1920 he declared: 'Since I have had much to do ... with the activities of the directorship ... I must protest vigorously ... against Zoltán Kodály alone being held responsible.' The case against Kodály ended with his full acquittal. Nevertheless the flood of defamation was slow to recede, and not until September 1921 was he able to resume his teaching activities.

Understandably Kodály's creative ability suffered as a result of these experiences. Between 1919 and 1920 he wrote only one *Serenade*—for two violins and viola. He also gave up his work as a critic in April 1919 to devote more time to his ethnological studies of music.

The *Psalmus Hungaricus* for tenor solo, mixed choir, children's choir, orchestra and organ which received its first performance on 19 November 1923, in the same programme as Béla Bartók's *Dance Suite*, brought Kodály his first world success. All his music is primarily vocal in feeling and invention; even the important works for orchestra or his chamber music are based to a large extent on folk-songs. Despite the modernities of his musical language, links with traditional folk-music are ever-present. Kodály's music certainly owes much of its character to his encounter with French Impressionism, and particularly with the music of Claude

Debussy, an experience he was quick to share with his friend Bartók. But whereas Bartók's compositions remained mainly instrumental and often emphasized short-lived stylistic trends, always involving experimental adventures, Kodály pursued an independent line with innumerable choral works, songs and pieces written for different combinations of voices with instruments. Amongst these are such important works as the *Te Deum* and the 'ballad operas': *Háry János* 1926, *The Spinning Room* of 1932 and *Czinka Panna* of 1948.

When the waves of political upheaval had subsided Kodály was again able to take up his old connections throughout the world. In 1924 he was appointed to the jury of the ISCM as its Hungarian representative, and four years later he set up the Hungarian section together with Bartók, Alexander Jemnitz and Antal Molnar.

The original success of the *Psalmus Hungaricus* was repeated in 1926 at a performance in Zürich under Volkmar Andreae. Since then the work has been translated into eight languages and performed all over the world. In October of the same year the colourful, folk-style ballad opera *Háry János* was performed in Budapest. Slowly the composer's fame increased. In 1927 Kodály was invited to Amsterdam, London and Cambridge to conduct his own works, and the *Psalmus Hungaricus* was given the same rapturous reception as in Hungary and Zürich. Suddenly Kodály's orchestral and choral works were found in programmes with all the leading conductors. Ernest Ansermet in Geneva, Pablo Casals (who had now started to conduct) in Barcelona, Wilhelm Mengelberg in Amsterdam, Wilhelm Furtwängler in Berlin, Eugene Ormandy in New York, Victor de Sabata in Milan and Arturo Toscanini in New York—all these became enthusiastic advocates of Hungary's national composer. During these years, his compositions turned increasingly away from instrumental towards choral music. As early as 1925 and 1926 he had written children's choruses to traditional texts and in later years he added to their number, using songs in a folk idiom, partly unaccompanied and partly with organ accompaniment. These now formed the focal point of Kodály's writing. After a whole programme had been devoted to such children's choruses in Budapest in April 1929, a development began to take place in Hungary towards which Kodály himself had been deliberately working. The Arts Faculty of the University gave him a teaching appointment in folk music. This was the more remarkable since there was no Chair of Music at the University, all study of musicology being at that time confined exclusively to the Academy of Music. A large number of scholarly and literary articles resulted from these lectures.

The *Marosszek Dances* for orchestra which were written during this period soon achieved the same international popularity as had the *Psalmus* seven years earlier. Kodály also resumed work in 1932 on a ballad opera, begun in 1924, based on poems and tunes of the Szekls (a race of people in Transylvania). Performed under the title *The Spinning Room* this work too enjoyed as popular a success on its first performance in Budapest as had *Háry János*. In the *Dances from Galanta* written in 1933 Kodály revealed his symphonic skill even more clearly than in the *Marosszek Dances*.

Kodály's fame was two-sided. Whilst the musical worlds of Europe and America showered praise on his work in particular on the orchestral pieces and chamber music, Kodály was quietly working on a large number of choruses and songs which were more enthusiastically received in his Hungarian homeland. Only later, at a greater distance from the immediate impact of his music, has it been possible to recognise its inherent unity. For even in his chamber music and orchestral works, nationalistic and folk-lore elements make their appearance, not only as melodic or rhythmic material but as a sincerely felt and sublimated motivating force. Kodály, with his calmer temperament, did not feel the growth of fascism in Central Europe as a direct threat as much as his friend Béla Bartók. Nevertheless after 1933 both withdrew further into their ethnographic research. They collaborated once again in a study of the folk-song, undertaken for the Budapest Academy, resulting in 1934 in a grouping and cataloguing of the available material. Soon after this Kodály composed a number of church works, among them the *Te Deum* for solo quartet, mixed choir, organ and orchestra which, after its first performance in Budapest, soon became famous and has been performed throughout Europe. The most important result of his studies, Kodály's book on Hungarian folk music, was published in 1937 and appeared later in German, English and Russian translations.

In 1938 the danger of fascism drew nearer to Hungary. Austria had already been annexed and the freedom of Hungary was at stake. The Concertgebouw orchestra of Amsterdam commissioned a work from Kodály and this was the origin of the orchestral variations on *The Peacock*. The melody is among the most beautiful in primitive Hungarian folk-music. It is pentatonic and is considered in Hungary as expressing the will for freedom, just as the peacock itself is an ancient symbol of liberation. Kodály worked on the score from 1938 until 1939. In the intricate variations and in his commentary on the composition, Kodály reveals an encyclopaedic knowledge of links, origins and ethnological relationships. The song is indeed related to the folk music of distant races, such as Mongolian tribes in Asiatic Russia, members of the Finno-Hungarian family of languages. Thirty years before, Bartók had already used the peacock song at an emotional climax in his first string quartet. Kodály's *Variations* were performed for the first time in Amsterdam in 1939 under Mengelberg. They are full of great musical beauty, his most mature orchestral work before the *C Major Symphony* of 1961.

In 1940 Kodály gave up teaching and devoted himself primarily to the collection of folk songs, which he later published under the sponsorship of the Academy of Sciences. In the same year his friend Bartók, turning his back on fascist Europe, took leave of him. The following year Kodály retired after a teaching career lasting thirty-five years. The year of his sixtieth birthday was celebrated as Kodály Year for all Hungarian choirs; he received an Honorary Doctorate of the University of Kolosvar, the freedom of the city of Galanta, and a year later, was elected a member of the Hungarian Academy. Apart from choral works, the concerto for orchestra and a *Missa Brevis* for choir and organ, most of his compositions at that time were purely pedagogic in intent, being connected with the teaching of music in schools. As Hindemith had done before him in the twenties, Kodály, although much more methodically, now wrote two-part singing exercises, choral exercises and the *Bicinia-Hungarica* as an introduction to two-part singing. The results of this practical work have become more convincing and more astonishing from year to year: after a quarter of a century, musical education in Hungarian schools is now second to none in the world.

In 1944 Hitler's troops occupied Hungary. For Kodály and his aged wife, who came of a Jewish family, the situation was dangerous. A convent took them both in and granted them asylum until the liberation. To show his gratitude Kodály wrote his choral work *The Feast of St Agnes* for women's voices. After leaving the convent Kodály and his wife had to spend the first few months of 1945 in basement rooms of the Budapest Opera House. News of the death of their friend Bartók in New York came as a severe blow, and in March 1946 Kodály spoke at a concert in his memory.

The Hungarian Academy of Sciences elected Kodály as its President in July 1946. Three months later he travelled through Switzerland, France and England to America, giving concerts. He received a special welcome in November 1946 when he conducted the Pittsburgh Symphony Orchestra in his *Dances from Galanta*. His tour of America was followed by an equally successful tour of Soviet Russia.

The fact that Kodály never bowed to any totalitarian regime and fearlessly maintained his individuality testifies to his stature and strength of character. At an interview in New York he answered a question by saying 'The National Socialists wanted to get rid of the Jews and the Communists would like to do the same with the Christians'. He defied both parties yet they let him be. Thus even after 1948 he was able to hold leading positions in the cultural life of Hungary with no one disputing his right to them.

In 1948 the Swedish Academy elected Kodály to its membership. In the same year he was awarded the Hungarian Kossuth Prize and his new ballad opera *Czinka Panna* was performed at the Budapest Opera. During the following years concert tours took him to France and England. On his return home in 1950 he resigned the Presidency of the Academy. He was then engaged in writing new choral works, including the *Geneva Psalms* and more pieces of an educational nature.

In 1954 Kodály's wife fell ill as the result of an accident and remained an invalid for the rest of her life. She died in 1958 and according to her wish Kodály married again the following year. His second wife, Sarolta Peczely, was sixty years younger than he. He accepted distinctions such as an Honorary Doctorate of Music in Oxford in 1961 with calm dignity, accompanied by his new young wife, who seemed to rejuvenate him. In 1961 he composed his *First Symphony*, of which his former pupil Ferenc Friscay was an enthusiastic interpreter.

Kodály outlived several of his large circle of pupils. Among the best-known composers who studied under him are Istvan Arato, Paul Kadosa, Gyorgy Ranki, Sandor Veress and Matya Seiber. He dedicated his *Media Vita* to Seiber on his death in a car crash in Johannesburg in 1962. Hungary celebrated Kodály's eightieth birthday as a national holiday.

In 1964 Kodály and his wife visited Germany. In Weimar he was awarded the Franz Liszt medal and nominated as an honorary senator of the Liszt Academy. After East Germany he paid a short visit to West Germany in order to visit Alain Danielou's International Institute for Research into Comparative Music. The present writer met him there amongst a small circle of friends. The conversation took place in English, German and French. Kodály was fluent in all three languages but preferred English which his wife could understand better. He seemed fresh and relaxed and had just come back from seeing and admiring Hans Scharoun's Philharmonic Concert Hall on the border of West Berlin, near to the East Berlin wall.

Suddenly he asked whether we had read Ernest Ansermet's book *Les Fondements de la Musique dans la Conscience Humaine*. Ansermet, an old friend, had sent it to him and he was full of approval. Kodály whole-heartedly agreed with the theoretical rejection of all music which turns its back on tonality, Schoenberg's twelve-note music in particular. The point was made that many of Hungary's young musicians were going the way of Schoenburg. Kodály smiled: 'They are already finding Schoenberg old-fashioned and are worshipping Anton Webern. Young people who have not yet found their own style like to imitate something ultra-modern.' The conversation then turned to equal temperament. Danielou rejected it completely: for him the development of music after Bach was an aberration. To this Kodály replied: 'We use natural intonation in singing and piano accompaniments are forbidden for choral singing. But for instrumental music we use equal temperament. One must distinguish carefully between natural intonation and equal temperament in music-making.'

Kodály wished to have nothing to do with the most recent trends in music. However, he supported those whose ways he could not believe in, if it was a question of defending the autonomy of art and intellect. Among his friends were Benjamin Britten and Yehudi Menuhin. Both admired him, not only as a composer, but also as an incomparable educator. 'Musical education must begin', as Kodály once maintained, 'not only nine months before the birth of a child, but even before that of its mother.' It was he who introduced daily singing lessons into hundreds of schools in Hungary. His method of teaching, based on the sol-fa system and the pentatonic scale, achieved astonishing results in pure intonation, rhythm and sight-singing.

When he died on 6 March 1967, at the age of eighty-five, he left behind, in addition to his compositions, a legacy of musical education which shows the way for far-reaching development.

25 Leoš Janáček

On 30 April 1926 a group of prominent musicians, writers publishers and journalists met at Claridge's Hotel in London. Their hostess was Rosa Newmarch, seventy-year old musicologist. She was an established expert on Russian music, had written a biography of Tchaikovsky and translated operas by Moussorgsky and Smetana. During her journeys through the Slav world, she had deepened her knowledge of Czech music. Her guest of honour on this April afternoon was a white-haired old man with a bushy moustache and the brilliant eyes of youth. His name was Leoš Janáček and he was one of the celebrities of the young Czechoslovak state; his London ambassador, Jan Masaryk, had fetched him from the station the day before. The concert a few days later, attended by London's most knowledgeable and musical experts, was a triumphant success for Janáček. He wrote to his friend Kamilla Stössl: 'They are on strike here. Today there was no milk to be had in London. Everything is suddenly getting dearer. A bad atmosphere for a concert, but I accomplished my mission satisfactorily.'

Janáček's career was highly unusual. He was born on 3 July 1854, in the village of Hukvaldy in the Moravian part of Czechoslovakia, and was the son of the village schoolmaster. The countryside formed his personality, that of a peasant of unmistakable West-Slavonic type, who could be compared in many traits of character to the much older Anton Bruckner (a musician whom he greatly surpassed in intellectual and critical faculties). Janáček was the ninth of thirteen children and was born in a room in the school-house whose windows looked out over the church and a brewery. Life in the parental home was modest in the extreme. The boy was introduced to music-making by his father at an early age and attended the village school from 1859 to 1865. He also sang in the church choir. In 1865 his father took him to the choir-master of the monastery of Old Brno for an audition. The ten year old boy became a pupil at the monastery in September of that year. A fellow-pupil has described his appearance: curly brown hair down to his shoulders, top-boots and the national Sokol-cap. In the monastery he developed into a brilliant pianist, made his first attempts at composition, learned to play the organ and took part in choral performances under the musical director, Pavel Krizkovsky.

In 1874 Janáček's training was completed. Furnished with an excellent testimonial by Krizkovsky the nineteen-year-old left the monastery school for the famous College of Organists in Prague where he hoped to acquire further knowledge qualifying him for admission to the State Teacher's Training College. The director of the College of Organists, F. Z. Skuhaersky, gave him an enthusiastic testimonial:

> He possesses talent, intelligence, perseverance and enthusiasm, united in the best harmony. Janàček has already reached a level worthy of respect as a productive and reproductive artist. A wide knowledge of the musical repertoire, a good ear and a full mastery of musical theory and aesthetics qualify him as a conductor and critic.

The hard childhood in the parental home and hunger in the monastery-school had yielded a rich harvest.

Janáček had a certain restlessness. Like many of his countrymen he loved to travel and he had curiosity and a desire for knowledge. Although he had obtained his teacher's diploma in 1878 the musical training in his country seemed to him inadequate. He went abroad, first to St Petersburg, hoping to study with Anton Rubinstein and, then, when this plan misfired, to Leipzig. There he found the traditionalist spirit of the Conservatory uncongenial. After five months he went, via Brno, to Vienna, but once again left after a short stay.

Earlier, in Brno, he had formed a deep attachment to Zdenka Schulz, the beautiful daughter of the director of the Teacher's Training College. In numerous letters to his fiancée he related his experiences in the great musical cities. Janáček had grown into a small and slender young man with rapid graceful movements and quick physical and intellectual reactions. His large head with its high forehead was surrounded by an unruly shock of curly hair. From the age of twenty-four he wore a luxuriant beard. This is what he looks like on a photograph taken at his wedding to Zdenka Schulz in 1881. The young couple look like a painting by Renoir, romantically elegant but not without a touch of provincial sentimentality.

Janáček was capable of dionysiac outbursts of rage, especially in relation to artistic matters. He had an impetuous and dramatic temper and was a strict teacher and an extremely difficult marriage partner. The tensions of many years of quiet work and study were accumulating in his mind without having yet found their proper release. The artistic and moral force with which he embraced life, man and nature, lay dormant until the years of his maturity. Then this force broke free, impetuous and magnificent, a fiery stream or masterworks that rejuvenated Janáček in the very act of creation.

His earliest compositions consist of orchestral works, chamber music and liturgical choral pieces. These works already show the influence of Moravian folksongs, which he collected and studied together with Frantisek Bartos almost twenty years before Bartók's and Kodály's field-work in Hungary and the Balkans. During the nineties these studies led to Janáček's theory of speech-melody, the basis of all his later vocal music. Even orchestral works like the *Lachian Dances* of 1890 are based on melodic and rhythmic elements of the ancient music of the Western Slavs. Politically Janáček was a nationally conscious Czech, a fact which concerned and alarmed his father-in-law, who was a supporter of the Habsburg Monarchy. Janáček's nationalism broadened into Pan-Slavism. He spoke Russian fluently and belonged to the Russian circle in Brno. In 1896 and 1902 he travelled three times to various Russian and Polish cities.

In his early youth Janáček had envisaged a College of Organists in Brno which was to become the centre of musical education for the whole of Moravia. This school was opened in September 1882, and Janáček remained its foremost teacher and organizer until 1919. A number of highly trained creative and executive musicians received their musical education from him. His untiring energy enabled him to increase his output of music year by year despite his teaching commitments, and an active private life centred round his family and an extended circle of friends.

During his years of study in Prague he had met another musician who, like him, led an active life as teacher and composer and who embodies the musical genius of the Czechs: Antonin Dvořák. Dvořák was primarily a composer of chamber and orchestral music. His great operatic output won only hesitant recognition and is only kept alive in the opera houses of Czechoslovakia. Janáček, too, was attracted by the stage relatively early in his career. His later fame is based on a composition that is generally considered his masterwork, the opera *Jenufa*. But long before this he wrote the opera *Beginning of a Novel*, a village idyll placed in the mythical and legendary haunts of the Bohemian amazon, Sarka, and containing some mild social criticism. *Jenufa* was written between 1894 and 1903 and first performed in Brno in 1904.

Despite its local success, Prague refused for twelve years to perform this work of the Moravian composer, who was mocked as a peasant. The crucial intuition of the poet Max Brod discovered the genius of Janáček in 1916. He translated *Jenufa* into German and so initiated after its performance in Vienna the opera's victorious progress across many operatic stages. Until then the composer had lived in provincial quiet, though not without dramatic moments and artistic and literary disputes. Tragedy and passion dominate his opera *Jenufa*, in which the powerful and puritanical step-mother menacingly dominates all his other characters. Janácek's choice of subjects was determined by his closeness to nature and was alien to the spirit of the modern metropolis. Not only *Jenufa* but also *Katya Kabanova, The Cunning Little Vixen* and *From the House of the Dead* are an expression of his love and closeness to nature. Only once, in his bizarre play *Fate* did he approach the seedy musical and theatrical world of the art nouveau period.

Life remained difficult for him. His teacher's salary was insufficient for the needs of his small family. For many years Janáček had to earn his living as a choral conductor and organist, occasionally as a critic and writer of highly original essays. He was an avid reader of the classics, of the Russian novelists, whom he possessed in the original, and of contemporary Czech literature. In the writings of a favourite author, the poet and novelist Svatopluk Czech, who belonged to the generation of Strindberg, Janáček came across the character of Brouček, the epitome of the petit bourgeois and philistine who has come into money, gets drunk, chases women, and always supports the winning side, carefully avoiding taking risks. Czech makes him travel in space and time: one journey takes him to the moon, the second into the fifteenth century and the Hussite wars. Janáček was enthusiastic about the idea of a two-fold unmasking of the shabby character of a philistine. In 1917 he finished his two part opera: *Mr Brouček's Excursions to the Moon and into the Fifteenth Century*. It is the most bizarre and comic of his stage-works. He compared the protagonist to Oblomov in Ivan Gontcharov's novel: 'There are as many Broučeks to be found among our people as there were Oblomovs in Russia. I wanted to make such a man repellent, so that we annihilate and strangle him at every step—above all in our own natures.'

In 1896 Janáček spent his summer holidays visiting Nizhny Novogrod. In 1902 he followed the course of the Volga and visited the steppes. The impressions from these journeys took shape in his next dramatic work *Katya Kabanova* (after Ostrovsky's *Storm*) composed between 1919 and 1921. By the time the opera was performed in Brno in 1921, Janáček had become famous. In 1919 he was appointed professor of the master-class in Prague. Following the performance of his violin sonata in Salzburg in 1923, his music had been played increasingly at the festivals of the International Society for Contemporary Music and soon his operas were staged in Berlin, Cologne and many other musical cities in Germany. In his sixties the organ teacher from Brno finally achieved the success that had long been his due.

Meanwhile a woman had come to exert a profound influence upon his whole life and work. Since the death of his younger daughter in 1903, Janáček had felt estranged from his own family. During a stay at the Spa Luhacovice in 1917 he met Mrs Kamilla Stössl who was nearly forty years his junior and who became his most intimate friend and correspondent until his death.

The tension of his new-found love found release in the *Diary of a Man who Disappeared* for tenor, contralto, piano and three women's voices. The anonymous author of these twenty-two poems describes the love of a village boy for a dark gypsy, and his tragic fate. 'Perhaps it will make a pretty little musical novel', he wrote to Kamilla in August 1917. It became not a novel but a compressed drama, the expression of another relationship which equally defied both convention and legality. With this work, which was completed only in 1919, Janáček's output became entirely autobiographical. Musically, a motivic cell built around the interval of an ascending or falling fourth predominates. In the *Diary* the melodic idiom is frequently based on primitive pentatonic forms which are derived from folk-music.

The subject of *Katya Kabanova,* the Russian Madame Bovary as Max Brod calls her, can equally be claimed to be autobiographical. The young woman destined to die tragically could be the portrait of the rich, unhappily married Jewess living in the Bohemian province with whom Janáček fell passionately in love at the age of sixty-three. Even the names Katya and Kamilla show an assonance. 'I have never known greater love than mine for her. To her I dedicate this work' he wrote in Kamilla's vocal score of the opera.

The wide landscape far from any town, with the slow-flowing Volga and the outbreak of a thunderstorm defines the setting in which Janáček recreates Ostrovsky's human beings. Nature dominates even more in his next stage work, *The Cunning Little Vixen.* It is a strange tale of the small comedies and tragedies in the forest, where man and animal not only live together but occasionally exchange their existence, and where a friendship like that between the gamekeeper and the vixen is made possible. Even reincarnation is suggested by the reappearance of the mother in her child.

Janáček always made use of the phonetic observations he had been making daily over many years. He had long been in the habit of taking down the cadences of human speech as well as those of bird-calls and other sounds of nature in his small sketch-books. This enormous archive led to distillation of a new musical language expressing every shade of emotion. This language is the basis of all his vocal music but nowhere is its richness more impressive and nearer to reality than in this epic of the Moravian woods. Janáček became the great Pan himself when he wrote this score from 1921 to 1923.

Meanwhile new plans had matured. During November 1923 the first string quartet was written, under the spell of Tolstoy's *Kreutzer-Sonata,* and was enthusiastically acclaimed at its first performance during the ISCM festival in Venice.

Shortly before his seventieth birthday Janáček was invited by the Prussian State Opera in Berlin to attend a performance of his *Jenufa*. Erich Kleiber, the conductor, received a cordial letter of thanks, praising the many virtues of the excellent performance. Work continued. Janáček read Karel Capek's play *The Makropoulos Affair*. He was fascinated by the idea of extending the life of a beautiful woman for many centuries by the use of an elixir. 'The poor three-hundred year old beauty', he wrote to Kamilla. 'People thought her a thief, a liar, an animal without feeling. . . . And her guilt? That she had to live so long. I was sorry for her.'

New honours arrived, new suffering, new works. In January 1925 an honorary doctorate was conferred on him by the Masaryk University in Brno. Janáček was very proud of this distinction. Meanwhile he had written two purely instrumental works, the *Concertino* for piano and chamber-ensemble, which met with resounding success at its performance in Frankfurt in 1927, and the wind-sextet *Mladi* (Youth), one of his gayest works. At a London concert in April 1926 the work was enthusiastically acclaimed in a performance by English wind players.

From 1924 Janáčk visited the small South Bohemian town of Pisek where Kamilla Stössl often stayed, and became friendly with the local musicians. He attended concerts and loved to listen to the military band which played in the park on Sundays. This band gave him the idea of writing his *Sinfonietta,* a highly original work with the unforgettable sound of its twelve trumpets. It is a suite in five movements whose origin in waltz, polka and Moravian folksong is easily discernible. A three-note motif at the beginning is contained within the space of a falling fourth. It is a paradigm of early music of a kind to be found in the works of Bartók, Kodály and Stravinsky.

The *Sinfonietta* was composed in 1926. In the same year Janáček wrote his *Glagolithic Mass*, a Slav Festival Mass to words in archaic old-Slav, an expression of his ideas of the Eastern Church, 'this atmosphere of Kyrill and Methodius' as he described it, with reference to the two Greek Apostles of the ninth century. Written for soli, chorus, orchestra and organ, the mass avoids musical pietism but is full of strong, irresistible faith. It is the expression of an intense religiosity known to everyone who has witnessed the prayers of Slav people in their churches. In place of a *Dona nobis pacem*, Janáček included a stormy organ solo based on a Gregorian theme. The mass ends surprisingly with a jubilant and splendid *Intrada*. It seems as if figures of the *Ecclesia Triumphans* enter this world with choirs of strings and wind replacing psaltery and harp.

Once more Janáček's amazing, creative Indian summer yielded a new harvest. In February 1927 he discovered in Dostoyevsky's *Siberian Diary* the outlines of a dramatic composition. Work on this project occupied him until shortly before his death. In between he wrote his last piece of chamber music, a passionate hymn to his beloved Kamilla in the form of a string quartet. 'It shall be called *Love Letters,*' he wrote to her and continued: 'You are behind every note, alive, near, radiant with love.' When the four movements were finished during the summer of 1927, he called them *Intimate Letters.*

He received new honours: a memorial tablet on the house of his birth and membership of the Berlin Academy of Arts. The old man cared little for all this. Feverishly he worked at his Dostoyevsky opera which was to be called *From the House of the Dead,* and which he prefaced by the epigraph: 'In every creature there is a spark of God'. The opera is the most passionate avowal of freedom and humanity, consisting of action without any definable dramatic rule, without a love story, almost without a glimmer of light on the dark gloom of the prison. The music too defies all conventions. One recognizes Janáček's style in repeated motifs, in wind instruments, polkas, short gay or sad songs, echoes of hymns, soli on the xylophone, pointillistic glitter by the celesta.

In the morning the old man would go to his desk or to the sunny terrace of his house. He would write, go for walks or shopping and have an early supper. Then he would write letters and go to bed. He would work in his garden and play with his two dogs whose barking he carefully transcribed in musical notation.

On 1 July 1928, he travelled to Luhacovice and spent a month there. In August he met Kamilla and her eleven year-old son in Hukvaldy. Although he had always enjoyed the best of health, he caught a cold during an excursion. On 10 August he was admitted to hospital in Moravska-Ostrava with pneumonia. Two days later he died.

Everything that he created, music, his prose writings, his letters of love and anger, seems to have originated under the open sky. Nature, the landscape of the countryside, everything that is hidden from our eyes in the ravines of the city streets, permeated his work. The changing of the hours and of the seasons, the voices of the elements and of the animals provide the background. Janáček's childhood and his early intellectual development are as impregnated by them as was that of Gustav Mahler by the sound of trumpets in the nearby barracks. All his life Janáček remained faithful to the landscape of his homeland, and returned to it to die.

Index

Index

Index

Fauré, Gabriel, 157
Friscay, Ferenc, 111, 198, 238
Furtwängler, Wilhelm, 46–7, 86, 102–3
   148, 158, 198, 227, 234

Gershwin, George, 145
Goll, Iwan, 140, 141

Hába, Alois, 10, 85, 196
Hartmann, Karl Amadeus, 10, 57, 105,
   213–20
   works,
    Anno 48 – Peace, 214
    Cantata No. 2, 215
    China at War, 216, 217
    Gesangsszene, 220
    Laments, 219
    Miserae, 214
    Music for Mourning, 214
    L'Oeuvre, 214
    Simplicius Simplicissimus, 213–15,
     217–18
    Symphony No. 1, 214–15, 217
    Symphony No. 2, 216, 218
    Symphony No. 3, 217, 218
    Symphony No. 4, 217, 218
    Symphony No. 5, 218
    Symphony No. 6, 219
    Symphony No. 7, 219–20
    Symphony No. 8, 220
Hauer, Josef Matthias, 9–10, 45, 71–80
   works,
    Apocalyptic Fantasia, 72, 77
    First Suite (Opus 31), 75
    Hyperions Schicksalslied, 72
    Kyrie eleison, 72
    Nomos in seven parts (Opus 1), 72
    Nomos (Opus 2), 72
    On the Essence of Music, 75
    On Tonal Colour, 73, 75
    Piano Studies (Opus 22), 73
    Salammbô, 76, 77
    Die Schwarze Spinne, 76
    *Suite for Orchestra No. 7 (Opus
     48)*, 77
    *Twelve-Note Theory, the Study of
     Tropes*, 76–7
    Vom Melos zur Pauke, 73, 75
    Wandlungen, 77
Hegar, Friedrich, 155, 166, 175
Henze, Hans Werner, 10, 87, 167,
   183–191, 203, 206, 217
   works,
    Antifone, 187, 190
    Apollo and Hyacinth, 184
    The Bassarids, 191
    Being Beauteous, 189
    Chamber Music 1958, 187
    Concerto per il Marigny, 187

    The Country Doctor, 206
    Elegy for Young Lovers, 187–9
    The End of a World, 188, 189
    Five Neapolitan Songs, 186
    The Idiot, 186
    King Stag, 185–7, 189
    Das Kleine Wundertheater, 189
    Manon Lescaut, 185
    Maratona di Danza, 186
    Muriel, 189
    Nocturnes and Arias, 187
    Novae de Infinito Laudes, 189
    The Prince of Homburg, 187
    Sonata per Archi, 187
    Symphony No. 4, 189
    Symphony No. 5, 189
    Three Dithyrambs, 187
    Undine, 186, 187
    The Young Lord, 159, 190
Hesse, Herman, 21, 166, 167, 172, 173
Hindemith, Paul, 10, 18, 40, 86, 97–
   106, 107, 129, 138, 140, 153, 161,
   184, 193, 194, 197, 198, 204, 208, 236
   works,
    Canons, 102
    Cardillac, 100, 103
    A Composer's World, 104
    Cupid and Psyche, 104
    The Demon, 100
    The Four Temperaments, 104
    Frau Musica, 102
    Funeral Music, 104
    Die Harmonie der Welt, 105, 161
    Hérodiade, 104
    Hin und Zurück, 99–100
    Kammermusik (Opus 24), 99
    Lehrstück, 101
    The Long Christmas Dinner, 105
    Ludus Tonalis, 104
    Das Marienleben, 99, 103, 165
    Mathis der Maler, 102, 103, 105,
     181, 190
    Neues vom Tage, 99, 101–2
    Noblissima Visione, 104
    Nusch-Nuschi, 99
    Piano Suite 1922, 99
    Requiem, 104, 215
    *Schulwerk fur Instrumental-Zusam-
     menspiel*, 102
    Seranaden, 100
    Sinfonia Serena, 104
    Solo Sonata for Viola, 103
    Symphonic Metamorphoses, 104
    Triadic Ballet, 99
    Das Unaufhörliche, 101, 102, 104
    Unterweisung in Tonsatz, 103
    Viola Concerto, 103
Honegger, Arthur, 10, 119, 155–63, 166
   170
   works,

252

Index

Index

Index

Index